HUMAN RIGHTS OF
AMERICAN MINORITIES

HUMAN RIGHTS OF AMERICAN MINORITIES

FIRST EDITION

Edited by M. Nicole Warehime

University of Central Oklahoma

Bassim Hamadeh, CEO and Publisher
Mazin Hassan, Acquisitions Editor
Amy Smith, Project Editor
Casey Hands, Associate Production Editor
Jackie Bignotti, Production Artist
Sara Schennum, Licensing Associate
Natalie Piccotti, Director of Marketing
Kassie Graves, Vice President of Editorial
Jamie Giganti, Director of Academic Publishing

Cover image copyright © 2014 Depositphotos/Rawpixel.

Printed in the United States of America.

ISBN: 978-1-5165-3974-1 (pbk) / 978-1-5165-3975-8 (br)

To the children, so that they learn to treat all humans as humans
with basic human rights.

CONTENTS

INTRODUCTION

M inority. *Majority.* Understanding these terms provide the foundation of this textbook. A minority and a majority can be defined in multiple ways, as will be discussed later in this book. However, what is important to understand and study is the outcome of the definitions. How are individuals treated and understood as a result of being labeled a minority or a majority?

Many scholars have argued that the mere distinction of minority or majority causes a good deal of social problems in the American society. Others argue that because researchers cannot agree on a simple definition of these terms, it is impossible to actually study these individuals. Yet, others show concern that the definitions create more questions than solutions.

Sociologists systematically study the interactions and group behavior of humans. Sociologists study nuclear families where everyone in the family knows the other members of the family. Every member is shaped and influenced by the other family members. Sociologists also study gender groups where not everyone in the gender group knows other members of the gender. Despite not knowing each other, members are shaped and influenced by the other members of the gender group. This is a bit tricky to identify and understand. In Unit 2, more distinction will be made on the historical change in focus, from the similarities of individual group members as being biological to the similarities being understood from a sociological perspective. Are you born knowing how to be a lady or gentleman (biology), or are you taught to be a lady or gentleman (sociology)?—not to mention the discussion that can a person be something beyond a lady or a gentleman (to be discussed in Unit 4).

Several sociologists have attempted to create a definition of minority. One most often used is the definition by Wagley and Harris, introduced in 1967:

> (1) Minorities are subordinate segments of complex state societ-
> ies; (2) minorities have special physical or cultural traits which
> are held in low esteem by the dominant segments of the society;
> (3) minorities are self-conscious units bound together by the
> special traits which their members share and by the disabilities

which these bring; (4) membership in a minority is transmitted by a rule of descent which is capable of affiliating succeeding generations even in the absence of readily apparent racial, cultural or physical traits; (5) minority peoples, whether by choice or necessity, tend to marry within the group. (Wagley & Harris, 1967, p. 10)

So, Wagley and Harris identify five broad categories that a minority group must have to be considered a minority: inequality, visibility, awareness, ascription (characteristics or traits an individual is born with), and intimate relationships. Another definition is provided in 1978 by van Amersfoort:

[A] minority has three constituent properties. ...

(1) A minority is a continuous collectivity within the population of a state. This continuity has two important aspects: (a) the minority consists of several generations, (b) membership of the minority has priority over other forms of social categorization.

(2) The numerical position of a minority excludes it from taking effective part in the political process.

(3) A minority has an objectively disadvantageous position in ... the four following 'public' fields: (a) the legal system (b) the educational system (c) the labour market (d) the housing market. (Amersfoort, 1978, p. 233)

So, van Amersfoort (1978) builds on Wagley and Harris (1967) to introduce the importance of the outcomes of being identified as a minority. This definition highlights another struggle with defining a minority, statistics. Although in statistics, a numerical minority means that there is less than the majority, from a sociological discussion, this may not always be the case. Women, statistically, represent the majority in the world; however, women, socially, represent the minority in the world, meaning men have more power and control compared to women. The top 1% of the world's richest people (statistical minority) arguably have more political and economic power compared to the lower 50% (statistical majority). So, how do we, as new scholars to this field, identify and study a minority?

Smith (1987) concludes a discussion of the definitions of minorities by stating:

Besides comparing the specific disabilities and conditions of existence that distinguish disadvantaged collectivities in common and differing societies, to understand the situation of any collectivity, whether privileged or disprivileged, it is necessary to situate that unit firmly in its social and historical context. To do so, we need first to study the unit's formal and informal relations with other units in the society to determine how those relations serve or have served to shape or maintain its distinctive attributes, including its relative size, location, resources, occupations, wealth, language, culture, religion, legal and political rights and development. (p. 360)

With this in mind, we begin our analysis of the American minority and majority social systems. We begin this book with a discussion of the declaration of human rights. We conclude this book with a discussion of social policy and how this policy would best serve to create equality among all individuals.

References

Smith, M. G. (1987). Some problems with minority concepts and a solution. *Ethnic and Racial Studies, 10*(4), 341–362.

van Amersfoort, H. (1978). "Minority" as a sociological concept. *Ethnic and Racial Studies, 1*(2), 218–234.

Wagley, C., & Harris, M. (1967). *Minorities in the new world*. New York, NY: Columbia University Press.

Basic Rights, Minority and Majority

While visiting major cities around the world, it is interesting to hear people's discussions at crosswalks about the homeless problem the city faces. Oftentimes, the discussion highlights the mentality that these individuals in the socioeconomic <u>minority</u> are somehow <u>less than</u> human. The United States has a long history of treating various racial and ethnic <u>minorities</u> as <u>less than</u>. Although women around the world are the statistical majority, women have been considered a <u>minority</u> and <u>less than</u> men. Homosexuals and other sexual orientation <u>minority</u> groups still face struggles around the world as <u>less than</u> heterosexuals. New to the sociological study of minority groups, obese individuals are being identified as a <u>minority</u> and the study of the inequalities shows that obese individuals face being seen as <u>less than</u> healthy.

While thinking of a <u>minority</u> from a statistical perspective, the concept is defined as "<u>less than</u> majority." While thinking of a <u>minority</u> from a demographic perspective, the concept is defined as "<u>less than</u> majority." While thinking of a person in the <u>minority</u> from a sociological perspective, the concept is defined as having "<u>less</u> power than the majority," despite numerical calculations. While thinking of a <u>person in the minority</u> from a society standpoint, humans tend to think of these people as "<u>less than</u>."

It has long been tradition for our society to rank individuals from a stratified perspective. <u>A stratified perspective simply refers to the social ranking of members of our society.</u> For example, when considering sex and gender, our society thinks of males, and masculinity has preferable characteristics over females and femininity. This, of course, is a fluid ranking, meaning it needs to be studied in a continuum, rather than a category. We will discuss this more throughout the book.

To address this <u>less than</u> mentality from the start, this book begins with a discussion of human rights. One of the major goals of this study of minority groups in the United States is to have people think of the individuals in the minority group as a HUMAN, not as <u>less than</u> human. Although the United States has not ratified the Universal Declaration of Human Rights (UDHR), many of the components are represented in the Declaration of Independence. For the purpose of this section, we will not get bogged down into the theories of why the United States has not ratified the UDHR (most notably, the US does not want another governing body having control over the sovereignty of the United States). However, we want to focus on what the human rights are as individuals. Are individuals in the minority group afforded the rights as humans?

HOMELESS > HUMAN
WOMEN > MEN
HOMOSEXUALS > HOMO
OBESE > HEALTHY

- STRATIFIED PERSPECTIVE: SOCIAL RANKING OF MEMBERS OF OUR SOCIETY

- FLUID RANKING STUDIED IN CONTINUUM

Universal Declaration of Human Rights

Preamble

United Nations

Whereas recognition of the inherent dignity and of the equal and inalienable rights of all members of the human family is the foundation of freedom, justice and peace in the world,

Whereas disregard and contempt for human rights have resulted in barbarous acts which have outraged the conscience of mankind, and the advent of a world in which human beings shall enjoy freedom of speech and belief and freedom from fear and want has been proclaimed as the highest aspiration of the common people,

Whereas it is essential, if man is not to be compelled to have recourse, as a last resort, to rebellion against tyranny and oppression, that human rights should be protected by the rule of law,

Whereas it is essential to promote the development of friendly relations between nations,

Whereas the peoples of the United Nations have in the Charter reaffirmed their faith in fundamental human rights, in the dignity and worth of the human person and in the equal rights of men and women and have determined to promote social progress and better standards of life in larger freedom,

Whereas Member States have pledged themselves to achieve, in cooperation with the United Nations, the promotion of universal respect for and observance of human rights and fundamental freedoms,

Whereas a common understanding of these rights and freedoms is of the greatest importance for the full realization of this pledge,

Now, therefore,

The General Assembly,

United Nations, "Universal Declaration of Human Rights," *United Nations*. 1948.

Proclaims this Universal Declaration of Human Rights as a common standard of achievement for all peoples and all nations, to the end that every individual and every organ of society, keeping this Declaration constantly in mind, shall strive by teaching and education to promote respect for these rights and freedoms and by progressive measures, national and international, to secure their universal and effective recognition and observance, both among the peoples of Member States themselves and among the peoples of territories under their jurisdiction.

Article 1

All human beings are born free and equal in dignity and rights. They are endowed with reason and conscience and should act towards one another in a spirit of brotherhood.

Article 2

Everyone is entitled to all the rights and freedoms set forth in this Declaration, without distinction of any kind, such as race, colour, sex, language, religion, political or other opinion, national or social origin, property, birth or other status. Furthermore, no distinction shall be made on the basis of the political, jurisdictional or international status of the country or territory to which a person belongs, whether it be independent, trust, non-self-governing or under any other limitation of sovereignty.

Article 3

Everyone has the right to life, liberty and security of person.

Article 4

No one shall be held in slavery or servitude; slavery and the slave trade shall be prohibited in all their forms.

Article 5

No one shall be subjected to torture or to cruel, inhuman or degrading treatment or punishment.

Article 6

Everyone has the right to recognition everywhere as a person before the law.

Article 7

All are equal before the law and are entitled without any discrimination to equal protection of the law. All are entitled to equal protection against any discrimination in violation of this Declaration and against any incitement to such discrimination.

Article 8

Everyone has the right to an effective remedy by the competent national tribunals for acts violating the fundamental rights granted him by the constitution or by law.

Article 9

No one shall be subjected to arbitrary arrest, detention or exile.

Article 10

Everyone is entitled in full equality to a fair and public hearing by an independent and impartial tribunal, in the determination of his rights and obligations and of any criminal charge against him.

Article 11

1 Everyone charged with a penal offence has the right to be presumed innocent until proved guilty according to law in a public trial at which he has had all the guarantees necessary for his defence.

2 No one shall be held guilty of any penal offence on account of any act or omission which did not constitute a penal offence, under national or international law, at the time when it was committed. Nor shall a heavier penalty be imposed than the one that was applicable at the time the penal offence was committed.

Article 12

No one shall be subjected to arbitrary interference with his privacy, family, home or correspondence, nor to attacks upon his honour and reputation. Everyone has the right to the protection of the law against such interference or attacks.

Article 13

1 Everyone has the right to freedom of movement and residence within the borders of each State.

2 Everyone has the right to leave any country, including his own, and to return to his country.

Article 14

1 Everyone has the right to seek and to enjoy in other countries asylum from persecution.

2 This right may not be invoked in the case of prosecutions genuinely arising from non-political crimes or from acts contrary to the purposes and principles of the United Nations.

Article 15

1 Everyone has the right to a nationality.

2   No one shall be arbitrarily deprived of his nationality nor denied the right to change his nationality.

Article 16

1   Men and women of full age, without any limitation due to race, nationality or religion, have the right to marry and to found a family. They are entitled to equal rights as to marriage, during marriage and at its dissolution.

2   Marriage shall be entered into only with the free and full consent of the intending spouses.

3   The family is the natural and fundamental group unit of society and is entitled to protection by society and the State.

Article 17

1   Everyone has the right to own property alone as well as in association with others.

2   No one shall be arbitrarily deprived of his property.

Article 18

Everyone has the right to freedom of thought, conscience and religion; this right includes freedom to change his religion or belief, and freedom, either alone or in community with others and in public or private, to manifest his religion or belief in teaching, practice, worship and observance.

Article 19

Everyone has the right to freedom of opinion and expression; this right includes freedom to hold opinions without interference and to seek, receive and impart information and ideas through any media and regardless of frontiers.

Article 20

1   Everyone has the right to freedom of peaceful assembly and association.

2   No one may be compelled to belong to an association.

Article 21

1   Everyone has the right to take part in the government of his country, directly or through freely chosen representatives.

2   Everyone has the right to equal access to public service in his country.

3   The will of the people shall be the basis of the authority of government; this will shall be expressed in periodic and genuine elections which shall be by universal and equal suffrage and shall be held by secret vote or by equivalent free voting procedures.

Article 22

Everyone, as a member of society, has the right to social security and is entitled to realization, through national effort and international co-operation and in accordance with the organization and resources of each State, of the economic, social and cultural rights indispensable for his dignity and the free development of his personality.

Article 23

1   Everyone has the right to work, to free choice of employment, to just and favourable conditions of work and to protection against unemployment.

2   Everyone, without any discrimination, has the right to equal pay for equal work.

3   Everyone who works has the right to just and favourable remuneration ensuring for himself and his family an existence worthy of human dignity, and supplemented, if necessary, by other means of social protection.

4   Everyone has the right to form and to join trade unions for the protection of his interests.

Article 24

Everyone has the right to rest and leisure, including reasonable limitation of working hours and periodic holidays with pay.

Article 25

1   Everyone has the right to a standard of living adequate for the health and well-being of himself and of his family, including food, clothing, housing and medical care and necessary social services, and the right to security in the event of unemployment, sickness, disability, widowhood, old age or other lack of livelihood in circumstances beyond his control.

2   Motherhood and childhood are entitled to special care and assistance. All children, whether born in or out of wedlock, shall enjoy the same social protection.

Article 26

1   Everyone has the right to education. Education shall be free, at least in the elementary and fundamental stages. Elementary education shall be compulsory. Technical and

professional education shall be made generally available and higher education shall be equally accessible to all on the basis of merit.

2   Education shall be directed to the full development of the human personality and to the strengthening of respect for human rights and fundamental freedoms. It shall promote understanding, tolerance and friendship among all nations, racial or religious groups, and shall further the activities of the United Nations for the maintenance of peace.

3   Parents have a prior right to choose the kind of education that shall be given to their children.

Article 27

1   Everyone has the right freely to participate in the cultural life of the community, to enjoy the arts and to share in scientific advancement and its benefits.

2   Everyone has the right to the protection of the moral and material interests resulting from any scientific, literary or artistic production of which he is the author.

Article 28

Everyone is entitled to a social and international order in which the rights and freedoms set forth in this Declaration can be fully realized.

Article 29

1   Everyone has duties to the community in which alone the free and full development of his personality is possible.

2   In the exercise of his rights and freedoms, everyone shall be subject only to such limitations as are determined by law solely for the purpose of securing due recognition and respect for the rights and freedoms of others and of meeting the just requirements of morality, public order and the general welfare in a democratic society.

3   These rights and freedoms may in no case be exercised contrary to the purposes and principles of the United Nations.

Article 30

Nothing in this Declaration may be interpreted as implying for any State, group or person any right to engage in any activity or to perform any act aimed at the destruction of any of the rights and freedoms set forth herein.

Post-Reading Activities

1   In your opinion, which article of the Universal Declaration of Human Rights (UDHR) is the most important? Why? How have you seen this in the real world?

2   Think of a minority group in the United States (i.e., race/ethnic groups, illegal immigrants, legal immigrants, homosexuals, women, homeless people, obese people, disabled people, and religious groups). Which article of the UDHR most affects this minority group? How does this article affect the minority group?

3   Do you think the American society treats all humans as humans? If yes, why do you think Americans treat humans as humans? If no, how can we change the American society to actively treat all humans as humans, as defined by the UDHR? Be specific.

4   From your university's library, select a peer-reviewed scholarly journal article on your minority group of choice (see #2). After reading the article, how do the researchers define your minority group? How does this definition relate to the definitions discussed in the Smith article? What, if any, human rights are addressed in the study of the minority group?

Basic Identities, Minority and Majority

How do we agree to the terms needed to study American minorities? Because we have such terms of race, sexuality, gender, and class, do we thus create an emphasis on being a minority or a majority? How do these terms interact and affect our day-to-day lives? As Americans, we tend to want to categorize all people we meet. We do this often and quickly, many times unaware of the cognitive process. In other words, we size up those we meet. How do we compare? Not always do we use this information in a negative form; we oftentimes use the information to find similarities or common ground to interact with the individual. Other times, we use the information to explore differences. It is when we use the information to divide individuals and create inequalities that these categories cause social problems. Or, we use these differences to justify which individual shall receive the guarantees of basic human rights and which shall not.

Key Definitions to Understanding the Concepts

Race. Historically, racial identification was described by census workers who made the determination by simply looking at an individual. In the 2000 census, Americans were able to self-identify a racial category. Technically speaking, the darkest skin individual could self-identify as a White individual on the census and vice versa. Sociologists identify race as a *socially constructed* term. This means that race within a society is simply what the society claims race to be. In the United States, we tend to create races based on skin color or eye shape (i.e., Black, White, Native American, and Asian). We also incorporate ethnicity, a *culturally constructed* term. This means that ethnicity within a society refers to similar cultural backgrounds. In the United States, we tend to create ethnicity based on country of origins (i.e., Hispanic). Ethnicities tend to share language, food, history, and religion. Because humans can interbreed among races and immigrate extensively, these categories are becoming less distinct over time. Thus, social problems arise on the need of racial and ethnic categories and the applications of such categories.

Class. Numerically speaking, all individuals can be ranked according to their yearly income to create classes. We can place these individuals into quintiles, or five groups of 20% of the population by yearly income. However, this is not a clean definition. As translated by Gerth and Mills, Weber(1998) discusses, there is more to a person's social class than simply the yearly income. Social class also incorporates status or mannerisms (i.e., knowing what fork to use with each course in a seven-course meal) and power (i.e., the ability to express control over others). Many college students come from a middle-class background with middle-class behaviors and expectations of power. However, if these college students were studied simply by their yearly income, many of these students would be at the poverty class level. But, they do not behave in ways that are conducive to the poverty level; instead, these students continue to behave as if they live in the middle-class. Also within the United States, there is a cultural belief that everyone has the ability to achieve high class (social mobility). What is often overlooked is the structural obstacles that society throws at the individual. For example, yes, the United States provides mandatory, "free" education to all children. However, because the "free" education is provided to the students through funding from property taxes, some school districts have more resources than other school districts. Also, some school districts have great resources such as libraries, sports programs, music programs, and drama programs, while other school districts struggle to provide basic resources such as current textbooks. Class inequality is oftentimes multigenerational because of this. It is hard to make it in the United States when the starting line is already behind others.

Gender and sex. Gender and sex, like race and ethnicity, incorporate both culture and biology. Gender refers to the *cultural* distinctions of masculine, feminine, and androgynous. Traditionally, two gender categories were identified, which linked to the two sex categories, *biology* distinctions (i.e., chromosomes, sex glands, hormones, genitalia). Now, with greater research and understanding, many researchers refer to these categories as more spectrum based, rather than categorical based. Gender is oftentimes discussed as "doing gender." Doing gender refers to "acting like a lady" or "being a man." What exactly does this mean? Are we taught to be a lady or are ladies naturally (born) more caring and nurturing? Do ladies need gentlemen to protect them and to provide for them? We are now identifying transgender and transsexual individuals. Transgender refers to individuals whose behavior does not match the society's accepted conventional behaviors of an assigned sex—for example, a young man who lives and presents himself as a female in society. He does the expected behavior of a female, despite the biology of the male. Transsexuals physically alter their sexual biology to match that of another sex through surgery and/or hormonal treatment. Intersexuals are individuals who are biologically a mixture of both male and female biological characteristics, have incomplete sexual development, and have unclear sexual identification based on biological markers. Many jurisdictions are trying to accommodate the changing understanding of sex and gender by adding bathrooms, changing rules of sports participation, etc. However, other jurisdictions are staunch in remaining a dichotomy of sex and gender. Individuals must identify as either/or in these jurisdictions. And, if these individuals do not fit one of the categories, they are oftentimes mistreated or risk losing universal human rights.

Sexuality. Sexual orientation refers to the romantic *attraction* one has toward another individual. Sexual identity refers to the way one expresses the sexual orientation. For example, if one individual is sexually and romantically attracted to an individual of the opposite sex, then that individual would be identified as having a sexual orientation of heterosexual. Continuing, if one individual is sexually and romantically attracted to an individual of the same sex, then that individual would be identified as having a sexual orientation of homosexual. However, if that person presents him- or herself in society as heterosexual, the sexual identity of the person would be heterosexual, despite the sexual orientation being homosexual. Although occurring less today than in the past, the United States remains a heteronormative culture. This refers to the idea that the culture assumes first that heterosexuality is normal and expected behavior. Many laws and policies are written to favor heterosexual couples. Although the marriage laws have changed in the United States, many adoptions favor heterosexual couples, many insurance policies favor heterosexual couples, many probate laws favor heterosexual couples, and the list continues.

Intersections. BUT, individuals do not live in a bubble of their classification. However, the classifications intersect and create sub-classifications of minorities. For example, not all women have similar lifestyles. Being a Black woman is different than being a White woman. Being a rich woman is different than being a poor woman. Being a lesbian woman is different than being a heterosexual woman. Patricia Hill Collins (2016) introduces the idea of *intersectionality*, referring to the idea that the relationships between these identities cannot be viewed in isolation. Although most recognize the differences, very few can articulate these ideas into practice or social policy. Thus, we have a discussion of the deserving and the undeserving of social provisions. Traditionally, our society is willing to help women and children, but we fail to recognize men in need of services. Today, we distinguish between those we believe to be able-bodied workers and those who are not; thus, we have new outposts of inequality affecting day-to-day lives and human rights of Americans.

Additional minorities. When considering the definitions of minority introduced previously, it can be difficult to recognize religion, age, disability, and obesity as categories of minority. However, when considering the Universal Declaration of Human Rights, one can identify where some members of these categories face inequality and discrimination based on the characteristics. More discussion of these groups will be in Unit 4.

Identity Within the Concepts

Buechler (2014) introduces the reader to the historical view of identity theory from a sociological perspective. Prior to people viewing people as individuals, people viewed people as a collective. This is a very important introduction to understanding minorities. It not only assists an individual to understand how and he or she is identified, but also how he or she identifies others. The United States is notoriously identified as one of the most individualistic societies in the world, so it is imperative for a scholar of minority relations to understand the historical context and development of this identity so that a scholar can understand the majority-minority relationships established.

Next, Wieringa (2002) introduces the concepts of essentialism and constructivism. Traditionally, racial differences are based on skin color, hair texture, and eye shape. With these biological distinctions, biology plays a heavy role in determining race; however, social attributes such as athleticism, intelligence, and wealth become mixed in to the idea that it must be biologically determined. For example, a common stereotype is that Asians are the most intelligent students in the American education system. Is this to a biological advantage or a social advantage? Are Asians "born smarter" or are Asians taught to be studious, disciplined, and to value education? Another common stereotype is that Blacks are better athletes. Is this a biological advantage or a social advantage? Are Blacks "born athletic" or are Blacks taught to be athletes, to be disciplined, and to value athletics? If we go down this path, we run into stereotypes of minorities that are more likely to be criminal, "born criminal." How do these ideas affect an individual's identity in American society? *Essentialism*, or natural emphasis, focuses on the explanations that individuals are born with characteristics that give individuals a clear advantage or disadvantage. But, with this line of thought, it is assumed that ALL individuals within the category also have the advantages or disadvantages. But, what about the Asian who struggles with academics or the Black who is not athletic? This forces another thought of *constructivism*, or societal emphasis, and focuses on explanations that recognize the role of society or culture in the development of one's characteristics, highlighting one's advantages and disadvantages. BUT, as Wieringa (2002) highlights, this line of theoretical understanding may not be the best explanation either.

Finally, Smith (2015) unifies the discussions in this unit by further explaining the key concepts and placing them in the context of identity. He also discusses the outcomes of such identity in terms of diversity and inequality.

References

Buechler, S.M. (2014). How we become who we are. In *Critical Sociology*. London: Paradigm Publishers.

Hill Collins, P. & Bilge, S. (2016). *Intersectionality*. Cambridge: Polity Press.

Smith, D.G. (2015). The role of identity in diversity. In *Diversity's promise for higher education*. Baltimore: Johns Hopkins University Press.

Weber, M. (1998). "Class, Status, Party." In H.H. Gerth & C.W. Mills (eds.), *From Max Weber: Essays in Sociology*. London: Routledge.

Wieringa, S. (2002). Essentialism versus constructivism: Time for a rapprochement? In *Gendered Realities*. Mona: University of the West Indies Press.

How We Become Who We Are

Steven M. Buechler

The previous chapter traced the history of the individual. We learned that the individual is a late arrival who appears only with the rise of modernity. All societies contain people, but only modern ones have individuals.

This chapter traces the biography of the individual. Here, the individual arrives late in a different sense. We become individual only through socialization. We begin this process utterly dependent on others. Only after extensive social support do we develop self-awareness, become individuals, and acquire identity. In both historical and biographical terms, individuals only emerge through social connections with others. We are always social before we are individual (Lemert 2008).

When we ponder what makes one person different from another, there are at least two types of answers. A psychological answer seeks unique traits to explain personal differences. A sociological answer examines the relationships people have with others. Here individuality arises not from something internal, but rather from our external ties to others. A classic version of this idea sees the individual existing at the center of a "web of group affiliations" (Simmel 1908).

A modern variant is the sociograph. You can construct your own. Draw a small circle in the center of a piece of paper to symbolize you. Now draw spokes radiating out to other circles that represent the people in your life. Your relationships with those people differ in many ways: the length of time you have known them, the closeness or intensity of your bonds with them, and the like. Imagine drawing spokes in differing colors, thicknesses, or lengths to capture such nuances.

If you took this exercise seriously, the resulting sociograph would be different from those constructed by others. Sociographs illustrate how no two people occupy the same location in a web of group affiliations. Put differently, we all have unique locations in social networks.

A sociological perspective thus explains the uniqueness of individuals not by focusing inward on personal traits but rather by focusing outward on social networks. We differ from others because we occupy different locations in different networks. Even individuality is not "personal" as much as it is "social."

Take the exercise a step further. Imagine moving to some other circle in your sociograph and constructing that person's sociograph. Their web would include you and some people you know in common, but it would also include people who aren't in your web. Now imagine constructing a sociograph for everyone in your sociograph. As the number of spokes multiply exponentially, the circles representing individuals become less prominent than the ties linking them together. Indeed, the circles representing people come to look like fleeting interruptions in a flow of social forces and connections between them.

This imaginary exercise dramatizes how individuals don't exist apart from social ties with other individuals and groups. Moreover, individuality itself (even with its connotation of uniqueness) is best seen as a product of our distinctive ties with others rather than a purely personal set of traits.

In what follows, we explore how individual selves emerge through social processes. The exploration begins with C. H. Cooley's looking-glass self and proceeds to the synthesis of George Herbert Mead. We then examine symbolic interactionism and identity theory. The chapter closes with observations about how human beings are reflexive actors who bring self-awareness to every situation they encounter.

Cooley's Contributions

Charles Horton Cooley made two vital contributions to understanding how selves emerge through a social process. His work anticipates that of George Herbert Mead, who inspired the symbolic interactionist tradition, which remains sociology's best guide to unraveling questions about self and society.

The first of Cooley's (1998) contributions concerns the role of primary groups in social life. Primary groups involve intimate, face-to-face interaction with others. Within primary groups, we know others and are known to them as whole people, because our involvement is ongoing, all-inclusive, and central to our sense of self.

People also belong to secondary groups, but their connections to such groups are less personal, less intimate, more formal, and often shorter lived than with primary groups. In the sociograph you imagined a moment ago, your primary group consists of the people with whom you have the strongest (and often longest) bonds. They are probably the people closest to you in the sociograph. Farther away from you and your primary group, there are probably other nodes and networks that represent your secondary groups.

The vast majority of people begin their lives within a primary group of family members and perhaps others who are regarded as "family." For better or worse, whether "functional" or "dysfunctional," such familial primary groups are the first and most important social group through which most of us are socialized and develop a sense of self and individuality.

As our self develops, we venture out and join other groups. On the first day of school, we become members of a secondary group of other students. What might start as a frightening social encounter with strangers often develops into another primary group. As we come to know, interact, and play with the same circle of kids, we might form increasingly intimate bonds that become primary relationships.

In adolescence, such peer groups often become more primary and intimate than our family groups. When young people feel as if their friends understand them in ways their parents no longer do (and when parents feel the same way), it is a good indication of multiple primary ties (and tension between them). A more intense emotional tie might then arise, as a romantic partner displaces both the peer group and the family. And somewhat later, we might marry one of those partners and begin a family that will become our next primary group.

Throughout the life cycle, our web of group affiliations consists of shifting combinations of primary and secondary groups. But primary groups remain central to who we are. Our sense of self is intimately connected to these groups. In somewhat different sociological language, primary groups are crucial reference groups; we refer ourselves to these groups to judge who we are, what to do, how to act, and where to find validation for the people we have become. For all these reasons, our webs are held together by our thickest social ties to primary groups.

Cooley's second major contribution is his notion of the self, which is closely tied to primary groups. The key point is simply that there is no self or individual apart from our relationships with other people. "From Cooley's vantage point, then, the self is a social product, a product 'produced' largely in the primary group. It is a product best labeled a 'looking-glass self', in that a child obtains an identity only with the realization that his or her picture, idea or image of himself or herself 'reflects' other people's picture of him or her" (Reynolds 2003, 63–64).

Imagination is crucial to Cooley's notion of the self. To say that we live in an imaginary world sounds like a put-down. But imagining involves basic processes of thought and cognition; to imagine is to think about the world, about people in the world, about our impressions of them, and about their impressions of us. In this sense, we inevitably live in an imaginary world, because we routinely try to understand the world by thinking about it. These processes are central to how we construct, maintain, or undermine our sense of self and identity.

When we combine primary groups and imagination, we can see the logic in Cooley's "looking-glass self." A crucial part of our imaginary lives involves speculation about the thoughts of others. The thoughts of others, in turn, contain impressions about who we are (and we're pretty disappointed if they don't). It is through this interactive process that we arrive at our sense of self.

This self has three components. First, we imagine how we appear to others. Second, we imagine how they evaluate our appearances. Finally, we construct a sense of self, based on our imaginary understanding of how others evaluate us (Reynolds 2003, 64). Put more succinctly: I am who I think you think I am.

Although the term *looking-glass* sounds quaint, the metaphor of a mirror still makes the point. Without others to reflect who we are back to us, we would have no reliable means of arriving at a sense of self. Common sense might dismiss this as "imaginary," but sociological insight says that this is all we have to base a self on.

We can even dispense with the metaphor. We use real mirrors when we want to assess, modify, or repair our physical appearance. The mirror is essential to get outside ourselves and see ourselves from the perspective of other people. In parallel fashion, our self only becomes known to us through the perspective of other people.

Cooley claimed we also develop strong, emotional responses to the selves that we construct through the looking-glass process. The emotions Cooley regarded as most central were pride and shame. When our judgments of others' judgments about us suggest we are viewed positively, then our self incorporates pride in who we are. When our judgments of others' judgments about us suggest we are viewed negatively, then our self incorporates shame about who we are. For Cooley, the looking-glass self was as much about emotional responses as cognitive processes (Scheff 2005).

Popular culture often tells people to "be positive" and "feel good about themselves," as if this could be accomplished by sheer will. More sociologically informed advice would say surround yourself with people who are positive about and feel good about you. Easier said than done, but if Cooley is right, our self-feelings do not arise on their own and cannot long exist in contradiction to the feelings we imagine others have about who we are.

Mead's Synthesis

Building on the work of Cooley and others, George Herbert Mead formulated a distinct perspective on self and society. Mead wrote little but was a gifted lecturer at the University of Chicago. Upon his retirement and death in 1931, his students assembled his ideas into a sociological classic titled *Mind, Self and Society* (Mead 1934).

Mead's work synthesized ideas prevalent in late nineteenth- and early twentieth-century social thought. Georg Simmel's web of group affiliations is one element. So is Max Weber's insistence that we can only understand social action if we see it from the perspective of the actor. Cooley's looking-glass self plays an obvious role. William James had also studied the social self. Mead also drew on the work of John Dewey, who approached mind not as a physical structure but as a process of interpretation and meaning. Finally, W. I. Thomas had discussed the "definition of the situation" and demonstrated that situations defined as real will be real in their consequences. The imagery of social actors imposing definitions on the world around them and acting on those definitions was central to Mead's work.

Mead's synthesis put him at odds with other sociological approaches. Many versions of sociology analyze social structures as static entities, but Mead saw society as a dynamic process of change and fluidity. For Mead, the social world is less like still pictures and more like a movie playing at multiple frames per second. Moreover, although some versions of sociology explain the world through casual relationships of independent and dependent variables, Mead saw social elements as interrelated and interdependent. Each part gained its meaning from its relationship to others and to the whole, so it is difficult to isolate elements that can be analyzed as cause and effect.

Having said that, Mead is clearly in the sociological camp by recognizing that society precedes and shapes the individual. Although grammatically awkward, a more conceptually accurate title for Mead's book might have been "Society, Mind, Self and Society," to suggest the priority of society as a social environment in which minds and selves develop in individuals who only then become competent social actors.

Mead's exploration of minds and selves develops some of the core ideas of interactionist sociology. The first challenge is to understand the development of individual minds. Mead's concern is not with the physical structure of the brain but with the social process of the mind. The focus is not neurons and synapses but rather consciousness and meaning.

Mead begins with behaviorist logic but quickly moves from static psychological behaviorism to symbolic social psychology. He defines a gesture as any action that serves as a stimulus and provokes a response. The response becomes a stimulus for the initial actor who then responds to it, which in turn becomes a new stimulus for the second actor. In this way, a conversation of gestures is an interactive spiral of stimuli and response between two or more actors.

Whereas behaviorists applied this logic to all human behavior, Mead thought conversations of gestures were primarily found in the nonhuman animal world (which is the basis for much behaviorist research going all the way back to Pavlov's salivating dogs). Such nonhuman animal behavior is largely rooted in instincts, meaning that animals are pre-wired to act in certain ways and do not rely on symbolic interpretations to do so. Mead's favorite example was a dogfight in which the behavior of each dog becomes a stimulus provoking an instinctive response in the other dog, leading to an escalation of barking, snarling, flattened ears, bared teeth, biting, and the like.

Mead departed from behaviorism by arguing that the vast majority of human action—and certainly the most sociologically interesting action—could not be understood as instinctual, unthinking patterns of stimulus and response. Humans differ from other animals because they formulate, interpret, and attribute *meaning* to actions and to people in their environment. This is why a boxing match is very different from a dogfight. Unlike dogs, boxers interpret, imagine, anticipate, and deceive as part of their strategy. It is this complex mental world—even in the brutality of the boxing ring—that qualitatively distinguishes human *action* from animal *behavior*.

To capture human action, Mead proposed different terminology. In contrast to the simple gestures of animals, human interaction involves significant symbols. Simple gestures become significant symbols when they meet two requirements. First, they carry a specific meaning.

Second, that meaning is shared within some community of people. Although this might sound obtuse, the best example is right here on the page. Human languages are vast collections of significant symbols known as words, which in turn can be put together in larger, meaningful units like phrases, sentences, paragraphs, and even books. Physical gestures (handshakes, applause, the finger) can also be significant symbols if they carry a specific, shared meaning.

Significant symbols arise from interaction, because it is only through interaction that they achieve significance. Consider that the meaning is in the response. If you utter a phrase that elicits immediate recognition, the odds are it is a significant symbol that carries the same meaning for others as it does for you. If your phrase is met with a blank stare, the odds are it's not a significant symbol, because it is not calling up a similar meaning in those around you.

Here's a simple example. I live with a cat that freaks out when someone rings the doorbell. After an especially traumatic episode, I tried a stopgap measure of taping a small piece of paper over the doorbell. To me, the paper meant "don't ring the doorbell—knock instead." The next day, a delivery person rang the doorbell (traumatizing the cat). The day after that, someone selling something I didn't need rang the doorbell (further traumatizing the cat). Neither person interpreted the paper over the doorbell in the way I intended. It was not a significant symbol, because there was no shared meaning between me and my visitors. The day after that, a neighbor came to borrow something and gently knocked on the door. In this instant, the piece of paper became a significant symbol, because she assigned the same meaning to it that I did and acted accordingly. She did so because she had also tried to keep people from ringing her doorbell and disturbing her child's afternoon nap.

The simple example illustrates several larger points. Significant symbols are not static; they emerge through interaction only when it becomes evident that people assign the same meaning to some part of their environment. Moreover, what is a significant symbol to some people might not be a significant symbol to other people. This is most obvious when speakers of different languages attempt to communicate; it is a struggle to find even a minimal set of significant symbols so they can understand one another. But even within the same language group, there are subcultures of people who speak distinctive sublanguages known to them but not to outsiders. Indeed, the identity of many subcultures depends precisely on who "gets it" (that is, shares their significant symbols) and who doesn't have a clue. The abbreviations and shortcuts that comprise the vocabulary of texting (well understood by those who text and often impenetrable to those who don't) is merely a recent example of this long-standing aspect of human communication.

This demonstrates the social roots of individual minds. Here's the logic. "Mind" is shorthand for the process of thinking, involving consciousness and meaning. Thinking is really an internalized conversation of significant symbols. The focus of our thought could be anything: how to spend the weekend, whether we should call an elderly relative, pondering the motivation behind a friend's snide comment, or whatever. Regardless of the topic, to think is to have a silent conversation with oneself about that topic. Whereas interaction is an externalized conversation of significant symbols with others, thinking is an internalized conversation of significant symbols with ourselves.

Mead implies we cannot think without significant symbols; they are the building blocks of the internalized conversations that compose thinking. But if the symbols that comprise thinking are significant, this means they carry a shared meaning. Such shared meanings can only arise from interactions with others. The conclusion seems obvious: Humans are born with a physical brain but not a social mind. Minds are only acquired through social interaction with others. That social process provides us with the shared meanings of the significant symbols that allow us to think. When it comes to minds—as with so much else—we must first be social before we can be individual. Sociologically speaking, socialization makes us human by developing the capacities that distinguish us as a species.

Mead's argument might seem convoluted, but it resonates with common sense. Imagine encountering someone on a city street who is babbling incomprehensibly. What conclusions do we draw about their mental state? Now imagine that people who speak this person's language appear, and they have an animated discussion in Norwegian about how to find the subway station. We are likely to revise our opinion of their mental state when we recognize that they share meanings and a language with a group of people (just not us). But if no one ever comes along who understands our urban babbler, we are likely to conclude that they have "lost their mind." Even everyday language links making sense, shared meanings, and having a mind.

For Mead, the distinctive qualities of human interaction emerge from our ability to create, learn, and communicate significant symbols. They allow us to interpret stimuli and respond in meaningful ways. They allow us to develop abstract concepts that go beyond immediate experience and classify experiences into categories. This allows imaginative reflection on past experiences and future possibilities rather than learning only through trial and error. In the end, this makes intelligent action possible, as we use significant symbols, shared meanings, and abstract concepts to learn from the past, interpret the present, anticipate the future, and link them all together.

If minds only emerge through a social process, the same is true for selves. We are not born with a self but rather acquire one through socialization. Cooley's looking-glass self is an early statement of this position, and Mead builds on it.

The self has two components; one is there from the beginning. The "I" refers to impulses to act toward the world. This inborn "I" is later joined by a socialized "Me" to form a fully developed social self. Selves thereby involve interaction between the "I" and the "Me."

Although the impulses of the "I" are channeled by the socialization of the "Me," it never disappears. The "I" persists as an active subject; it is the part of us that acts in the moment. The persistence of the "I" even in the mature self means that people are always capable of spontaneous, creative, unpredictable actions. The self is never completely determined by larger social forces, because we always retain the capacity to act back upon those forces.

To have a self means to see oneself as an object. It is the capacity to be self-aware or self-conscious. The "I" can never achieve such awareness because it is always acting in the moment. It is the "Me" that provides this self-awareness. The "Me" only develops through "taking the role of the other." This is Mead's version of Cooley's looking-glass self. The underlying idea is quite similar: We arrive at a sense of self by imaginatively taking the role of other people in our social environment.• From their perspective, we are an object in their world. When we imaginatively adopt their perspective, we are able to see ourselves as an object. We develop self-awareness.

•Once again we must be social before we can be individual. Until we interact with others whose roles we imaginatively take, we cannot develop a concept of ourselves as an object. We need others whose roles we take to provide the mirrors that tell us that we have a self and who we are. Immersion in sustained interaction with others is the only way we develop a mind and a self; it is the way we become human.

To have a self is to be capable of observations, judgments, and feelings about the self that only become possible by taking the role of the other. If we act in ways that surprise others (and ourselves), this demonstrates the capacity of the "I" to act in novel ways. If we explain such action by saying "I'm not myself today," we are displaying a fully developed self. The statement is logically ludicrous but sociologically sensible. We are saying that some momentary action is inconsistent with a well-established sense of who we are based on a long process of role taking. Only the "Me" can offer such observations about the self.

The "Me" is thus the perspective of others internalized by the self. The "Me" is a developmental product of interaction that emerges in stages. As infants in the pre-play stage, we are incapable of getting outside ourselves and taking the role of others. Infants are all "I" and no "Me." As young children, however, we begin to develop both a mind and the ability to take the role of the other. In the play stage, we take the role of significant others in our social environment. These are specific people who are familiar to us. As we play, we model their behavior and imaginatively see the world from their perspective. This is the earliest version of seeing ourselves as an object; by imaginatively seeing ourselves through the eyes of our parents or primary caretakers, we begin to develop a sense of self.

As we become more skilled at role taking, we enter the game stage and simultaneously take the roles of multiple others in more complex situations. The famous example is playing baseball, but any team sport will do. To play such games well, each player must anticipate the actions of everyone else on the team. By anticipating their actions in different situations, good players align their actions to fit with overall team strategy. Such game playing presupposes an ability to take multiple roles that only emerges over time. This is why young children can handle some interactive play but are incapable of more complex team games.

As we progress from taking the role of significant others to multiple others, we eventually take the role of the generalized Other. This is not a particular person or group but rather the larger society and its norms and values. Returning to Cooley's language, the development of the self proceeds by switching mirrors. As very young children, it is particular, significant others who provide the mirror that tells us who we are. As older children, it is multiple others who provide that mirror. As socialization continues, the mirror becomes all of the attitudes, values, and beliefs that compose our society itself. The constant is that we look outside ourselves to know who we are. The variable is which "others" are most central in reflecting our self back to us.

The ability to take the role of the generalized Other signals a fully developed self. This "Other" is initially outside us, but it becomes incorporated inside us in the form of the "Me." The mature self combines the acting "I" and the socialized "Me." Because the self requires a "Me" and the "Me" requires taking the role of the other, the self only emerges through social interaction with others.

The development of mind and self go hand in hand. The internal conversation that comprises the mind can only occur with a corresponding self-awareness that signifies a self. Both emerge through interaction with others that provides shared meanings and role-taking opportunities. Although later sociologists have pursued many variations on these themes, Mead's synthesis provides a vital sociological understanding of the relationship between self and society.

..Symbolic Interactionism

Mead's student Herbert Blumer took the lead in publishing Mead's (1934) ideas. Blumer also coined the term *symbolic interactionism* to underscore the importance of symbolic meanings in interpreting human action. The phrase sounds awkward, but conveys much about the assumptions of this approach.

Blumer (1969) subsequently claimed that symbolic interactionism could be summarized in three basic premises. The first is that human beings act toward things on the basis of the meanings things have for them. What is important is not the things but rather the meanings that we (and others) attach to them.

This seemingly subtle distinction makes a big difference. Consider the contrast between psychological behaviorism and symbolic interactionism. Behaviorists explain what we do as responses to stimuli in the environment. The environment determines behavior by providing stimuli that mechanistically lead us to seek rewards and avoid punishments. The stimuli, response, rewards, and punishments are assumed to be transparently self-evident to both the organism and the behaviorist. There is no need to explore the subjective "black box" of the mind; behaviorism rather seeks an external explanation linking behavioral responses to environmental stimuli.

This makes sense if people respond directly to things. It makes much less sense if they respond to the meanings of things, as Blumer claims. Interactionism sees action as a process of self-indication. Actors select which aspects of their environment are meaningful for them. Because they assign meanings to their surroundings, it could be said that actors determine their environment rather than the other way around. Because meanings vary across persons and situations, we must examine how minds shape meanings. Interactionism thereby seeks an internal explanation of action by linking minds, meanings, and actions.

The first premise establishes that meanings are central. The second is that meanings are derived from social interaction. This locates meanings between two polar opposites. They are not purely objective qualities attached to things in the same way in all times and places. But they are also not purely subjective choices of individuals outside interaction. Meanings are rather intersubjective accomplishments of social interaction. Like Mead's significant symbols, objects acquire meanings as a result of ongoing social interaction.

This premise explains variability in the meanings of objects over time and across groups. Why do people disagree about the appropriateness of Indian mascots for sports teams? How do people interpret the meaning of the Civil War in the South and the North? What does the word *gay* mean to different generations of people? When is graffiti a marker of gang affiliation, and when is it art? What does it mean to have a tattoo or a piercing? Such meanings are not fixed and objective; neither are they purely subjective and idiosyncratic. It is interactions in different groups that define the "same event" like the Civil War as a humiliating defeat or a glorious victory. Both meanings are "true" in different social worlds that sustain those definitions through interaction.

The variability of meanings reflects the pragmatist heritage of symbolic interaction in which things acquire meaning by how they are used or how people interact with them. Thus, a tree has different meanings and becomes a different object for the botanist, the timber company, and the poet. Take another example. A woman nursing an infant is interacting in a way that defines her breasts as nourishment and nurturance. That same woman making love with her sexual partner is interacting in a way that defines her breasts as erotic stimulation and gratification. That same woman undergoing an exam by her doctor is engaged in an interaction that defines her breasts as potential sites of disease and malignancy. Same woman, same breasts—but drastically different meanings arise from different interactions with different people.

The ways that interactions create and sustain meanings also establish the definition of the situation. Such definitions are intersubjective, cultural creations that provide cues about what to expect and how to behave in a given situation. Differing definitions of the situation create different meanings in "objectively" similar situations. A woman who bares her breast in public to nurse her infant might meet with acceptance, whereas a woman who does so in a strip joint might be condemned or even arrested (depending on local ordinances). A male doctor examining a female patient is engaging in behavior that could be construed as sexual assault in other settings, but is regarded as normal as long as the medical definition of the situation is maintained.

Blumer's third and final premise is that meanings are handled and modified through an interpretive process. This means that even when meanings are well established (and especially when they are not), people still tailor them to the specific situation at hand. This work begins with the process of self-indication in which people "create" their environment on the basis of intersubjective meanings.

The process continues because no two situations are exactly the same and general meanings must be adapted to specific settings. People are active throughout this process. "The actor selects, checks, suspends, regroups, and transforms the meanings in the light of the situation in which he is placed" (Blumer 1969, 5). This process of interpretation is a formative one in which meanings are used, revised, and modified as the actor fashions action that will be meaningful to all concerned.

Blumer's formulation of symbolic interactionism puts it at odds not only with psychological behaviorism but also with more structural approaches in sociology. Blumer insists that concepts like structure, system, function, or institution are really shorthand abstractions for people interacting with one another. Although the shorthand is convenient, it becomes a trap when we speak as if these abstractions act or even exist apart from the interactions that sustain them. For Blumer, good sociology avoids structuralist abstractions by focusing on the meanings and interactions that create, sustain, and modify social patterns.

Identity Theory

Interactionist theory provides sociology with its best understandings of identity. The starting point is that the self is the ability to see oneself as an object, evidenced by self-awareness or self-consciousness. This awareness originally emerges from, and subsequently depends on, interactions with other people.

We move from self to identity by asking what kind of object we see ourselves to be. If self is the object, identity is the meanings attached to that object. Identity emerges when meanings are attached to the object we call the self.

Blumer's first premise is that it is not objects but their meanings that are important. This applies to identity as follows. Everybody acquires a self. We couldn't interact with people if they didn't have a self through which to organize interaction. What is of interest in interactions is not the generic selves everyone possesses, but the particular identities or meanings of those selves. This is how we identify ourselves and others; who people are is a function of the meanings or identities linked to selves.

Blumer's second premise is that meanings arise through interactions with others. They are intersubjective accomplishments. The same applies to the meanings we call identities. Just as Mead's symbols become significant when they call up the same meaning in others as they do in us, identities become real when there is a shared understanding about who someone is. "One's identity is established when others *place* him as a social object by assigning him the same words of identity that he appropriates for himself or *announces*. It is in the coincidence of placements and announcements that identity becomes a meaning of the self" (Gregory Stone, cited in Vryan, Adler, and Adler 2003, 368; italics in original).

Take an extreme example. I might believe, and then announce to the world, that I am the second coming of Christ. If I persist in this claim, I will be dismissed as a nutcase. If I convince a small band of devoted followers of my claim, we will all be dismissed as mentally unstable (but perhaps dangerous because of our numbers). But if I somehow convince hundreds, then thousands, and finally millions of people around the world of my identity claim, and they relate to me as if I am that person, then don't I become that person? If my announcements and others' placements concur, does that not become my identity? In less extreme cases, the process is clear: identity emerges when an actor's announcements and others' placements coincide.

Blumer's third premise is that meanings are handled and modified through an interpretive process as people tailor meanings to fit specific situations. Applied to identity, this means that we continually reinterpret, select, check, regroup, suspend, and transform our understandings of who we and others are as part of ongoing interaction. For example, we understand that people (including ourselves) have different identities in different situations. When we encounter them in a certain situation, we selectively present some of our identities and expect them to do the same. If everyone enacts identities appropriate to the situation, interaction will proceed smoothly.

Each of Blumer's premises about meaning thus applies to identity itself. Interactionism also distinguishes several types of identities, including social, situational, and personal identities (Vryan, Adler, and Adler 2003, 367–372).

Social identities arise when we announce and others place us in positions within social structures. Identities based on class, race, gender, religion, or sexual orientation exemplify social identities. They are broad social categories that link us to others with similar traits and separate us from those with different traits. Social identities shape how people are enabled or constrained by social order; differing opportunities emerge from the statuses granted to or withheld from these identities.

Situational identities arise when we engage in face-to-face interactions with others and organize our action through situationally appropriate roles and definitions of the situation. Although they might be repetitive and patterned, situations are relatively short-lived. When we attend a baseball game, we become a fan; when we go on vacation, we become a tourist; when we leave for work, we become a motorist or commuter. We thus acquire a situational identity in a particular context. The ways we enact this identity are constrained by cultural norms and situational definitions, but there is always room for some individual creativity in enacting situational identities.

Personal identities arise when we construct biographical narratives about who we are. They distinguish us from others in the same positions or situations. Thus, part of my story is that when I was an undergraduate, I made my living (and more) as a drummer in a rock-and-roll band. Even though I stopped playing when I went to graduate school more than thirty-five years ago, it is part of who I am, because it is who I once was. Moreover, it helps establish my distinctiveness: not many college professors are former rock drummers, and not many rock drummers become college professors (and it's probably just as well that they don't).

Situational identities like baseball fan, grocery shopper, or wedding party member are short-lived and don't necessarily reveal much about who we are. Social identities are more permanent because they are difficult or impossible to change, although people can either embrace them or hold them at arms' length. Personal identities are more lasting in a different way, because they rest on a person's accumulated biography. Although we can distinguish different types of identity, the basic principles of identity theory still apply. Identities of all types are meanings attached to the self that emerge through announcements by self and placements by others.

Like all meanings, identities are socially constructed, maintained, and transformed. Most identity transformations are gradual, developmental transitions through the life cycle.

Even though parenthood or retirement might feel sudden to the individual, they are routine in that they happen to many people and it is possible to anticipate and plan for them in advance. Other, less common identity transformations are quick and radical in nature. When prisoners of war are brainwashed, when people undergo a conversion experience, or when individuals are radicalized by extremist websites, they might renounce former identities and embrace dramatically different ones very quickly.

Another type of identity transformation involves "suspended identity" (Schmid and Jones 1991). This occurs when people must leave one identity behind while adopting another identity. If they intend to reclaim their former identity, it is not so much terminated or transformed as it is suspended. It's as if they hang that identity in the closet until they can wear it once again. When citizen soldiers are called up as army reservists or National Guard troops, they suspend their citizen identity and adopt a soldier identity. Unlike regular army troops, however, they are likely to see their citizen identity as the "real" one, which is temporarily suspended during military duty.

A classic case is people who go to prison. Before going to prison, people have a "pre-prison identity." Like the civilian anticipating becoming a soldier, these citizens anticipate becoming a prisoner as they move through the criminal justice system. A common response is self-insulation by minimizing contact with others, avoiding conflict or violence, and avoiding any situations that might undermine their preprison identity.

Despite these resolutions, inmates cannot take their pre-prison identity with them, nor can they live in complete isolation. They have to create a prison identity to relate to staff, guards, and other prisoners. Short-term inmates see this prison identity as temporary and situational, although they worry that it might displace their pre-prison identity. While serving time, inmates experience a dualistic self. They try to sustain a pre-prison identity, which is temporarily suspended, privately held, and rarely affirmed. They simultaneously enact a prison identity, which is self-consciously learned, enacted for self and others, and affirmed through prison interactions.

Toward the end of their sentence, prisoners develop a release identity that sets aside their prison identity and revives their suspended identity. Like earlier stages, this involves much self-talk about who they really are, how they might have changed, and how they can become the person they used to be. Upon leaving prison, former inmates acquire a post-prison identity that distances them from their prison experience and helps restore their suspended identity (Schmid and Jones 1991).

Prison thereby poses a particular identity challenge. Although most of us will not go to prison, all of us undergo processes of identity formation, maintenance, and transformation. Interactionist theory provides powerful tools for understanding them.

People as Reflexive Actors

Interactionist theory underscores how human action is guided by reflexivity. People are conscious of the meanings of selves, others, and objects in their world, and they use this knowledge to organize actions and pursue goals. The premise of reflexivity is shared by other theoretical perspectives as well.

As we saw in Chapter One, there is a debate in sociology over the relationship between structure and agency. Structure-based approaches emphasize large social patterns that seem to dwarf individuals. Agency-based approaches stress individual choices and seem to deny the weight of external factors. Neither approach is completely satisfactory; the challenge is to strike a balance between the two.

One attempt is structuration theory (Giddens 1984). It rejects a view of structures as merely external and constraining forces that exist on their own. Rather than structures, it speaks of "structuration processes" as a way of linking structure and action. Here, structures are no more than the outcomes of past actions and the means for organizing current ones.

Seen this way, structuration processes sometimes constrain action because they are obstacles to what we want to do. But they can also enable action when they provide resources and means to pursue goals. Rather than seeing structures as external, controlling forces, we should see structuration processes as providing opportunities to act (within certain limits). Moreover, when people act, they unintentionally reproduce (and sometimes transform) those very structures.

This approach assumes people are reflexive actors. People in society "are vastly skilled in the practical accomplishments of social activities and are expert 'sociologists.' The knowledge they possess is not incidental to the persistent patterning of social life but integral to it" (Giddens 1984, 26). In other words, people routinely use practical consciousness in daily life to monitor their actions and the actions of others and to align both. This consciousness contains much practical knowledge about how things work in a particular society and culture.

People also incorporate sociological knowledge into practical consciousness; ideas like self-fulfilling prophecies, unintended consequences, or group-think have migrated from social science to everyday consciousness. It is difficult to appreciate the importance of this practical consciousness, because it becomes second nature once we're socialized. But if you've had any experiences with other cultures or languages that made you feel "dumb," it underscores how "smart" you are about your own culture and language and how unconsciously you call upon knowledge of it to do things.

Another way of describing reflexivity is sociological competence. "This seemingly native, highly practical, virtually ubiquitous capacity sustains us individually, but it also contributes mightily to our ability to form and keep social relations with others. Without it, social life would be impossible. Without it, every time we entered a new and different social situation, we would be forced to learn anew what to think of it and how to behave. But, most of the time, we understand what is going on and where we fit in" (Lemert 2008, 5). Like linguistic competence, sociological competence seems to be an inherent capacity to understand the social world. When it is matched with socialization, we use it in an almost effortless way.

Although acquiring sociological competence is *almost* effortless, it nonetheless requires practice. Charles Lemert (2008) draws on Pierre Bourdieu's (1977) notion of habitus to understand how sociological competence is sustained through practice. The concept of habitus underscores how much of social life involves habitual actions that once had to be learned but then became second nature—things that we do unthinkingly, and usually quite competently. Like Giddens's structuration, Bourdieu's habitus is where agency and structure meet and their seeming contradiction is resolved. Habitual practices simultaneously result from social rules (structures) and individual flourishes (agency) that produce action (Lemert 2008, 43).

From another angle, habitus is the intersection between actions experienced as novel by the individual while simultaneously conforming to social patterns. This is most evident when we first learn things that have yet to become habitual. The first time we drive a car, have a sexual encounter, or work at a job, the event is new to us but part of a larger pattern that happens in roughly similar ways for millions of people. The awkwardness that characterizes each of these original experiences demonstrates that these competencies must indeed be learned and practiced. At a certain point, driving, sex, or working are accomplished with much less awkwardness, signifying that we have learned and habitualized them. We have acquired sociological competence.

In everyday life, we focus on immediate concerns. We rely on sociological competence and acquired habits. It rarely occurs to us that our actions help sustain the society around us. Nonetheless, habitual actions performed by socially competent actors do precisely this. Giddens's structuration, Lemert's competence, and Bourdieu's habitus all point to the same conclusion. Social order rests upon the reflexivity of actors who use existing structures to do things while simultaneously (if unintentionally) sustaining, re-creating, and transforming those very structures. Without reflexivity, social order itself would be impossible.

Conclusion

Interactionist theory provides rich insights into mind, self, identity, and reflexivity. It is a good example of humanistic sociology. As such, it is critical in two ways. First, it is critical to an accurate understanding of the complex, dialectical connections between self and society, structure and agency, and micro and macro levels of society.

Second, it is critical by revealing that things are not always what they appear to be (Berger 1963). If we want to see beyond appearances to underlying realities, this theory is like a backstage pass in the theater of social life. Consider individualism one more time. As noted earlier, US culture is probably the most individualistic in human history. If any culture assumes we are individual before we are social, it is ours. Interactionist theory is thus critical to seeing all the ways we are unavoidably social before we can become individual (Lemert 2008).

The third sense of critical sociology explicitly examines power, domination, exploitation, and oppression. Here, interactionism has been largely silent. It critically examines US individualism, but it uncritically accepts US egalitarianism.

US culture has always emphasized its distance from European traditions, where rank, status, class, and distinction are crucial. US ideology describes a "classless" society where everyone gets a chance and no one is held back by artificial social barriers. Although not necessarily embracing these specific ideas, interactionism's image of society also downplays vertical hierarchies and emphasizes horizontal life-worlds. The interactionist image of society is multiple social worlds of distinctive meanings and identities coexisting alongside one another. It implicitly sees society as a pluralistic conglomeration of such worlds.

What is lacking in this image is the role of power in social life. Although it is true that different social worlds construct different meanings, it is also true that some worlds have the privilege and power to make their meanings normative while marginalizing others. The meanings central to interactionist theory are often hierarchically organized so that some groups benefit at the expense of others.

This is nicely captured in the notion of ideology as meaning in the service of power (Thompson 1990). Interactionism has provided a rich vocabulary for analyzing meanings in social life, but it will only reach its fully critical potential when it examines the relationships between meaning and power.

References

Berger, Peter. 1963. *Invitation to Sociology.* New York: Doubleday.

Blumer, Herbert. 1969. *Symbolic Interaction: Perspective and Method.* Englewood Cliffs, NJ: Prentice Hall.

Bourdieu, Pierre. 1977. *Outline of a Theory of Practice.* London: Cambridge University Press.

Cooley, Charles Horton. 1998. *On Self and Social Organization.* Chicago: University of Chicago Press.

Giddens, Anthony. 1984. *The Constitution of Society.* Berkeley: University of California Press.

Lemert, Charles. 2008. *Social Things.* 4th ed. Lanham, MD: Rowman & Littlefield.

Mead, George Herbert. 1934/1962. *Mind, Self and Society.* Chicago: University of Chicago Press.

Reynolds, Larry T. 2003. "Early Representatives." In *Handbook of Symbolic Interactionism,* ed. Larry T. Reynolds and Nancy J. Herman-Kinney, 59–81. Lanham, MD: AltaMira.

Scheff, Thomas. 2005. "Looking Glass Self: Goffman as Symbolic Interactionist." *Symbolic Interaction* 28(2):147–166.

Schmid, Thomas J., and Richard S. Jones. 1991. "Suspended Identity: Identity Transformation in a Maximum Security Prison." *Symbolic Interaction* 14(4):415–432.

Simmel, Georg. 1908/1955. *Conflict and the Web or Group Affiliations.* New York: Free Press.

Thompson, John. 1990. *Ideology and Modern Culture.* Stanford, CA: Stanford University Press.

Vryan, Kevin D., Patricia A. Adler, and Peter Adler. 2003. "Identity." In *Handbook of Symbolic Interactionism,* ed. Larry T. Reynolds and Nancy J. Herman-Kinney, 367–390. Lanham, MD: AltaMira.

Essentialism Versus Constructivism

Time for a Rapprochement?

Saskia Wieringa

There have been two waves of feminism and two sexual revolutions since the beginning of the twentieth century. The first one ended in and was drowned by the establishment of essentialism by the sexologists. The second one is still going on and has produced constructivism as the dominant paradigm by which to analyse sexuality.

The first wave of feminism is better known for its struggle for women's rights in the field of the vote, education and employment. That feminist women in those years also fought against what they saw as male sexual aggression is almost obliterated from memory. In Britain their campaigns were centred around the issue of "social purity", which included prostitution, traffic in women and abuse of girls. Male vice was seen to cause these problems, which resulted in what was at times dubbed "bodily slavery" of women. The sexologists, of whom Havelock Ellis was the best known, successfully deployed "natural sex" against feminism, by proclaiming the "scientific truth" of their findings.

There seems to be an unbridgeable rift between essentialism and constructivism or constructionism. If essentialism dominated the debate on "women's nature", human sexuality and human behaviour in general in the first sixty years of the twentieth century, present-day essentialists face heavy criticism. They are denounced as reactionary persons who attempt to continue women's subordination. When an argument is called "essentialist" no more discussion about the issue at stake is deemed necessary: doesn't essentialism mean that all women are seen as "natural" housewives and as masochists who delight in sexual humiliation?

No one wants to be regarded as such a backward person. Simone de Beauvoir's dictum that woman is made, not born, is generally regarded as the decisive blow against essentialism. And many more blows followed. Not women's nature but the construction of gender relations is the topic of the dominant type of research and debate. Yet, at the same time, specific rights for women are demanded. Women are seen as a distinct category, suffering from a special kind of subordination which requires specific policies and campaigns. Although feminists generally agree that there are wide differences between women in relation to class, race, ethnicity, sexual option and age, they still do talk about "women". What, then, *are* these "women"? What do women have in common? Only oppression? And what about their bodies, motherhood and sexuality?

The way sexuality has been conceptualized clearly demonstrates how far essentialism and constructivism diverge. Essentialist scientists have argued since the beginning of the twentieth century that women's sexual difference from men is the cause of women's oppression. Wittig takes an extreme constructivist position when she argues that oppression produces sexual difference.

In this chapter I explore the relations between these two positions. In so doing I suggest that we may need a *rapprochement* between the two. I argue that instead of resorting to an either/or position it may be most fruitful to find the interconnections between the two and where each of them can be most strategically deployed.

I first discuss essentialism, and stress that it arose partly in response to a strong feminist movement. Next I discuss the two major contributions to the unmasking of essentialist thought as it existed in the 1960s and 1970s: Foucault and the women's movement. In the conclusion I insist that although constructivism is a decisive step forward from essentialism, we should not completely denounce essentialism.

Essentialism

Essentialism arose in the first quarter of the twentieth century. The major theorists associated with this stream of thinking are Havelock Ellis, Kinsey, and Masters and Johnson. Although there are important differences between these three major sexologists, they are generally assumed to agree on the basic ideas of essentialism. They are presented as the ones who have liberated sexology from Victorian sexual repression. Admittedly, Victorian ideas about sexuality left a great deal to improve: a double morality (in which upper-class women, as opposed to men or working-class women, were seen as innocent beings who did not or at least should not know anything about sex), its class specificity and its legislative effects.[1] Essentialism is generally credited with "freeing" women as sexually active human beings.

But Havelock Ellis in particular, one of the major founding fathers of essentialism, waged his war not only against Victorian morality but also against the feminist movement of his day, with its strong critique of male domination. The feminists of his day were not only suffragists, they were also "spinsters", a term they carried proudly, rejecting and denouncing male sexual aggression. Around 1900 violent debates ensued against male violence, which, it was said, was used to control free women who refused these male ideas of sexuality. Sheila Jeffreys, in her excellent 1985 study of these debates, gives many examples of feminists who saw male sexuality as a weapon of male power. Elisabeth Wolstenholme Elmy, for instance, who worked alongside the radical suffragists Josephine Butler and Christabel Pankhurst and who founded her own Women's Emancipation Union in 1891, wrote in 1895, "[the Women's Emancipation Union] recognizes that the slavery of sex is the root of all slavery, and that injustice to womanhood, especially injustice within the family, is the perennial source of all other injustice ..." (Wolstenholme Elmy in Jeffreys 1985: 28).

Wolstenholme Elmy was also very active in a campaign surrounding the Criminal Code Bill, which was introduced in 1880. This bill aimed to embody in statute law the fact that a man could not rape his wife. She denounced this provision as an attempt to reduce wives to "bodily slavery" (Jeffreys 1985: 31). In fact, the struggle for the vote was seen by both men and women to be for the right of women to control their bodies and against the right of men to freely exercise their bodily lusts on women. As Christabel Pankhurst stated:

> The opposition argues thus: if women are to become politically free they will become spiritually strong and economically independent, and thus they will not any longer give or sell themselves to be the playthings for men. That, in a nutshell, is the case against votes for women. (Jeffreys 1985: 46)

Thus, feminists of the first wave did not see male sexual aggression as natural but as a weapon of male power.

In an attempt to counter these arguments, Ellis founded sexology as a science. Jackson, who has carefully studied Ellis's writings, concludes that he was seriously concerned about what he perceived to be the tendency of women to reject their maternal function and to "deny the laws of their own nature". Although he concedes that men were selfish and brutal lovers, he is confident that if they would engage in a more sophisticated "art of love", women would also get their own share of sexual pleasure. To this major task he vows to devote himself. He admits that this would be no mean task, with men behaving like "orangutan[s] playing the violin", yet he is confident of his success. He presents himself as the champion of women's erotic rights, for which he is regarded as adopting a progressive position (Jackson 1987: 56).

However, those erotic rights of women do not coincide with the ones that feminists like Wolstenholme Elmy advocated. As Jackson writes:

> For Ellis, then, every act of heterosexual intercourse was essentially a re-enactment of primitive, animal courtship; the male sexual urge was essentially an urge to conquer, and the female sexual urge an urge to be conquered: "The sexual impulse in woman is fettered by an inhibition which has to be conquered ... her wooer in every act of courtship has

the enjoyment of conquering afresh an oft-won woman." Thus the close association between male sexuality, power and violence was a biological necessity and therefore inevitable: "to exert power ... is one of our most primary impulses, and it always tends to be manifested in the attitude of a man towards the woman he loves". (1987: 57)

Jackson continues that Ellis tries to prove that "women 'really enjoy' being raped, beaten and sexually humiliated and brutalized. He concluded that in women pain and sexual pleasure were virtually indistinguishable" (Jackson 1987: 57).

It is no wonder, then, that feminists of the present wave of the women's movement denounced these ideas of a man who became the founding father of modern sex research and one of the major exponents of essentialism. The more so as Ellis clearly set his ideas up as the scientific proof to discredit feminist ideas of his time. Jackson again provides the relevant quotation:

I am well aware that in thus asserting a certain tendency in women to delight in suffering pain—however careful and qualified the position I have taken—many estimable people will cry out that I am degrading a whole sex and generally supporting the "subjection of women". But the day for academic discussion concerning the "subjection of women" has gone by. The tendency I have sought to make clear is too well established by the experience of normal and typical women—however numerous the exceptions may be—to be called into question. I would point out to those who would deprecate the influence of such facts in relation to social progress that nothing is gained by regarding women as simply men of smaller growth. They are not so: they have the laws of their own nature; their development must be along their own lines, and not along masculine lines. It is as true now as in Bacon's day that we only learn to command nature by obeying her ... We can neither attain a sane view of life nor a sane social legislation of life unless we possess a just and accurate knowledge of the fundamental instincts upon which life is built. (Ellis in Jackson 1987: 57–58)

As Ellis and his followers apparently were not fully convinced that the "academically accurate laws of nature" that they had "discovered" were equally clear to women, they proceeded to produce sex manuals. One of the most influential marriage manuals was the one by Van de Velde, first published in English in 1928. It became enormously influential: by the late 1970s over a million copies had been sold. Based on Ellis's ideas, the book set out to "teach wives not only how to behave in coitus, but, above all, how and what to feel in this unique act" (Van de Velde in Jackson 1987: 59). ⌐SEXUAL INTERCOURSE

Sexual disharmony was seen as the root cause of marital discord, threatening the basis of modern society. In order to avert this evil, members of the medical profession, psychoanalysts, took it upon themselves to teach women and men the proper laws of nature. One of the major tasks to which they devoted themselves was to eroticize women's submission to men and to teach men how to give their women pleasure in this sexual order. The final reward would be sexual bliss. A last quote from Van de Velde:

> woman is a harp who only yields her secrets of melody to the master who knows how to handle her ... the husband must study the harp and the art of music ... this is the book of rules for his earnest and reverend study ... his reward comes when the harp itself is transformed into an artist in melody, entrancing the initiator. (Van de Velde in Jackson 1987: 62)

A far cry indeed from the autonomous sexuality, free from male domination, for which the feminists of those days fought. The sex manuals were particularly directed against the spectre of lesbianism. As another writer of a well-known sex manual wrote:

> If a married woman does this unnatural thing she may find a growing disappointment in her husband and he may lose all natural power to play his proper part ... No woman who values the peace of her home and the love of her husband should yield to the wiles of the lesbian whatever her temptation to do so. (Cited in Jeffreys 1985: 120)

Yet, despite the tremendous efforts to educate women to "yield their secrets of melody to the hands of the master", many refused to do so. The problem of the frigid woman was widely discussed and generally seen as a sign of resistance, generated by feminism.

Writing a few decades later, Kinsey and Masters and Johnson, although allowing a much greater space for women's sexual desires and the role of the clitoris, did not depart very far from the basics established by Ellis.

Characteristics and Limitations of Essentialism

Essentialism takes as its starting point a position that human behaviour is "natural", predetermined by genetic, biological and physiological mechanisms which are essentially the same in all humans and only need to be uncovered by science. These mechanisms are not subject to change.

Second, it posits a polarity between "female" and "male", which is seen as "natural". In this "natural" order man is the hunter and woman the hunted. Third, sexual desire is seen as a basic, biological drive, which demands satisfaction. If the dominant male sexual drive is denied outlet, men will resort to illegitimate methods such as rape and the abuse of girls. Thus, it is biology which urges men to become rapists. If, on the other hand, women are denied their "normal" sexual lives, they may become neurotic. Fourth, heterosexuality is seen as the only "natural" mode of sexuality; all other forms of sexuality are seen as perversions. An aggressive male model of sexuality is deemed to be the most "natural" way to behave sexually for human beings. Fifth, essentialism leads directly to biological determinism, the belief that biology is destiny. This line of thinking rests on the premise that women's subordination and masochism are "natural", as is male aggression, and that women are "naturally" better homemakers, peacekeepers and environmental managers, while men are better politicians, industrial producers and polluters.

Essentialism also feeds the assumption that forms of human behaviour which show some similarity are the same, the expressions of underlying biological drives or tendencies. This belief has fed many research projects into the "causes" of sexual behaviour. For instance, the following question is often asked; is it hormones, genes, or a variation in the human brain which causes human homosexuality? Thus, essentialist scientists are unable to account for cultural and transhistorical variations. In their explanations for sexual behaviour they always remain within the medicobiological debate. A consequence of this line of thinking is that sexual behaviour which was characterized as a sexual perversion (such as homosexuality) could eventually be cured, either medically or with psychiatric treatment. Or, alternatively, that it could be prevented (by teaching boys to become "real men" and girls to follow their "true nature").

Last of all, the only sexual act which essentialists regard as "natural" for both sexes is intercourse, copulation. Thus the primacy of the penis is established for both sexes. Even Kinsey and Masters and Johnson, who located the site of female pleasure in the clitoris, end up, in their final analysis, with the penis as the major sexual organ for both women and men. Masters and Johnson went to great pains to demonstrate that penile thrusting indirectly stimulates the clitoris. Miller and Fowlker point out that although Kinsey found higher orgasmic achievement among committed lesbians compared to married women, he nevertheless propagated heterosexuality for women: "Kinsey the zoologist told us that lesbianism was an attractive, adult alternative; Kinsey the moralist moved discussion to 'moral restraints' and magical phalluses" (Miller and Fowlker 1980: 268).

Yet, despite its limitations, I suggest that essentialism does have some positive points as well. If essentialism is stripped of its biological determinism and its heavily biased, sexist and racist moral statements, the following fundamental issues emerge. In the first place essentialism did open up the area of sexuality for scientific research. With the feminist movement (which it attacked so vehemently), it lifted the taboo on female sexuality which existed in the Victorian era in the West. Although Foucault (1978) demonstrated that sexuality, far from being simply repressed in the Victorian era (as the sexologists claimed), was sustained in a particular regime of power-knowledge-pleasure, bourgeois women especially were socialized to control their sexuality. Since the intervention of the sexologists valuable research has been carried out which should not be dismissed lightly. Biology and medical research do have important views to add to the debate on sexuality. Second, essentialism does have political weight. The finding that homosexuality is just one biological variation among others provides a strong argument against legal restrictions of homosexuality.[2] Likewise, the argument that women by their "nature" need special policies to give them "normal" rights is a strong feminist weapon which is heard in a wide variety of feminist settings. These were considered "special" as against male rights, which were viewed as the norm. I will return to these arguments after a discussion of constructivism.

Constructivism

Since the end of the 1960s essentialism and biological determinism have been heavily attacked from various sides. The French philosopher Foucault with his theories on power and discourse, the women's movement with its attack on patriarchy, and especially the black women's movement with its insistence on diversity, as well as the gay movement with its exposure of the medicalization of homosexuality, combined to discredit essentialism. A new body of theories arose which, in all its diversity, generally became known under the name of "constructivism".

This theoretical approach is characterized by the following insights. In the first place it does not conceptualize sexuality as a medicobiological phenomenon but stresses that it is mediated by historical and cultural factors. That is, constructivist theorists reject transhistorical and transcultural definitions of sexuality, and instead stress that sexual behaviour is the fluid and changeable product of human action in its historically determined forms. Thus, sexuality is seen not as the invariant result of the body, biology or an innate sex drive, but as the product of sociohistorical variables.

Second, the constructivist debate on sexuality and human behaviour no longer takes place within medicobiological circles but in the fields of social enquiry and linguistics. This paradigm shift has led to novel questions about differences between women and men and sexuality, challenging widely held assumptions about human behaviour.[3] The constructivist vocabulary has dumped the words "normal" and "natural" in relation to sexuality and relations between women and men.

In the last place, constructivism has an enormous political advantage. By showing how certain forms of behaviour, certain norms and certain institutions have been historically constituted, the constructivist analysis implicitly leads to debates on transformation. That which has been historically constructed can be politically deconstructed.

In the following paragraphs I will briefly chart some of the major contributions to constructivist thought, focusing on the contribution of the women's movement to the debate. As many feminist writings of the last decades have been influenced by Foucault, I will start by introducing some of the elements of his thinking which are relevant for this discussion.

Foucault's intention was to understand the discourses around certain themes, the "ritualized stories which entire societies have in common" and which shape or constitute human thought and behaviour.[4] Deconstructing the history of sexuality, he concludes that sexuality should not be seen as constituted by an uncontrollable biological urge or innate drive, but as a form of behaviour and thought which is malleable by power relations, which are employed in the interests of other ends than sexuality itself (Foucault 1978).

Using Foucault's own instruments against him, I have various problems with his theories, however fascinating and insightful they are. My major hesitation arises from the fact that Foucault only talks about the male body and male sexuality. Where does his androcentrism come from? If we see Foucault as a person who is also the product of his time and space, can we ask what his interest is in neglecting women?[5] Would it be possible for a female philosopher to so exclude women, and to so stress the social in relation to sexuality? It is striking indeed that in his analysis of the serologists he does not refer to their opposition against feminism as one of the motivations from which they worked. Why does he sociologize sexuality to such an extent that the biological dimension is virtually excluded from analysis? And then, by focusing on male sexuality, the power asymmetry between women and men—especially in the area of sexuality—is ignored. Yet, for women, this is a major issue for analysis and political action. Elsewhere (Wieringa 1999) I explored the notion of "desire" in Foucault's work. I decided that it is possible to understand the manifestations of "deviant desires" using Foucault's analysis.

The second wave of the women's movement gained momentum in the 1970s. Women realized that suffrage, and the other legal and educational reforms women had gained since the beginning of the twentieth century, were not enough to liberate women from their subordination. Adherents of the women's liberation movement engaged in debates on patriarchy and clearly pointed to sexuality as a major site of men's power over women. The sexologists were heavily attacked for legitimizing certain myths: that men rape women because of their uncontrollable sexual urge;[6] or that the vagina is the main site of sexual pleasure for women; or that heterosexual intercourse is the only "natural" model of sexual behaviour.

The first author who departed from biological determinism and essentialism was Simone de Beauvoir, with her thesis that "woman is made, not born". She demonstrated that women's "otherness" is historically constructed, and she advocated that women become subjects by speaking out on behalf of humanity and transcending their sex, their bodies.

The next theoretical step was made fifteen years later when Gayle Rubin introduced her concept of a "sex-gender system" in which biological sex is transformed into a sociocultural system of gender relations. Creatively combining elements of Freud, Marx and Lévi-Strauss, she argues that the sex-gender system is a power system that aims at concentrating material and symbolic capital in the hands of the fathers, the older men of a society. She conceptualizes the sex-gender system as a political economy, with the institution of heterosexuality supporting the dominant male homosocial bond. This position—the view that heterosexuality is an institution intended to support the prevailing sex-gender system in any given society—is directly opposed to that of Ellis, who saw heterosexuality as the only "normal" model of sexuality.

Since its introduction, the concept of gender as a major ideological and political system of power mechanisms, regulating individual, socioeconomic and political relations, has gained wide acceptance. Numerous feminist theoreticians have taken up the concept. I will highlight here just a few moments of what has become a substantial body of social theory.

Adrienne Rich attempted to deconstruct a subject which has long been considered "natural" for women: motherhood. She analysed motherhood as an institution, constructed as a normative enforcement of one model of sexual behaviour: reproductive heterosexuality. She differentiated between motherhood as an experience, which she views as enriching, and as an institution, when it becomes a means of oppression.

Another valuable contribution by Rich to constructivism is her observation that gender is not a unitary phenomenon experienced similarly by all women, but that it is intersected by a number of other experiences, such as race, class, age and sexual orientation. In this she was inspired by black feminism, to which I will return shortly. Haraway (1991) would later formulate the consequences of this insight in the following manner: we have to "situate" ourselves to know ourselves. But Rich retains more than a streak of essentialism when she writes:

> We need to imagine a world in which every woman is the presiding genius of her own body. In such a world women will truly create new life, bringing forth not only children (if and when we choose) but the visions, and the thinking, necessary to sustain, console and alter human existence—a new relationship to the universe. (Rich 1976: 285–86)

A major impetus to the women's movement was given by black feminist writers such as Lorde and Morrison and theoreticians such as Johnson-Odim (1991), Giddings (1984), and Hill Collins (1991). Although the roots of the women's movement in the United States can be traced back to the militant black consciousness-raising movement of the 1960s, those "black" roots were downplayed by the white middle-class women who dominated the women's movement from the late 1960s onwards. Both black women and poor white women denounced the "bourgeois whiteness" of the movement, and the homogenizing call for solidarity based on women's "common" experiences which white middle-class women insisted on. As Huggins expressed it: "black women, who have worked for necessity, are apt to view women's lib as a white middle-class battle irrelevant to their own often bitter struggle for survival" (Huggins 1991: 8). Giddings (1984) demonstrates how the participation of black women in gender struggles has been downplayed in the historiography of the women's movement so far.

Third World women, too, were disappointed by the minimal relevance of this kind of feminism to their own struggles. Johnson-Odim reminds her readers that there is a "widely accepted perception" among Third World women that the feminism emerging from white, middle-class Western women "narrowly confines itself to a struggle against gender discrimination" (Johnson-Odim 1991: 315). This "widely accepted perception" is due to a neglect of the history of early Third World feminism, rather than to the absence of struggles by Third World women against colonial exploitation and subordination (Wieringa 1988, 1995).

Yet many Third World feminists also realize that, in spite of so many differences, women all over the world do have certain experiences in common: "we were wary of the tendency to generalize about women; although in their biological reproductive roles women experience a commonality of functions and responsibilities, they are less cohesive in their experiences of domesticity and the extent to which the double burden of nurturing and productivity come into daily conflict" (Afshar 1991: 3). If solidarity between Third World and Western women should become a reality, it would have to be constructed on the basis of both the commonalities and the specific experiences of women's oppression. This is borne out by the experiences in Beijing in 1995, where some forty thousand women from all over the world gathered for the Fourth World Women's Conference and the attending nongovernmental organization forum. One of the issues that came out most clearly is that the divide between women from the South and from the North seems to be becoming less striking. The differences between progressive and conservative women, which cut across religions, regions and countries, came much more to the foreground (Moghadam 1996). The critical intervention of black women was one of the major factors which blew up the myth of a homogenous women's identity. The realization that women's identities are multiple, constituted by intersecting, at times contradictory, variables, has been one of the most creative insights of the last decades in feminist theorizing.

Wittig (1991) takes the ultimate step of deconstructing womanhood altogether. She asks herself what is a woman? Does *woman* exist? Her answer is that a *woman* is just an ideological construct of male domination, that there is nothing real or essential about women, nor about men for that matter. In her view, there is no such thing as a biological reality of the two sexes, constructed as they are by patriarchy. This is a long way from de Beauvoir, who held on to the idea of two biological sexes. Wittig rejects this altogether, arguing that patriarchy, as the system of male domination, requires binary thinking, the division of the social and biological into two categories. As such, the gender system, the ideological construct of patriarchy, is imbued with masculine ideas. We cannot know it, but only politically deconstruct it. Woman is not, there are only human beings formed by the cultural and political system in which they are placed. But the problem remains from where patriarchy may have originated.

Although Wittig calls for the ultimate rejection of patriarchy and thus for concrete political action, her ideas have not easily been accepted by large parts of the women's movement. Her rejection of the commonality of women's experiences has the effect of disempowering the call for female solidarity by which many women are inspired. But new calls for "strategic alliances" may have come up (Dean 1996).

The approaches of Scott and de Lauretis have gained wider acceptance during the last decade. Scott (1988), drawing on poststructuralist analyses of power and discourse, conceptualizes gender as a network of power relations interacting with other power networks. This enables her to approach the initial question:

> We need theory that can analyze the workings of patriarchy in all its manifestations—ideological, institutional, organizational, subjective—accounting not only for continuities but also for change over time. We need theory that will let us think in terms of pluralities rather than of unities and universals. We need theory that will break the hold, at least, of those long traditions of (Western) philosophy that have systematically and repeatedly construed the world in terms of masculine universal and

feminine specificities. We need theory that will enable us to articulate alternative ways of thinking about (and thus acting upon) gender without either simply reversing the old hierarchies or confirming them. And we need theory that will be useful and relevant for political practice. (Scott 1988: 33)

Two of the most important theoretical tools that recent poststructuralist theory has provided, in her view, are the concepts of difference and deconstruction. Difference, she writes, is related to "the notion ... that meaning is made through implicit or explicit contrast, that a positive definition rests on the negation or repression of something represented as antithetical to it" (Scott 1988: 36–37). This establishment of contrast turns into hierarchical, fixed oppositions. Following Derrida, she stresses the need for feminist thinkers to deconstruct those oppositions: "Deconstruction involves analyzing the operations of difference in texts, the ways in which meanings are made to work ... It shows them to be not natural but constructed oppositions, constructed for particular purposes in particular contexts" (Scott 1988: 37–38).

However, it is not difference as such that feminist analyses should oppose, but the hierarchical structures built upon it. Feminist political practice should be based on the careful assessment of differences and their operations. Thus, we should both deconstruct the differences upon which hierarchies are built and take them as the basis upon which to create solidarity: a solidarity based not on sameness, but on respect for the different locations in which we find ourselves. Scott again:

the critical feminist position must always involve two moves. The first is the systematic criticism of the operations of categorical difference; the exposure of the ... hierarchies it constructs, and a refusal of their ultimate "truth". A refusal, however, not in the name of an equality that implies sameness or identity, but rather (and this is the second move) in the name of an equality that rests on differences—differences that confound, disrupt, and render ambiguous the meaning of any fixed binary opposition. (Scott 1988: 48)

Another important insight into the workings of gender is provided by Teresa de Lauretis. In her influential book *Technologies of Gender* (1987), she conceptualizes gender not only as a product of discourse (of the meanings produced in the power constellation that a discourse is), but also as itself a constructing process. Thus, one not only "receives" one's gender identity within a given discourse, but also, by assuming it, by enacting it, one creates the gender relations within such a discourse, producing and reproducing categories such as men, women, gays and lesbians. This is not an isolated process. As de Lauretis suggests, "the female subject is engendered across multiple representations of class, race, language and social relations" (de Lauretis 1986: 14). The intersecting normative variables of gender, race, class, ethnicity and age produce together the formidable construct of "normality".

Constructivist theorists thus conclude that there is no "true self", no inner essence of womanhood that can be uncovered. The feminist search for identity which had been carried out so vigorously in consciousness-raising groups, starting in the 1970s, led to the realization—which became especially acute after the intervention of black feminist thinkers—that there is no universal female identity. That, instead, women's identity is multiple, shifting, even contradictory at times. Feminist practice thus shifted from denouncing the definitions of the "normalcy" prescribed by Ellis and his successors, to denouncing and destabilizing the very category of "normalcy" itself.

Conclusion

Constructivism is a major departure from essentialism and biological determinism. It places sexuality on the social map and demonstrates that it is mediated by historical and cultural factors, that it is as fluid and changeable a product of human action and history as other forms of human behaviour.

The introduction of this concept of gender has opened new and intriguing avenues of research. In particular, the realization that gender as a cultural construction is a historical variable, intersected by and cross-cutting other variables, should be seen as one of the most innovative insights of the last decades. The insistence on flexibility and diversity of experiences has stimulated many creative research projects.

Politically too, constructivism has great relevance, as I indicated earlier. The realization that neither male dominance nor female subordination is "natural", but that both are instead the products of a long historical process, has swept aside the arguments of those conservatives, men and women alike, who are opposed to gender policies on the grounds that they would disrupt the "natural harmony of the sexes".

Yet constructivism does not convince as the all-encompassing paradigm some of its adherents claim it to be. My concern focuses on two problems. First of all, I am struck by the danger of sociologizing the body and the individual temperament of human beings. Second, I wonder whether it is at all possible to do away completely with essentialism—apart from the question of whether it would be politically desirable.

Although constructivists insist that discourses create their own counterdiscourses, the mechanisms of this process remain vague. If, as Foucault and many of his followers attempt, sexuality is completely deconstructed, there is no or hardly any space left for individual choices. How then do we account for rebellion, for resistance, for the rejection of the dominant sexual or social model? To illustrate this point I will quote a few lines of a poem by Una Marson, an important Jamaican feminist and poet:

I am afraid of that which lies within
My very soul and like a smoldering fire
Seems on the verge of bursting into flame

And so consume my very being's might.
I try to fathom what the urge may be,
and sometimes it reveals its presence there
Like fluttering of the tiny wings that grow
Upon the fledgling and with which it soars
To heights in later years.

(in Ford-Smith n.d.)

Where does Marson's "smoldering fire" come from? How is it possible to relate that to the sociocultural conditions of her time? How is she able to translate that powerful "urge" into a "flame" with which she makes some impact upon her society? The dominant discourse she finds herself in undoubtedly influences or even determines the content of her anger., but it is not the source of her "fire". This example makes clear that the relationship between "sex and society" is not solved once and for all by the constructivist insistence on the overall power of discourse.

In other words, what are the boundaries between the social and the individual, both in a psychological and in a sexual sense? It would be counterproductive to completely do away with sciences like biology and psychology, for several reasons. In the first place, important research is being carried out which is also directly relevant to women's lives. And in the second place, it is dangerous for feminists to completely ignore those sciences, as it would mean feminists renouncing the power to influence them. We cannot allow men only to carry out all research in genetic engineering, for instance.

A major question remains, where do we locate our bodily experiences, our desires, our moods? How can we insert the body, or the individual temperament, into constructivist analysis without resorting to some elements of essentialism?

Another issue which points to the need for a careful rethinking of some essentialist premises is the possibility of certain sexual and social patterns which repeat themselves historically and cross-culturally (see also Blackwood and Wieringa 1999). Without the possibility of asking such questions we would be unable to engage in comparative research. Historical narration and description might take the place of analysis.

That essentialism and constructivism should not be seen as oppositional, that indeed many essentialist elements are contained in constructivist writing is demonstrated by Fuss (1989). She warns against the danger of constructing another binary opposition, the two elements of which are seen as incompatible with each other.

In conclusion I would like to stress that I view constructivism as a major step forward, both theoretically and politically, from essentialism. But we should not reduce essentialism to biological reductionism. From the very start essentialism has been abused for political purposes. The problem, however, is not so much the questions essentialism addresses, but the answers many of its adherents have provided, and the way it has been deployed politically. There are many essentialisms. Fuss even argues that constructivism operates as a more sophisticated form of essentialism. She rightly asks the question, how can we speak about the social if we reject the natural?

Grounding the social in a historicized natural, taking into account the way each element influences the other, may yield important new insights. Biologists such as Birke and Vines have pointed out that "nature" is not always "naturally given" either, that nature and culture are engaged in mutually transformative processes (Birke and Vines 1987). An approach like this may open up new avenues of research in which social scientists engage in fruitful debates with biologists or adherents of medical and psychological sciences about issues related to sexuality, the body and behaviour.

Apart from that, essentialism can also be highly valuable politically, if it is not based on the dominant group seeking a justification of its power, but on the subordinate groups who demand an end to their oppression. It is important that women of all races, classes and sexual orientations recapture our bodies, our diverging experiences, and deploy them for our own political strategies. Not because we *are* all the same, but because we all share certain experiences of oppression.

Notes

1 Although male homosexuality was prohibited, female homosexuality was not, for, as Queen Victoria is reported to have said: "What can the poor things do, anyway?"

2 Jeffreys (1985) points out that this issue carries less weight for lesbianism, as it was never punishable in Britain to start with. Instead, the sexologists succeeded in making the tradition of spinsterhood and female friendships which flourished in the last decades of the nineteenth and the first two decades of the twentieth century look very suspicious, as being tinged with lesbianism. Single women came to be seen as mannish and homogenic. See also Faderman 1981.

3 Notions that were challenged by constructivist analysis include, for instance, the assumption that "normal" men behave aggressively sexually, or that "normal" women like their men to be dominant, or are "naturally" more caring.

4 See Braidotti 1991, McNay 1992 or Bordo 1989 for an introduction of the major themes of the work of Foucault in relation to feminism.

5 See the excellent biography by Miller (1994) for an exploration of certain themes in Foucault's life, such as his sadomasochism.

6 Kathleen Barry (1981) called the dominant ideology a system of cultural sadism in which women were held in sexual slavery.

References

Afshar, Haleh. 1991. *Women, Development and Survival in the Third World,* Harlow; Longman.

Barry, Kathleen. 1981. *Female Sexual Slavery,* New York: Avon.

Birke, Lynda, and Gail Vines. 1987. "Beyond Nature Versus Nurture: Process and Biology in the Development of Gender". *Women's Studies International Forum* 10, no. 6.

Blackwood, Evelyn, and Saskia E. Wieringa, eds. 1999. *Female Desires, Same-Sex Relations and Transgender Practices Across Cultures.* New York: Columbia University Press.

Bordo, Susan R. 1989. "The Body and the Reproduction of Femininity: A Feminist Appropriation of Foucault". In *Gender ¡Body ¡Knowledge, Feminist Reconstructions of Being and Knowing,* edited by A.M. Jaggar and S.R. Bordo. New Brunswick, NJ: Rutgers University Press.

Braidotti, Rosi. 1991. *Patterns of Dissonance; A Study of Women in Contemporary Philosophy.* Cambridge: Polity Press.

Dean, Jodi. 1996. *Solidarity of Strangers: Feminism after Identity Politics.* Berkeley: University of California Press.

de Lauretis, Teresa, ed. 1986. *Feminist Studies ¡Critical Studies.* Bloomington: Indiana University Press.

_____. 1987. *Technologies of Gender: Essays on Theory, Film and Fiction,* London: Macmillan.

Faderman, Lilian. 1980. *Surpassing the Love of Men: Romantic Friendship and Love between Women from the Renaissance to the Present.* London: Junction Books.

Ford-Smith, Honor. N.d. "The Value of an Angry Woman: The Importance of Una Marson". Mimeo.

Foucault, Michel. 1978. *The History of Sexuality.* Vol. 1, *An Introduction.* New York: Pantheon.

Fuss, Diana. 1989. *Essentially Speaking: Feminism, Nature and Difference.* New York: Routledge.

Giddings, Paula. 1984. *When and Where I Enter: The Impact of Black Women on Race and Sex in America.* New York: Bantam Books.

Hill Collins, Patricia. 1991. *Black Feminist Thought: Knowledge, Consciousness and the Politics of Empowerment.* New York: Routledge.

Huggins, Jackie. 1991. "Black Women and Women's Liberation". In *A Reader in Feminist Knowledge,* edited by S. Gunew. London: Routledge,

Haraway, Donna J. 1991. *Simians, Cyborgs and Women: The Reinvention of Nature.* London: Free Association Books.

Jackson, Margaret. 1987. "Facts of Life' or the Eroticization of Women's Oppression? Sexology and the Social Construction of Heterosexuality". In *The Cultural Construction of Sexuality,* edited by P. Caplan. London: Tavistock.

Jeffreys, Sheila. 1985. *The Spinster and Her Enemies: Feminism and Sexuality, 1880–1930.* London: Pandora.

Johnson-Odim, Cheryl. 1991. "Common Themes, Different Contexts: Third World Women and Feminism". In *Third World Women and the Politics of Feminism,* edited by C.T. Mohanty, A. Russo and L. Torres. Bloomington: Indiana University Press.

Miller, James. 1994. *The Passion of Michel Foucault.* London: Flamingo.

Miller, Patricia J., and Martha R. Fowlker. 1980. "Social and Behavioural Constructions of Female Sexuality". In *Women, Sex and Sexuality,* edited by C.R. Stimpson and E.S. Pearson. Chicago: University of Chicago Press.

Moghadam, Valentine M. 1996. "Notes from the Field: The Fourth World Conference on Women—Dissension and Consensus". *Bulletin of Concerned Asian Scholars* 28, no 1.

Rich, Adrienne. 1976. *Of Woman Born: Motherhood as Experience and Institution.* New York: Norton.

Rubin, Gayle. 1975. "The Traffic in Women: Notes on the 'Political Economy' of Sex". In *Toward an Anthropology of Women,* edited by R.R. Reiter. New York: Monthly Review Press.

Scott, Joan W. 1988. "Deconstructing Equality-Versus-Difference: Or, the Uses of Poststructuralist Theory for Feminism". *Feminist Studies* 14, no. 1.

Shaffer, Elinor. 1980. "*The History of Sexuality,* vol. 1: *An Introduction*" (review essay). In *Women, Sex and Sexuality,* edited by C.R. Stimpson and E.S. Pearson. Chicago: University of Chicago Press.

Wieringa, Saskia, ed. 1988. *Women's Struggles and Strategies.* London: Gower Press.

_____. 1995. *Subversive Women: Women's Movements in Africa, Asia, Latin America and the Caribbean.* New Delhi: Kali for Women.

Wittig, Monique. 1991. *The Straight Mind and Other Essays.* New York: Harvester Wheatsheaf.

The Role of Identity in Diversity

Daryl G. Smith

The concept of identity is core to the issues surrounding diversity. While a fuller discussion of the definition and conceptualization of diversity in higher education will come in chapter 3, I want to make explicit the significant role that identity plays in virtually all conversations about diversity. Human diversity takes many forms—in personality, points of view, appearance, background, genetic makeup, biological origins, and culture, to name but a few. However, specific kinds of individual and group identity formed by race, ethnicity, gender, class, culture, religion, sexual orientation, gender identity, language, and ability emerge as significant not only for individuals and groups, but for institutions and society as well. Questions about identity underlie virtually all diversity-related issues, and certain identities emerge as salient.

What is identity? Which forms of identity matter, and under what conditions do they matter? Is paying attention to identity good or bad for institutions? Is it necessary or optional? How should one address identities that have been historically stigmatized? Having constructive conversations about diversity in higher education and in society relies on informed and knowledgeable answers to these questions; but informed discussions are not common.

Emerging Developments in the Concept of Identity

The nature, importance, and role of identity cannot be fully addressed in this book. However, I provide here a summary of some emerging developments in our understanding of identity that will provide a foundation for the higher education context to follow.

Kinds and Sources of Identity

Scholars have categorized identities in different forms, often to make clear that these may have different meanings. Identities may emerge from personal qualities, such as roles and personality, or from voluntary associations, such as sports teams or interest groups. They may be rooted in culture or religion. Identities also emerge through ascriptive (i.e., nonvoluntary) characteristics, such as race/ethnicity and gender (Gutman, 2003). To demonstrate how complex even this form of categorization can be, there is still debate as to whether sexual orientation is ascriptive or whether it is a voluntary preference. Other scholars distinguish between *personal* identity and *social* identity, contrasting characteristics that connect the individual with the group (social identity) with those that distinguish individuals from others (personal identity) (Carter, 2008; Monroe, Hankin, & Van Vechten, 2000; Parekh, 2008).

The category of race, though static in so much of the literature, is clearly quite complex in its relation to culture, biology, law, and even religion even as the inequities associated with race in a number of countries remain urgent (Bensimon & Bishop, 2012; Brodkin, 2004; Cornell & Hartmann, 1998; Harper, 2012; López, 1996; Mukhopadhyay, Henze, & Moses, 2013; Sanjek, 1994; Smedley & Smedley, 2005). Further, race and ethnicity are conceptually both distinct and interconnected, especially in the U.S. context. Often, ethnicity is connected to issues of language, culture, and history (Adams, 2001; Ferdman & Gallegos, 2001).

While visible forms of identity are the most obvious and are studied more often, invisible forms are extremely significant as well. Invisible forms of identity can place people in jeopardy, as sexual orientation has been known to do in the workplace. It can create perceptions of inclusion or exclusion, as has happened to persons who have disabilities that are not seen (Beatty & Kirby, 2006; Clair, Beatty, & MacLean, 2005; Herek & Capitanio, 1996). Moreover, invisible identities, especially those that bear a social stigma, create a number of unique stressors and experiences (Preves, 2005; Quinn, 2006; Yoshino, 2006).

Multiple and Intersecting

There is a growing recognition that any given individual has *multiple* identities and that these identities must be seen as they *intersect* one another (e.g., Carter, 2008; Dill & Zambrana, 2009). The list of identities associated with an individual may be long and may include race, ethnicity, class, gender, sexuality, gender identity, abilities, and so on. Early literature in psychology emphasized the development of identity as a single and coherent concept (Erikson, 1997). With the emergence of ethnic and women's studies and other fields, however, the literature began to make explicit the multiplicity of identities for any given individual (Ali, 2003; Anzaldúa, 2002; Beemyn & Rankin, 2011; Carter, 2008; Collins, 1990; Espiritu, 1997; Frable, 1997; Hull, Scott, & Smith, 1982; Lott, 1998; Omi, 2001; Omi & Winant, 1994; Sleeter & Grant, 1988; Takagi, 1998; Torres, Howard-Hamilton, & Cooper, 2003; Wilson, 1996; Woodward, 2000).

Sometimes identities have been seen as competing with one another for significance in a social context. Early scholarship developed by women of color responded that framing identity in terms of gender *or* race was inappropriate and inaccurate. Higginbotham (1993) pointed out that "race only comes up when we talk about African Americans and other people of color. Gender only comes up when we talk about women, and class only comes up when we talk about the poor and working class" (p. 14). Shirley Chisholm, the first African American woman to run for U.S. president, was constantly asked whether it was harder to be Black or to be a woman, a choice she refused to make. One of my favorite book titles in the early literature in ethnic studies, underscoring the intersection of race and gender, was created by Gloria Hull, Patricia Bell Scott, and Barbara Smith (1982): *All the Women Are White, All the Blacks Are Men, but Some of Us Are Brave: Black Women's Studies.*

The term *intersectionality*, developed by Williams (1994) in the context of international discussions of human rights, captures the importance of understanding the interrelationships of (for example) gender and race. As Hall (1996) has noted, "The essential issues of race always appear historically in articulation, in a formation, with other categories and divisions and are constantly crossed and re-crossed by categories of class, of gender, and ethnicity" (p. 444).

The notion of multiplicity of identity and intersectionality most often refers to different kinds of identity, such as gender, race, class, and sexuality. The concept of biracial identity, particularly with respect to race and ethnicity, can suggest multiplicity as well and must be understood as the relationship of multiple racial identities to one another (Lee & Bean, 2004). This is clearly becoming a topic of great interest as a result of the new census classifications that allow individuals to check more than one racial category, even though, as mentioned earlier, only 2.4% of the population in the 2010 census chose a multiracial category.

Context and Saliency

There is a growing understanding that identity and the degree to which it is salient are influenced and even defined by context (Crisp & Hewstone, 2007; Friedkin, 2004; Horse, 2001; Marable, 1995; Raskin, 2002; Rosunee, 2013; Taylor & associates, 1994). The kinds of identities that have emerged as salient for diversity conversations around the world emerge in large part because of their context—historical, political, social, and economic. Some forms of identity are more *socially salient* than others, and we can identify what they are. Identities may have positive saliency because in a given context, they are seen as relevant to the values, history, and culture of a given society. They may add to the vitality of a community and engender solidarity in a community or group. These forms of salience underlie the language of multiculturalism—phrases such as *the celebration of diversity*—and the ways in which identity contributes to self and society.

Those same histories that produce positive saliency also introduce saliency of identity through stratification, in which some identity groups maintain positions of power and dominance over other groups. How and why group identification emerges in ways that exclude and that even escalate into discrimination and violence has been the subject of decades of research. However, as Inzlicht and Good (2006) comment, "Social Psychological research shows us that our environments can be threatening. They can remind us of our social identities, activate negative stereotypes, and otherwise communicate that our groups are marginalized, devalued, and not accepted" (p. 146). The existence of stratification requires that power, equity, and discrimination be addressed in any discussion of diversity and identity.

Adams (2001) describes the contextual significance of identity in the following way: "Interdependence of fate (or 'historical consciousness' as Marable calls it) grows out of a group's shared and acknowledged experience of social inequality and oppression, the salience of which hardly rests on whether race or ethnicity is the accurate term to explain the visibility that allows for persecution based on difference" (p. 210). Thus, while having blue eyes could form a basis of identity, it probably does not, because it has not emerged in any particular society as relevant for significant ways of organizing or stratifying people.

The interplay of context, multiplicity, and inequity illuminates why and how identity becomes dynamic, complex, and significant. As Symington (2004) suggests, "People live multiple, layered identities derived from social relations, history, and the operation of structures of power. People are members of more than one community at the same time, and can simultaneously experience oppression and privilege" (p. 2). This can lead to sometimes contradictory behaviors in society. Frankenberg (1993), for example, points to the ways in which White women experience gender and then do or don't address race, which suggests that gender can be an important factor in racial dynamics and that race can influence gender dynamics. As Espiritu (1997) notes, "for women of color, gender is only part of a larger pattern of unequal social relations" (p. 5). Such an analysis need not stop with race, ethnicity, and gender (hooks, 2000, 2003).

We often think of identity as primarily an internal process through which an individual or group comes to be known. However, identity is fundamentally shaped in interaction with others and through response from others. The situation can be highly individualized, as when a token woman in a meeting with a group of men finds gender issues emerging more prominently than other parts of her identity. In a society in which racism and race have long histories and impact structures, as in the United States, race surfaces as extremely salient but still shifts depending on context (López, 1996; McGuire, McGuire, Child, & Fujioka, 1978). It is widely acknowledged that all groups are classified into racial categories, usually for purposes linked to gaining power or maintaining the status quo. Brodkin's *How Jews Became White Folks and What That Says About Race in America* (1994) and Tuan's *Forever Foreigners or Honorary Whites? The Asian Ethnic Experience Today* (2005) document the dynamic ways in which race has shifted through law and culture and continues to shift in terms of how groups are treated and classified and how individuals identify. Concerns about depicting Asian Americans as the "model minority" underscore the interplay of identity and social meanings (Lee, 1996; Takagi, 1998).

Identity development is an individual, group, and societal phenomenon, described well by Ferdman and Gallegos (2001) in their study of Latino identity: "Latino groupness emerges both from external factors ... and from within group factors, including common experiences and features among Latinos. ... A third element leading to Latino groupness, perhaps combining the external and internal factors, has been sociopolitical.... In sum, this sense of identification as a group is based on commonalities, treatment by others and utilitarian reasons" (p. 38).

Context, then, strongly influences how individuals both experience and act on their identity. A large and growing body of literature in social psychology underscores the important role that context plays in both the experience and the dynamics of identities that are stigmatized. Goffman, in his classic book *Stigma* (1963), focused on identities that are characterized as negative in a particular circumstance. This literature has drawn attention to how individuals experience, respond to, and interact with others as a result of being stigmatized (Inzlicht & Good, 2006; Mendoza-Denton, Page-Gould, & Pietrak, 2006). Research has also emerged concerning the behaviors and attitudes of those who are in the more privileged, unstigmatized position as they interact with others (Crocker & Garcia, 2006; Crocker, Major, & Steele, 1998; Levin, van Laar, & Foote, 2006).

Marcus, Steele, and Steele (2002) describe *identity threat* as a situation in which an individual or group perceives his/her/its identity to be the cause of threat from others—the responses and fear that emerge from hate crimes or violence, including threat from society or government agencies. The notion of identity threat will become more significant in later chapters. Here I will simply point out that issues of stratification, inequality, and threat explain why the study of identities is not simply a study of the multicultural richness of diverse people. A person in a subordinate position experiences identity quite differently than a person in a dominant position.

When identity intersects with power, privilege, or inequity, the experience of identity is likely to be *asymmetrical*, depending on where one is positioned socially. Holland, Lachicotte, Skinner, and Cain (1998) describe this positionality from the following perspective: "Social position has to do with entitlement to social and material resources and so to the higher deference, respect, and legitimacy accorded to those genders, races, ethnic groups, castes, and sexualities privileged by society" (p. 271).

The experience of being the only White in a group of Latinos may make Whiteness more salient and may make the individual uncomfortable, but it is probably not the same as being the only Latino in a group of Whites. The mother of a friend of mine grew up in the South at a time when threats from Whites—even lynching—were common. To this day, this gracious and confident woman experiences profound anxiety when she walks into a room filled with White people. An African American applying for an apartment in our society may have a different experience than a White person. For many Whites, individual qualities such as appearance or credit rating might matter in looking for a home, but not group membership. That is less likely to be true for many persons of color and gays or lesbians, who anticipate they might be treated differently as a function of their group identity. Depending on one's social position, then, ordinary behaviors and activities can be experienced quite differently.

Identity can also trigger internal responses, with expectations of discrimination or fear that interactions will trigger negative stereotypes in others. This is especially true in environments where one is in a numerical minority and associated with a stigmatized group (Aronson, 2002; Crocker, Major, & Steele, 1998; Steele, 1997). The large body of literature that describes patterns of response to stigma would probably resonate with most people who are part of stigmatized groups. These patterns include vigilance, stifling complaints, withdrawal, and, if the stigmatized identity is concealable, concealment (Crocker & Garcia, 2006). As Crocker and Garcia (2006) note, "The stigmatized often feel caught between two alternatives—confront or overlook prejudice—each of which has undesirable consequences" (p. 288).

Identity today represents a paradox. With our understanding of its complexity, the meaning of any single dimension of identity becomes less clear. At the same time, identity has powerful meaning because of its social salience. Fried (1995) expresses this paradox with respect to race: "Biologically race is an illusion. Sociologically it is a pervasive phenomenon" (p. 6). Thus, the personal meaning of identity may be highly individualized at the same time that the social salience of race, gender, or sexuality emerges for groups as very significant.

Comprehensiveness

In addition to sources of identity, multiplicity, intersectionality, and context, the literature on identity recognizes (though practice often does not) that for any given individual, single—or multiple—sets of identities are not comprehensive descriptors for the person. Knowing that a person is a woman, Latina, lesbian, and working class does not tell us everything about the individual. Indeed, it may tell us very little, depending on the person.

Moreover, one can discuss African American or American Indian culture, but one cannot assume that any given person has all the attributes ascribed to the culture. In reading the literature on identity, one has to be careful not to essentialize the identity—to attribute to the individual the general descriptions associated with the group. Assuming all women are caring, empathetic, and collaborative is an example of essentializing. This distinction is important both for the language used in writing about identity and for avoiding the tendency to stereotype individuals, even when it is well intentioned.

Institutional Identity

Identities manifest themselves as rich and critical aspects of the human experience of individuals. They become institutionalized as a function of the historical and social conditions under which institutions are formed. That is, institutional cultures take on norms, values, and practices from the people in the institution and the historical and social circumstances in which it was developed and in which it exists. Because of this connection, institutions also reflect the stratification and values of the larger society. How identity is introduced into an institution, therefore, is not simply a matter of the current membership of the institution and access to the institution. Institutional culture represents one of the deepest and most important elements of how institutions admit, value, and reward people. It is directly linked to identity.

Institutional Culture

Identity and culture are as dynamic and complex in institutions as they are in individuals and groups. As with identity of individuals and groups, described in the preceding sections, identity in institutions has many sources, takes multiple forms, is not comprehensive in capturing all characteristics of the institution, and is very much shaped by context. Institutional patterns in particular can be shaped by history, by location, and by mission. As with individuals and groups, the questions an institution asks often reflect deeply held values: How is excellence defined? What does beauty look like? What defines merit? How should selection be practiced? What defines a family? What kind of knowledge is important? What do different forms of expression mean, and what is appropriate? Thus, institutions can either develop in ways that reflect and reproduce the larger society or—as in the case of civil rights organizations, women's colleges, and historically Black colleges and universities—act as catalysts and challenge the inevitability of replication by creating environments that attempt to reduce inequities.

When an individual's identities align significantly with the cultural identity of an institution, there is usually a sense of comfort and a lack of awareness of certain salient features of institutional culture. Institutional and societal norms are taken for granted. The institution can appear to be a neutral, cultureless place whose values and practices are simply the way "one does business" and where "individuals are treated as individuals." As a result, many institutional elements related to identity can be rendered *invisible*. What is more, the alignment between an individual or group and the institution can translate into definitions of excellence that reward some groups and not others.

Acceptable ways of dressing, talking, and wearing one's hair, as well as patterns of working, can be translated from cultural norms into acceptable work norms quite easily. In some institutions, to be successful, people must align with dominant ways of speaking, dressing, or expressing themselves or their emotions. "People must not be 'too Black,' 'too Jewish,' or 'too gay'" (Goodman, 2001, p. 17). Research on "implicit bias" demonstrates the bias in evaluations when names are changed from male to female or to names that sound African American. Bertrand and Mullainathan's study on hiring (2004) shows that switching candidates names to be associated with being African American can affect a candidate's chances in a search process. As Ragins (1995) suggests, "Organizational culture is shaped and supported by the power-holders of the organization. These individuals influence the values, assumptions, and ideologies of the organization's culture" (p. 97). Unsurprisingly, the research evidence is clear that most people in an institution tend to hire people like themselves and perceive that those most like themselves are the most qualified (Elliott & Smith, 2004; Harper, 2012).

Until Section 504 of the Rehabilitation Act was passed in 1973, most institutions were designed for people who could walk up stairs, read signs, and so on. All too often, persons without disabilities were unaware that they were enjoying a privilege that was denied to others—the right of access. Even today, architecture programs must intentionally raise the issue of physical access with students who take it for granted. In historically male-dominated environments, facilities for women have often been afterthoughts. Once women enter these environments, the ways in which gender has been privileged become apparent. Early generations of women elected to Congress were soon introduced to this issue when they saw the inadequate lavatory and gymnasium facilities available to them on Capitol Hill. No woman who attends a large event and finds herself standing at the end of an interminably long line to the ladies' room doubts that the design of public restroom facilities is gendered.

Early airbags were developed around an erroneous gender assumption that presumed passengers to be the height of the average man, an assumption that led to airbags being a danger, rather than a safeguard, for many women and children. One explanation for why so few women astronauts have done space walks is that one-size-fits-all space suits are too large for all but the tallest women. Recently, doctors announced the development of a female knee to be used in knee replacements. It turns out that the structure of the "generic" knee previously used was designed for men. The new knee was finally developed because women were having more difficulty recovering from knee surgery. These examples underscore the relationship of diversity to excellence, not simply inclusion.

In the United States, Christmas and Easter are automatically built into institutional calendars, reflecting the centrality of Christianity to American society. Most Christians take the presence of these holidays on calendars for granted, while those who identify with other religions view the universality of the Christian holidays as a clear indication of embedded norms. Even today, the association of science with maleness continues to be an impediment to opening science up for women at all levels (Schiebinger 2006, 2008a, 2008b; Tobias, 1990; Tobin & Roth, 2007; Towers, 2008). Further, many elite institutions are associated with the practices, behavior, and trappings of groups that formed around privileges of wealth and Whiteness.

Power and Privilege

As Peggy McIntosh (2008) so aptly describes in her metaphor about wearing the "backpack of privilege," it is important for institutions to understand what is privileged and valued and accessible to some people, and what is not. Because terms such as *privilege* and *power* carry both political and emotional weight, they are often difficult to engage. Yet unwillingness to name privilege and power can communicate arrogance about the fairness of the institution and its practices (Chase, 2012; Chesler, Lewis, & Crowfoot, 2005; A. Hurtado, 1996; Johnson, 2001; Kendall, 2013; Maher & Tetrault, 2007; Thompson & Louque, 2005). Indeed, one of the consistent themes in the research literature on identity, particularly in organizational and societal contexts, is the importance of recognizing the asymmetry of identity when power or stigma is involved.

The literature in social psychology dealing with ethnic conflict throughout the world and intergroup relations demonstrates that intergroup teamwork can be experienced quite differently by individuals depending on their positionality and the context. A number of researchers point out the tendency of those in power positions to view group efforts in terms of individual competence and to assume neutrality or symmetry with respect to context and power. At the same time, those whose identity is associated with stigma or discrimination often wonder whether what takes place is a function of their identity in a particular group or something else (Dale, 2004; Dovidio, Kawakami, & Gaertner, 2000; Levin & van Laar, 2006; Rouhana, 2004; Steele, 2010). As Dale (2004) notes, "Identity and the experience of the parties [in conflict] is constructed differently given their relative high or low power position" (p. 189). This concept will be central to the discussion of the design of institutional intergroup efforts in chapter 6.

Maher and Tetrault (2007), in their study of three universities, suggest that an important element in institutional transformation with respect to diversity is to name and address the forms of privilege that are embedded in institutional norms and practices—forms of privilege that may be invisible to some but are very visible to those on the margins of that experience. White privilege. Class privilege. Gender privilege. Heterosexual privilege. For those who find the institution comfortable, it may be uncomfortable to name them; however, it is essential that forms of privilege be confronted. While it often takes people on the outside of privilege to point this out, those on the inside must be willing to listen and to act. Recent research on implicit bias—the ways in which bias is cognitively embedded, is unconscious, and must be interrupted—has focused attention on the deep and invisible ways bias is manifest (Banaji & Greenwald, 2013; Nosek, Greenwald, & Banaji, 2005).

Robert Merton described the "Matthew effect" in the 1960s as the process of "cumulative advantage" that accrues to people in already advantaged positions in science. He says, "The concept of cumulative advantage directs our attention to the ways initial comparative advantage of trained capacity, structural location, and available resources make for successive increments of advantage such that the gaps between the haves and have-nots in science (as in other domains of social life) widen until dampened by countervailing processes" (1988, p. 606). The concept of cumulative advantage can certainly be applied to the inequities that emerged from the implementation of the GI Bill described in chapter 1. Cumulative advantage also accrues when institutions conflate identity with acceptable norms and practices that privilege some over others.

It would be easy to assume, therefore, that to build cultures that are more inclusive, one must fundamentally change the culture of the institution in all ways. Indeed, it would be easy to imagine that the only way to build capacity for diversity is to create a new culture. Because cultures are not easy to change, and because the people who are in institutions are often drawn to them in part because of the institution's mission and culture, most scholars and practitioners of institutional change suggest a very different approach to cultural change. This perspective is expressed clearly by Edgar Schein, one of the major scholars who has studied organizational culture and change for years. He suggests, "Never start with the idea of changing culture. Always start with the issue the organization faces. ... Always think initially of the culture as your source of strength. Even if some elements of the culture look dysfunctional, remember that they are probably only a few among a larger set of others that continue to be strengths. If changes need to be made ... try to build on existing cultural strengths" (1999, p. 189). Ultimately, the culture must be defined and perceived in such a way that it is seen as empowering and inclusive (Banks, 1997; Darder, 1991).

Individual Experiences in Institutional Contexts

Apart from individual personality, the institutional context can dramatically influence a person's behavior and experiences. The following sections describe some of the adverse ways that an institution can influence individuals as a function of identity.

Threat

Depending on the environment and history of the institution, there may be the perception of threat. For instance, to be gay or lesbian in the military is to experience a constant fear of discovery. To be a Muslim after 9/11 is to wonder how one is seen. Many African Americans move through their days with heightened vigilance in institutions where racist incidents are common, just as those who are undocumented—as well as those who simply look like those who are undocumented—feel threatened in environments in which immigration and illegal immigration are being discussed with hostility.

Threat can also take the form of wondering whether the institution with its cultural norms and practices truly welcomes the perspective of someone from the outside. Is it really okay to criticize the assumptions behind a dress code? Will voicing a concern about breakfast meetings be welcome if one is a single mother? Can a lesbian put pictures of her domestic partner on her desk? Will a person of color be viewed negatively if she or he reports racist incidents? Why is there a common understanding among women of the times when one speaks and no one seems to listen?

There are many examples, large and small, where even in spite of inclusive rhetoric, people experience their identity as not welcomed or valued and where efforts to participate may be invalidated. A robust body of literature addresses the experience of stigma, often associated with exclusion, harassment, and denial of resources (Konrad, 2003). Being stigmatized can have powerful implications for identity, for relationships with others, for feelings of competence, and for health performance (Cohen & Sherman, 2014; Davies, Spencer, Quinn, & Gerhardstein, 2002; Eisenhardt, Kahwajy, & Bourgeois, 1997; Inzlicht & Good, 2006; Levin & van Laar, 2006; Steele, 2010).

Microaggressions

The growing literature on microaggressions describes how many of the experiences associated with discrimination do not take the form of major affronts. Rather, they are smaller incidents that occur perhaps unconsciously on the part of the other person but are experienced by minorities as insulting, degrading, or potentially threatening. Any one incident can be seen as minor, but the accumulation over time becomes significant (Rowe, 1990). A review of the literature in *American Psychologist* reflects the growing salience of microaggressions and the patterns of interaction related to them (Sue et al., 2007). The authors point out that microaggressions can emerge from human interaction but can also be communicated in institutional environments, through what is not said and through how the culture is represented. To the individual experiencing the microaggression, there is the time and effort spent questioning whether the event occurred and then whether to avoid saying anything for fear of being called oversensitive or paranoid. Identity and position in the institution inform a person's perspectives on the institution and can have implications for institutional dynamics (Crocker & Garcia, 2006; Inzlicht & Good, 2006; Levin & van Laar, 2006; Solórzano, Ceja, & Yosso, 2000; Sue et al., 2007).

Simply claiming inclusiveness will not be sufficient. In an institutional context, there is a powerful intersection between identity and the power and influence that are aligned with identity. When an issue arises in an institution, many will discuss concerns associated with race or gender or class, but the underlying issue may have been triggered by power dynamics or negative experiences associated with identity more than with the characteristics of people.

Despite years of research suggesting that women are more collaborative, for example, it is not clear that collaboration is a product of being a woman; rather, it may be a reflection of the fact that women are often in an environment where they are less likely to hold power, making collaborative strategies necessary. I have been in discussions where persons of color are angry and where Whites will ask, "Why do *they* have to be so angry?" When a group is seen as angry, is it because the *individuals* are angry people or because anger emerges from disempowerment, racism, sexism, or heterosexism? In the contexts of identity in institutions, questions of where the characteristic should be attributed are critical. Power dynamics, rather than individual characteristics, can explain many of the dynamics with respect to identity in an institution (Konrad, 2003).

Tokenism

The intersection of an individual's identity with institutions and societies is particularly relevant when an individual is a token, one of a few in an organization who share a salient identity. Some important themes resonate through the literature on tokenism (Agars, 2004; Garces & Jayakumar, 2014; Kanter, 1977; Yoder, 2002). For example, a person may be visible as a representative of the group but invisible as an individual. The first African American woman to lead a corporation is highly visible as an African American woman; as such, she will be studied and watched. Consequently, her successes and failures will often be attributed to the salience of race and gender in the corporate setting.

However, the fact that she is an individual who carries with her the same range of strengths, weaknesses, and characteristics that others carry, irrespective of race and gender, will be considered far less often. As a result, her failure or success will take on huge significance for the group (i.e., African American women) while placing an extra burden on her as an individual. How often has one heard comments like "We tried a Latina in that position and it didn't work out" or "Our last CEO was a woman. We won't do that again"? Such sweeping generalizations and conclusions are not made about White men because their sheer number in the upper echelons allows any one individual to be just that—an individual White man who possesses individual strengths and weaknesses.

Not only is there considerable stress in being the sole representative of a group, there is also difficulty in satisfactorily negotiating culture. A woman who tries to be "too male" will not be accepted, but being "too female" can place her at risk. Similar dilemmas occur in scenarios that involve race, sexual orientation, age, and class. Research has suggested that those in token positions may experience a limitation of roles and a restricted range of acceptable behaviors, increased pressure to perform, threats to performance, lack of access to important informational and social networks, and stereotypes (Inzlicht & Good, 2006; Kanter, 1977; Konrad & Gutek, 1987; Wharton, 1992). Moreover, there is some evidence that women in token positions may be less likely to mentor, in order to not be seen as favoring women (Yoder, Adams, Grove, & Priest, 1985).

In highly visible positions requiring significant leadership, individuals will find themselves negotiating identities not only from their own (and the institution's) perspective, but also from the perspective of the communities from which the individual comes. Take, for example, the multiplicity of identities carried by a Latina lesbian who comes from a working-class background. Add a college presidency to that picture. It would not be surprising to find these identity groups expecting her to pay particular attention to diversity agendas. Because she is also a token in the institution, this president will be challenged to demonstrate that her vision is broader than diversity and that she represents the whole institution.

While the research on tokenism is still limited, it is apparent from numerous studies that context matters. Research has consistently shown that the more one is outnumbered, the greater the likelihood that the environment will trigger negative stereotypes or awareness of one's marginal position (Agars, 2004; Kramer, Konrad, & Erkut, 2006; Thompson & Sekaquaptewa, 2002; Williams & O'Reilly, 1998). Being the token can occur for anyone—a White man in nursing, for example. However, Yoder and Schleicher (1996) have found that the impact on the individual and the dynamics in the organization vary considerably with gender role violations and are asymmetrical.

A man's experience in a traditionally woman's field is asymmetrical to that of a woman in a man's field. Here the status of the field and gender interact. Yoder and Schleicher's research results suggest a much more positive experience for a man in nursing than for a woman in engineering. In one study, women in engineering were seen as less likable, less attractive, and, significantly, more distanced from colleagues than men. In nursing, in contrast, men experienced little hostility and were more accepted as a "nontraditional person." Even so, some other research suggests that men may be unhappier in the minority than women and that Whites may be more uncomfortable in the minority than persons of color. Thus, while being "the only one" could apply to anyone, the dynamics vary and are asymmetrical depending on social norms, status, and expectations in society (Fagenson, 1993; Richard, 2000; Richard, Kochan, & McMillan-Capehart, 2002; Riordan & Shore, 1997; Yoder, 2002).

Critical Mass

Rosabeth Moss Kanter's early work on tokenism and the consequences of skewed demographics in an institution suggested that when a group constitutes 20% of the organization, the impact of tokenism is decreased (Kanter 1977). More recent research suggests that to limit the impact of skewed environments, 35% would be a better proportion for any group (Ely, 1994; Kramer, Konrad, & Erkut, 2006). With such representation, individuals are more likely to be seen as individuals, without the visibility and stress of being a token. At the same time, achieving a critical mass allows members of an identity group to come together and gain some measure of "voice" in an institution. Paradoxically, it also helps to dispel stereotyping. The larger the membership of an identity group, the greater the likelihood that there will be individual variation that will facilitate the breakdown of stereotypes. Greater proportionality can also create more positive views of the organization and more optimism about the possibilities for success for minorities in token positions (Ely, 1994).

Though it is clear that achieving a critical mass for a salient identity group and establishing the conditions for making it effective are crucial for the individual and for the institution, the concept of critical mass itself is not well understood (Garces & Jayakumar, 2014). It may be that the complexity of critical mass reflects the complexity of identity itself. In determining a critical mass, how and when can we aggregate groups so that we look at the numbers and percentages of persons of color in general? When do we need to disaggregate groups and look at racial, ethnic, and gender groupings separately? Does the location of a critical mass matter? Is the unit of analysis the institution, or does a critical mass have to be achieved in the location where individuals work or study? Is achieving a critical mass in a department more essential than simply looking at a critical mass at the institutional level? On the other hand, achieving a critical mass may matter a great deal at the institutional level. We know little about when a critical mass is reached. Because so few institutions have attained it in terms of race, ethnicity, and gender, there have been few opportunities to study the dynamics surrounding the conditions for achieving a healthy critical mass.

Institutional Isms

While racism, sexism, heterosexism, and other isms are often described from a psychological perspective as the behaviors and attitudes between individuals and groups, institutional forms of isms highlight the ways in which institutional structures, like culture, come to embody forms of inequity. Indeed, some identities, such as race, gender, and sexuality, become salient and often essentialized in part as a function of racism, sexism, heterosexism, and so on (Darder & Torres, 2003). Some scholars therefore urge shifting from the language of race, for example, to that of racism, to capture the social meanings for race, as distinguished from individual meanings (Baum, 2006). "It is racism as an ideology that produces the notion of 'race,' not the existence of 'races' that produces racism" (Darder & Torres, 2003, p. 257). Similarly, Minnich (2005) suggests converting nouns into active forms—for example, shifting from *race* to *racializing* and *gender* to *gendering*—to show the processes and means by which inequity is maintained.

These structural elements are significant precisely because the consequences in terms of inequality are not generally explicit. Institutionalized isms are standards, policies, and practices that are embedded in the institution, that have a disparate impact on particular groups, and that are not essential to fulfill the institution's mission. This last point is very important. Decisions about what is essential to fulfill institutional purposes are a necessary task for any institution. What makes something a form of institutional ism is that it limits access, success, or participation by individuals or groups who would otherwise be successful.

When police departments and fire departments had height requirements, this criterion—developed because a minimal height was assumed to be a necessary qualification—limited the number of women who could apply. Eventually, it became evident that women and men who did not meet the height standard could still pass rigorous tests for becoming a member of the police or fire department. This is an example of institutional sexism, as was the design of the airbags described earlier. The implementation of the housing policies of the GI Bill is a perfect example of institutional racism under cover of states' rights. Indeed, Sidanius and Pratto, in a review of empirical evidence (1999), have concluded that "institutional discrimination remains a very significant feature of modern 'democratic' states" (p. 303). These patterns are reflected in the workplace, schools, health care, housing, and the criminal justice system.

Chesler, Lewis, and Crowfoot provide a framework for the institutional elements that conceal or reveal structural inequity. They look at the institution's mission, culture, power, membership, technology, resources, and boundary management as places to be studied. Institutionalized isms are often not explicit but implicit, buried in the context of rules and norms that allow processes to be named as fair even when they are not (Chesler, Lewis, & Crowfoot, 2005; Sidanius & Pratto, 1999).

An institution that seriously wants to engage these embedded assumptions will have to determine which assumptions are essential to the institution and do not inappropriately deny access and success to particular groups, and which assumptions need to be changed in order to create a more inclusive environment. Some changes will cost money. Certain changes will affect everyone, and some of these will benefit everyone. The increasing number of companies implementing family-friendly policies that were originally introduced as "women's issues" has been positive for men as well. Change requires resources of time, people, and money. The willingness of an institution to make these investments is directly related to perceptions of a commitment to diversity. It appears that unless an institution understands these investments as being in its best interests, there will be considerable resistance to making significant changes.

Diversity and Divisiveness

Does an emphasis on diversity cause the kind of divisiveness that one witnesses throughout history and today? Would it be better to downplay identity groupings based on culture and religion? Would it be better to minimize ascribed identities such as race, gender, and ethnicity? One can understand why, as identity becomes more multifaceted and complex, some think we should not pay attention to identity at the societal level. This is the appeal of color blindness. We are happy to appreciate and celebrate the diversity of individuals and groups as long as, at the institutional or societal level, things are "neutral" (Bennett, 1998; Bonilla-Silva, 2014; Marcus, Steele, and Steele, 2002; Yoshino, 2006). Unfortunately, structural inequities in society make serious discussion of color blindness—that is, identity blindness—much more problematic than simply a call to consider individuals as individuals (Eagly, Baron, & Hamilton, 2004; Wise, 2006).

When identities are embedded in circumstances that are characterized by exclusion, inequity, discrimination, injustice, and lack of access to power, they assume significance beyond the functions they serve for individuals and groups. Most of the identities associated with diversity in society and on campuses are linked to these issues, and they are fueling the collective and individual actions that seek to produce institutional transformation. As Gut-man (2003) points out, "Socially salient parts of people's identities—such as their color, gender and physical disabilities—shape their interests, and their interests in turn shape their identities" (p. 133). She notes further that "the fewer the alternative means of representation available to disadvantaged individuals, the more powerful an ascriptive association is" (p. 137). In such cases, organizations often develop to represent the group's interests and participation in society.

In the United States, the legacy of race and racism in society and continued evidence of inequity leave race a highly salient part of identity. Even as women—particularly White women—have made progress, there are many contexts in which gender remains extremely salient for women (Blau, Brinton, & Grusky, 2006). Sexual orientation, gender identity, disability, and class, as well as the intersections among them, are also significant with respect to inequity. However, for each identity, the particulars of the saliency differ [...]. How one frames diversity and the conditions under which identity is developed have a great deal to do with whether identity will serve a positive or negative purpose.

When someone asks why we can't be color-blind and treat everyone as an individual, they are asking the wrong question. We should all be asking, instead, how we might create just institutions and societies that benefit from diversity and that embody a multiplicity of cultures and identities. Significantly, such a question moves beyond individuals and groups. It asks us to look at inequity and how those from specific identity groups are positioned to benefit from and experience institutions quite differently. Until these inequities that are built into the structures of institutions and society are addressed, the consequence of color-blind (or gender-blind, or ability-blind) policies is more likely to be the maintenance or exacerbation of inequity—as we have seen with the implementation of "color-blind" admissions policies in higher education, gender-neutral airbags, and so on. The view that identity needs to be understood, not hidden, will be echoed in the results of the empirical work in the field of intergroup relations reviewed in chapter 6.

Current research suggests that rather than downplaying identity, a more powerful strategy for society and institutions would be to build on the multiplicities of identities and allow individuals to look at the similarities and differences across them, as well as the social context in which identities emerge. To do that requires building institutions that signal and manifest diversity in their culture (Ibarra, 2000; Padilla, 2004; Ramirez & Castañeda, 1991; Sanchez, 2004). Amartya Sen (2006), a Nobel Prize–winning economist, notes, "The hope of harmony in the contemporary world lies in a clearer understanding of the pluralities of human identity, and in the appreciation that they cut across each other and work against a sharp separation along one single hardened line of impenetrable division" (p. xiv).

In the process of South Africa's emergence as a democracy, a former justice of the Constitutional Court, Albie Sachs, spoke eloquently about the relationship of diversity and community:

> Shared citizenship, far from being the enemy of difference, is the bedrock for the recognition of difference. It is only when culture, background, language and appearance become used as a means of controlling resources and political power—ethnic mobilization for the purpose of advantage—that culture in that sense becomes politicized and is precarious and antagonistic to the culture of others. Where common citizenship is profound and strong, then the expression of one's culture in no way requires the disrespect of another's. (Sachs, 1999, p. v)

The Challenges of Language, Labels, and Identity

The question of language arises the moment one sets out to write about diversity. Issues of language, especially naming, can be appropriately introduced in regard to every category and label used in this book. The use of the term diversity has been contested, and one can see the emersion of phrases like "diversity and inclusion" to represent offices and roles. Like so many other aspects of diversity, the nature of language itself is dynamic and ever evolving. For example, naming has profound political significance and is critical to identity and self-empowerment. Yet it is not always easy to know what names to use, and in what context. In 1986, I was working on the final edits of a monograph I had written on diversity when I began to hear Jesse Jackson refer to Blacks as African Americans. There had been no vote, no announcement of any formal decision; but it was clear that how we referred to Blacks was about to change—and indeed it did. For any author, the best approach to naming and other issues related to language is probably to identify the issues, make a decision, and go forward.

Because words can be seen as ideological or politically correct—or politically incorrect—the use of certain words can be catalytic, if not inflammatory. It is important to be historically, socially, and politically sensitive to words and names and their impact on individuals and groups. For anyone interacting in diverse settings, it is probably useful to keep in mind that regardless of how any one author or body of literature refers to specific groups, signifiers are seldom set in stone, and it is always best to ask and listen before making assumptions. Where possible, I try to honor self-identification, to be specific when there are other issues that emerge, to disaggregate large categories, and to recognize that these issues change all the time.

Naming

The significance of naming challenges both individuals and institutions to critically examine language, to disaggregate groups, and to avoid labels that, while convenient, may not be adequate. However, some clarification about my own use of certain terms may be helpful in understanding the text.

Race and Ethnicity

Throughout the text, I often combine the terms *race* and *ethnicity* (*race/ethnicity*). In the current U.S. census, race and ethnicity are not interchangeable. The census classifies "Hispanic" as an ethnicity because Hispanics may be of different races. At the same time, issues of ethnicity and culture are core to discussions about African Americans and Asian Americans. Race and facets of ethnicity such as language, culture, and history are inextricably intertwined, and scholars may use one term or the other or both to capture this complexity (Adams, 2001; Ferdman & Gallegos, 2001). Rather than choose one over the other, I have elected to use *race/ethnicity* to capture both elements together.

The phrase *women and minorities* is often used to deal with the intersection of race and gender. However, it has become clear to me that in many cases, women of color are included in minorities (especially with respect to institutional data) and "women" really means "White women." The use of "women and minorities" often reflects a reluctance to specify "White women" when that is what is meant. This is a perfect example of the discomfort in naming race. If I am referring to White women, I will be explicit in indicating that.

One word commonly used in virtually all scholarship on diversity is *minority*. While this word has relevance as a numeric reference, it also has great significance in regard to issues of power. As a result, there is an enormous amount of research on "minorities," with *minority* defined as the smaller part of a population with respect to a particular characteristic. In the United States, that characteristic may be tied to racial and ethnic groups, with Whites being associated with the majority and all groups of color being characterized as minorities. However, diversity within the United States has increased such that there are now some states, such as California and Texas, where Whites are not in the numerical majority. Most would agree, however, that even in those states, Whites still represent the majority of individual and institutional power, and non-Whites continue to be seen as minorities even though they are the majority.

While the term *minority* still has significance in some contexts, my feeling is that it is too generic when used to represent all non-Whites. Perhaps more importantly, its use places Whites at the center of the diversity discussion. Therefore, I use it only when necessary and prefer to use *persons of color* when referring to African Americans, Asian Americans, Latinos, and American Indians.

Another term that is used in federal information and appears pejorative is *non-resident aliens*. One wonders how long international residents and students will be referred to in this way.

Continuing waves of immigrants require us to pay attention to the suitability of those names that have become established and to use new or broader terms to include new groups. While the term *African American* has been used for the past two decades, there is a growing recognition that the ethnic and national origin of Blacks in this country is expanding. Blacks who trace their roots to places outside of Africa, such as the Caribbean, do not necessarily see themselves as African American. For the most part, I continue to use the term *African American* unless the context suggests that a different choice would be more appropriate.

Preferences for group names can vary from region to region. Because the term *Hispanic* was used by the U.S. census, some groups view it as a governmental label that was imposed on them. However, many people in Texas intentionally use the term. The word preferred by many Californians is *Latino*, while other people favor names that reference national origin (e.g., *Mexican American*) or historical and political positionality, such as *Chicano/Chicana* (González & Gándara, 2005; Za-vella, 1994). Considering the history and significance of these terms, I have chosen to use *Latino/a*, unless reference to specific subgroups, authors, or book titles is warranted or when the data are developed from government information using traditional labels such as *Hispanic*.

American Indians have gone through similar transitions in naming, and I have tried to honor those changes. Increasingly, American Indian authors self-identify through tribal affiliation. This is useful in highlighting the tremendous diversity among tribes, with each bringing its own history, traditions, culture, and language.

The term *Asian American* evolved through efforts of the civil rights movement to address the fact that Asian American issues were largely ignored in many diversity dialogues. Recognizing that there is power in numbers, Americans with ancestries rooted in the enormous Asiatic sphere have achieved some political clout by being combined into one category (Hune, 1995; Hune & Chan, 1997; Takaki, 1993). However, as with other pan-ethnic groupings, there is great diversity within the Asian American community, and the differences often outweigh the commonalities.

In the political and social context of the United States, where Whiteness has been dominant and where so much of the history of race has centered on what has been called the Black-White paradigm, pan-ethnic identities provide political and social communities where important issues can be addressed. However, in recognition of the heterogeneity within such groups, there are increasing references to particularity. A growing academic literature has developed for many such communities. Some of these efforts are now emerging in higher education, as researchers begin to delve into the experiences of specific national or ethnic groups in higher education. This disaggregation is also occurring in literature on White ethnic communities (Phinney, 1990, 1996). Researchers must not lose sight of the particular, even as we talk about the general.

In education, the issues associated with race have historically focused on African American, Latino/a, and American Indian students (Anderson & Kim, 2006). The term *historically underrepresented minorities* (URM) has emerged as useful in speaking of issues related to these three groups, who remain the most underrepresented in higher education relative to their share of the population. However, with increasing immigration and diversity, other groups have been, and will be, underrepresented and underserved in higher education. The term *nonimmigrant minorities* (Marcus, Steele, & Steele, 2002) may be a useful way to distinguish domestic diversity from immigrant diversity. Some have suggested broadening the term *URM* to include underrepresented people such as the Hmong and other Southeast Asian communities.

I recognize that the term *underrepresented minority* is not entirely adequate, but it is useful enough that I will employ it to refer to African American, Latino/a, and American Indian groups, keeping in mind all the caveats that suggest its limits. In the context of this book, referring to specific groups as much as possible and attending to disaggregated data are perhaps the most useful approaches. Doing so permits greater attention to American Indians, who often get lost in the data of aggregated discussions about URM because their numbers are small.

In the naming of groups, even spelling can come to have meaning. As Gonzalez (2006) notes, the spelling *Pilipino* has come to signify something associated with the roots of the Filipino community; the use of the initial *p* connects the word to indigenous cultures, where *f* did not exist, and also to progressive politics.

Sex, Gender, and Sexuality

There is a lack of consensus around the terms *sex* and *gender*. I prefer to use *gender*, because it takes into account biological, social, and cultural dimensions and reflects greater complexity.

Gay and lesbian terminology continues to emerge through efforts to deal explicitly with the intersection of gender and sexuality. What has been one of the most stable dichotomies, the sex dichotomy between male and female, is shifting with the growing recognition of transgender and bisexual identities. *LGBT* (lesbian, gay, bisexual, transgender) is commonly used as a way of acknowledging the complexities of sexuality, complexities that go beyond naming to the fundamental nature of sexuality itself. On many campuses, we will see variations such as *LGBTQ*, where *Q* stands for "queer." As part of this, even the use of gendered pronouns to describe individuals (he/she) is evolving, so that individuals are using a variety of pronouns to describe themselves, commonly known as personal gender pronouns (PGP) (DiBartolo, 2013).

Ability Groups

Concerning the concept of ability/disability, I have elected to use *ability* terminology (Hehir, 2005). The complexity involved in defining "disability" can be seen in the passionate discourse within the Deaf community. Advocates of sign language square off against those who promote spoken language. Endorsers of cochlear implants clash with those for whom being deaf is a way of life, rather than something that should be changed. The discussion of ability grouping has evolved into a debate that is articulated around two perspectives. One prefers to emphasize an individual who has a disability rather than someone who is a disabled person. The other suggests that differential abilities are present in everyone and that notions of disability are therefore overly simplified.

The word *ableism* is often used to mean "a pervasive system of discrimination and exclusion that oppresses people who have mental, emotional, and physical disabilities" and that, when combined with norms of excellence, ability, talent, potential, or appearance, creates environments hostile to those who have such issues (Rauscher & McClintock, 1997, p. 198). The topic of ability is at times given short shrift in diversity discussions. It is, however, quite important and requires attention.

Class

The use of socioeconomic status (SES) has a long history in the social sciences, and there is no question that economic and educational markers continue to be critically relevant to scholarship. However, these markers are too limiting in the context of this book. Therefore, I use *class*, not only to capture these identifiers, but to indicate the cultural aspects that are emerging in research (Borrego, 2004; Chan & Goldthorpe, 2007; Zandy, 1996, 2001).

Zandy describes class as "an aspect of shared economic circumstances and shared social and cultural practices in relation to positions of power" (1996, p. 8). This conception of class evokes not simply a person's economic circumstances, but also one's social and cultural capital, norms, and values—concepts that will be addressed in the following chapters.

The Politics of Language

Issues of language are not only questions about how to "name" individuals and groups. They also involve questions about how language is used and how it is received. As I write this chapter, I am very conscious that words such as *privilege*, *power*, *racism*, and other *isms*, along with phrases such as *White privilege* and *heterosexual privilege*, have become part of the culture wars in our society. Unless one is willing to ignore stratification and issues such as institutional racism, it is impossible not to use language that describes these conditions.

For me, this is not a matter of being "politically correct" in the pejorative way in which this term is used. It is important to try to accurately depict and engage issues that reveal embedded phenomena and to suggest ways in which change can occur. Because diversity is fundamentally about these issues, they must be addressed. There are few ways to avoid the use of words or phrases that will evoke reactions or risk putting my work in a box. Nonetheless, I have tried to be clear and to use terms as precisely as I can, even as I invite the reader to engage in considering the significance of language.

Diversity, Democracy, and Higher Education

It is in the broad national and global context, and with identity holding a central place, that diversity's role at the core of higher education emerges. In the mid-1990s, Peter Drucker (1993) began to describe a major transition in society as he named and forecast the rise of the *knowledge worker* as central to the future social, political, and economic organization of communities. The knowledge worker assumes a role that requires informational expertise more than, for example, physical strength. Knowledge workers come to their role in society through education. In that context, education in general—and higher education in particular—are critical.

Indeed, the mandate of higher education in the United States and its relationship to the future of democracy is emerging as a core context for diversity. In *The Quiet Crisis* (2004), Peter Smith talks about the connections between education, the aspirations of democracy, and the future of society. "What's really permanent?" he asks. "What really endures is the soul of our democracy. And deep in America's soul lies the promise of opportunity, of liberty and freedom for every person. ... With this commitment, we will survive. Without it, we will decline. ... Education is the path to the table of opportunity in 21st century America" (p. 6).

In their report *Now Is the Time* (2005), the American Association of State Colleges and Universities and the National Association of State Universities and Land-Grant Colleges declare that "the promise of a just and truly multicultural democracy made possible through a more diverse academy cannot wait for another generation. The challenge for change within higher education must be taken up and addressed boldly. And it must be addressed today" (p. 3).

And in *Grutter v. Bollinger* (2003), the Supreme Court affirmed the relationship between diversity, democracy, and higher education when it stated, "the diffusion of knowledge and op- ― INTERNET portunity through public institutions of higher education must be accessible to all individuals, regardless of race or ethnicity. ... In order to cultivate a set of leaders *with legitimacy in the eyes of the citizenry*, it is necessary that the path to leadership be visibly open to talented and qualified individuals of every race and ethnicity" (p. 20; emphasis added).

These statements speak to the relationship between diversity and democracy and to the need for higher education to represent the diversity of society. However, the complexities that surface through issues of identity and the strategies needed to create pluralistic communities that work are not discussed frequently enough or with sufficient depth at the policy level or within academe. These issues are not about changing individuals; they are about changing the institutions and structures that make identities salient. As such, they are deeply connected to the ways in which individuals interact and institutions function (Gutman, 2003; Putnam, 2007).

By extension, these issues are also deeply connected to the future of a democratic society. In "Culture, Identity and the Role of Higher Education in Building Democracy in South Africa" (1999), Cloete, Cross, Muller, and Pillay suggest that "a curriculum for common citizenship and sites for democratic practices could be a central role for higher education in South Africa's fledgling democratic practice" (p. 46). In the 1990s, a Ford Foundation–sponsored program called for a conversation about diversity, democracy, and higher education among teams from India, South Africa, and the United States. This three-year project underscored the importance of diversity for the vitality and viability of democracy and the role of higher education in this effort (Beckham, 2000, 2002; Cloete, Cross, Muller, & Pillay, 1999; Cloete, Muller, Makgoba, & Ekong, 1997; Cross et al., 1999). The connection between diversity and inclusion, institutional transformation, excellence, and healthy societies is beginning to emerge transnationally (Bagilhole, 2009; Sagaria, 2007; Shimahara, Holowinsky, & Tomlinson-Clarke, 2001; Smith, 2014).

While the focus of diversity has often been on people and their interpersonal relationships, diversity is manifested through our institutions and society at large. Higher education, then, rather than being seen as the elite terminus of the educational pipeline, can be seen as one of the *beginnings*. In addition to its crucial role in building the capacities of individuals from all sectors of society, higher education plays a strong role in defining knowledge, identifying and framing problems that need to be solved, allocating resources, developing and training teachers and faculty, and cultivating leaders for all sectors.

We might say that higher education is the source of a river that waters culture and society and has the potential to nourish as it rectifies. These are the purposes for higher education today, and they are centrally linked to the issues of diversity described above. This is the context that frames the chapters to come, in which we will see how institutions can build capacity for excellence in a pluralistic society.

References

Adams, M. (2001). Core processes of racial identity development. In C. L. Wijeyesinghe & B. W. Jackson III (Eds.), *New perspectives on racial identity development: A theoretical and practical anthology* (pp. 209–243). New York: New York University Press.

Agars, M. D. (2004). Reconsidering the impact of gender stereotypes for the advancement of women in organizations. *Psychology of Women Quarterly*, 28(2), 103–111.

Ali, S. (2003). *Mixed-race, post-race: Gender, new ethnicities and cultural practices*. Oxford: Berg Publishers.

American Association of State Colleges and Universities/National Association of State Universities and Land-Grant Colleges Task Force on Diversity. (2005). *Now is the time: Meeting the challenge for a diverse academy*. New York: Author.

Anderson, E., & Kim, D. (2006). *Increasing the success of minority students in science and technology.* Washington, DC: American Council on Education.

Anzaldúa, G. E. (2002, October 11). Beyond traditional notions of identity. *Chronicle of Higher Education,* 49(7), B11.

Aronson, J. (2002). Stereotype threat: Contending and coping with unnerving expectations. In J. Aronson (Ed.), *Improving academic achievement: Impact of psychological factors on education* (pp. 279–301). San Diego, CA: Academic Press.

Bagilhole, B. (2009). *Understanding equal opportunities and diversity.* Bristol: Policy Press.

Banaji, M. R., & Greenwald, A. G. (2013). *Blindspot: Hidden biases of good people.* New York: Delacorte Press.

Banks, J. (1997). *Educating citizens in a multicultural society.* New York: Teachers College Press.

Baum, R. (2006). *The rise and fall of the Caucasian race: A political history of racial identity.* New York: New York University Press.

Beatty, J. E., & Kirby, S. L. (2006). Beyond the legal environment: How stigma influences invisible identity groups in the workplace. *Employee Responsibilities and Rights Journal,* 18(1), 29–44.

Beckham, E. F. (Ed.). (2000). *Diversity, democracy, and higher education: A view from three nations.* Washington, DC: Association of American Colleges and Universities.

Beckham, E. F. (Ed.). (2002). *Global collaborations: The role of higher education in diverse democracies (India, South Africa, the United States).* Washington, DC: Association of American Colleges and Universities.

Beemyn, G., & Rankin, S. (2011). *The lives of transgender people.* New York: Columbia University Press.

Bennett, D. (Ed.). (1998). *Multicultural states: Rethinking difference and identity.* New York: Routledge.

Bensimon, E. M., & Bishop, R. (Eds.). (2012). A special issue: Critical perspectives on race and equity. *Review of Higher Education,* 36(1).

Bertrand, M., & Mullainathan, S. (2004). Are Emily and Greg more employable than Lakisha and Jamal? A field experiment on labor market discrimination. *American Economic Review,* 94(4), 991–1014.

Blau, F. D., Brinton, M. C., & Grusky, D. B. (Eds.). (2006). *The declining significance of gender?* New York: Russell Sage Foundation.

Bonilla-Silva, E. (2014). *Racism without racists: Color blind racism and the persistence of racial inequality in America* (4th ed.). Lanham, MD: Rowman and Littlefield.

Borrego, S. E. (2004). Class in the academy. *The Academic Workplace* (New England Resource Center for Higher Education), 15(2), 1–7.

Brodkin, K. (2004). *How Jews became White folks and what that says about race in America* (Rev. ed.). New Brunswick, NJ: Rutgers University Press.

Carter, R. (2008). *Multiplicity: The new science of personality, identity, and the self.* New York: Little, Brown.

Chan, T. W., & Goldthorpe, J. H. (2007). Class and status: The conceptual distinction and the empirical evidence. *American Sociological Review,* 72(4), 512–533.

Chase, K. (2012). *Deconstructing privilege: Teaching and learning as allies in the classroom.* New York: Routledge.

Chesler, M., Lewis, A., & Crowfoot, J. (2005). *Challenging racism in higher education: Promoting justice.* Oxford: Rowman & Littlefield.

Clair, J. A., Beatty, J. E., & MacLean, T. L. (2005). Out of sight but not out of mind: Managing invisible social identities in the workplace. *Academy of Management Review,* 30(1), 78–95.

Cloete, N., Cross, M., Muller, J., & Pillay, S. (1999). Culture, identity and the role of higher education in building democracy in South Africa. In M. Cross, N. Cloete, E. F. Beckham, A. Harper, J. Indiresan, & C. M.

Musil (Eds.), *Diversity and unity: The role of higher education in building democracy* (pp. 20–48). Cape Town, South Africa: Maskew Miller Longman.

Cloete, N., Muller, J., Makgoba, M. W., & Ekong, D. (Eds.). (1997). *Knowledge, identity, and curriculum transformation in South Africa.* Cape Town, South Africa: Maskew Miller Longman.

Cohen, G. L., & Sherman, D. K. (2014). The psychology of change: Self-affirmation and social psychological interventions. *Annual Review of Psychology*, 65, 333–371.

Collins, P. H. (1990). *Black feminist thought: Knowledge, consciousness, and the politics of empowerment.* New York: Routledge.

Cornell, S., & Hartmann, D. (1998). *Ethnicity and race: Making identities in a changing world.* Thousand Oaks, CA: Pine Forge Press.

Crisp, R. J., & Hewstone, M. (2007). Multiple social categorization. In M. P. Sanna (Ed.), *Advances in experimental social psychology* (Vol. 39, pp. 163–254). Orlando, FL: Academic Press.

Crocker, J., & Garcia, J. A. (2006). Stigma and the social basis of the self: A synthesis. In S. Levin & C. van Laar (Eds.), *Stigma and group inequality* (pp. 287–308). Mahwah, NJ: Erlbaum.

Crocker, J., Major, B., & Steele, C. M. (1998). Social stigma. In D. T. Gilbert, S. T. Fiske, & G. Linzey (Eds.), *Handbook of Social Psychology* (4th ed., pp. 504–553). Boston: McGraw-Hill.

Cross, M., Cloete, N., Beckham, E. F., Harper, A., Indiresan, J., & Musil, C. M. (Eds.). (1999). *Diversity and unity: The role of higher education in building democracy.* Cape Town, South Africa: Maskew Miller Longman.

Dale, R. (2004). Comments on chapters 9 and 10. In A. H. Eagly, R. M. Baron, & V. L. Hamilton (Eds.), *The social psychology of group identity and social conflict: Theory, application, and practice* (pp. 189–192). Washington, DC: American Psychological Association.

Darder, A. (1991). *Culture and power in the classroom: A critical foundation for bicultural education.* New York: Bergin & Garvey.

Darder, A., & Torres, R. D. (2003). Shattering the "race" lens: Toward a critical theory of racism. In A. Darder, M. Baltodano, & R. D. Torres (Eds.), *The critical pedagogy reader* (pp. 245–263). New York: Routledge.

Davies, P. G., Spencer, S. J., Quinn, D. M., & Gerhardstein, R. (2002). Consuming images: How television commercials that elicit stereotype threat can restrain women academically and professionally. *Personality and Social Psychology Bulletin*, 28, 1615–1628.

DiBartolo, A. N. (2013). *Is there a difference: The impact of campus climate on sexual minority and gender minority students' level of outness.* Unpublished doctoral dissertation, Claremont Graduate University.

Dill, B. T., & Zambrana, R. E. (Eds.). (2009). *Emerging Intersections: Race, class and gender in theory, policy, and practice.* New Brunswick, NJ: Rutgers University Press.

Dovidio, J. F., Kawakami, K., & Gaertner, S. L. (2000). Reducing contemporary prejudice: Combating explicit and implicit bias at the individual and intergroup level. In S. Oskamp (Ed.), *Reducing prejudice and discrimination* (pp. 137–164). Mahwah, NJ: Erlbaum.

Drucker, P. F. (1993). *Post-capitalist society.* New York: Harper.

Eagly, A. H., Baron, R. M., & Hamilton, V. L. (Eds.). (2004). *The social psychology of group identity and social conflict.* Washington, DC: American Psychological Association.

Eisenhardt, K., Kahwajy, J., & Bourgeois, L. (1997). Conflict and strategic choice: How top management teams disagree. *California Management Review*, 39, 42–62.

Elliott, J. R., & Smith, R. A. (2004). Race, gender and workplace power. *American Sociological Review*, 69(3), 365–386.

Ely, R. (1994). The effects of organizational demographics and social identity on relationships among professional women. *Administrative Science Quarterly*, 39, 203–238.

Erikson, E. H. (1997). *The life cycle completed*. New York: Norton.

Espiritu, Y. L. (1997). *Asian American women and men*. Thousand Oaks, CA: Sage.

Fagenson, E. A. (1993). Is what's good for the goose also good for the gander? On being white and male in a diverse workforce. *Academy of Management Executive*, 7(4), 80–82.

Ferdman, B. M., & Gallegos, P. I. (2001). Racial identity development and Latinos in the United States. In C. L. Wijeyesinghe & B. W. Jackson III (Eds.), *New perspectives on racial identity development: A theoretical and practical anthology* (pp. 32–66). New York: New York University Press.

Frable, D. E. S. (1997). Gender, racial, ethnic, sexual, and class identities. *Annual Review of Psychology*, 48, 139–162.

Frankenberg, R. (1993). *White women, race matters: The social construction of Whiteness*. Minneapolis: University of Minnesota Press.

Fried, J. (1995). *Shifting paradigms for student affairs: culture, context, teaching, and learning*. Alexandria, VA: American College Personnel Association.

Friedkin, N. E. (2004). Social cohesion. *Annual Review of Sociology*, 30, 409–425.

Garces, L. M., & Jayakumar, U. M. (2014). Dynamic diversity: Toward a contextual understanding of critical mass. *Educational Researcher*, 43(3), 115–124.

Goffman, E. (1963). *Stigma: Notes on the management of spoiled identity*. Englewood Cliffs, NJ: Prentice-Hall.

Gonzalez, A. (2006). *The racial manipulation of Asian Americans and the discourse of denial of success*. Unpublished manuscript, Claremont Graduate University.

González, C., & Gándara, P. (2005). Why we like to call ourselves Latinas. *Journal of Hispanic Higher Education*, 4(4), 392–398.

Goodman, D. J. (2001). *Promoting diversity and social justice: Educating people from privileged groups*. Thousand Oaks, CA: Sage.

Grutter v. Bollinger, 539 U.S. 306 (2003).

Gutman, A. (2003). *Identity in democracy*. Princeton, NJ: Princeton University Press.

Hall, S. (1996). New ethnicities. In S. Hall, D. Morely, & K. Chen (Eds.), *Stuart Hall: Critical dialogues in cultural studies* (pp. 441–449). New York: Routledge.

Harper, S. R. (2012). Race without racism: How higher education researchers minimize racist institutional norms. *Review of Higher Education*, 36(1), 9–30.

Hehir, T. (2005). *New directions in special education: Eliminating ableism in policy and practice*. Cambridge, MA: Harvard Education Press.

Herek, G. M., & Capitanio, J. P. (1996). "Some of my best friends": Intergroup contact, concealable stigma, and heterosexuals' attitudes toward gay men and lesbians. *Personality and Social Psychology Bulletin*, 22, 412–424.

Higginbotham, E. (1993). Sociology and the multicultural curriculum: The challenges of the 1990s and beyond. *Race, Sex, and Class*, 1, 13–24.

Holland, D., Lachicotte, Q., Jr., Skinner, D., & Cain, C. (1998). *Identity and agency in cultural worlds*. Cambridge, MA: Harvard University Press.

hooks, b. (2000). *Where we stand: Class matters*. New York: Routledge.

hooks, b. (2003). Reflections on race and sex. In A. Darder, M. Baltodano, & R. D.

Torres (Eds.), *The critical pedagogy reader* (pp. 238–245). New York: Routledge.

Horse, P. G. (2001). Reflections on American Indian identity. In C. L. Wijeyesinghe & B. W. Jackson III (Eds.), *New perspectives on racial identity development: A theoretical and practical anthology* (pp. 91–107). New York: New York University Press.

Hull, G. T., Scott, P. B., & Smith, B. (Eds.). 1982. *All the women are white, all the Blacks are men, but some of us are brave: Black women's studies*. Old Westbury, NY: Feminist Press.

Hune, S. (1995). Opening the American mind and body: The role of Asian American studies. In D. T. Nakanishi & T. Y. Nishida (Eds.), *The Asian American educational experience*. New York: Routledge.

Hune, S., & Chan, K. S. (1997). Special focus: Asian Pacific American demographic and educational trends. In D. J. Carter & R. Wilson (Eds.), *15th Annual Status Report on Minorities in Higher Education* (pp. 39–63). Washington, DC: American Council on Education.

Hurtado, A. (1996). *The color of privilege*. Ann Arbor: University of Michigan Press.

Ibarra, R. A. (2000). *Beyond affirmative action: Reframing the context of higher education*. Madison: University of Wisconsin Press.

Inzlicht, M., & Good, C. (2006). How environments can threaten academic performance, self-knowledge, and sense of belonging. In S. Levin & C. van Laar (Eds.), *Stigma and group inequality* (pp. 129–150). Mahwah, NJ: Erlbaum.

Johnson, A. G. (2001). *Privilege, power, and difference*. Boston: McGraw-Hill.

Kanter, R. M. (1977). Some effects of proportions on group life: Skewed sex ratios and responses to token women. *American Journal of Sociology*, 5, 965–990.

Kendall, F. E. (2013). *Understanding white privilege: Creating pathways to authentic relationships across race* (2nd ed.). New York: Routledge.

Konrad, A. (2003). Defining the domain of workplace diversity scholarship. *Group and Organizational Management*, 28(1), 4–17.

Konrad, A. M., & Gutek, B. (1987). Theory and research on group composition: Applications to the status of women and ethnic minorities. In S. Oskamp & S. Spacapan (Eds.), *Interpersonal processes: Claremont symposium on applied social psychology* (pp. 85–121). Newbury Park, CA: Sage.

Kramer, V., Konrad, A., & Erkut, S. (2006). *Critical mass on corporate boards: Why three or more women enhance governance* (Report no. 781 283–2510). Wellesley, MA: Wellesley Centers for Women.

Lee, J., & Bean, F. D. (2004). America's changing color lines: Immigration, race/ethnicity and multiracial identification. *Annual Review of Sociology*, 30, 221–242.

Lee, S. J. (1996). *Unraveling the "model minority" stereotype: Listening to Asian American youth*. New York: Teachers College Press.

Levin, S., & van Laar, C. (Eds.). (2006). *Stigma and group inequality*. Mahwah, NJ: Erlbaum.

Levin, S., van Laar, C., & Foote, W. (2006). Ethnic segregation and perceived discrimination in college: Mutual influences and effects on social and academic life. *Journal of Applied Social Psychology*, 36(6), 1471–1501.

López, I. F. H. (1996). *White by law: The legal construction of race*. New York: New York University Press.

Lott, J. T. (1998). *Asian Americans: From racial categories to multiple identities*. Walnut Creek, CA: Alta Mira Press.

Maher, F. A., & Tetrault, M. K. T. (2007). *Privilege and diversity in the academy*. New York: Routledge.

Marable, M. (1995). *Beyond black and white: Transforming African-American politics*. New York: Verso.

Marcus, H. R., Steele, C. M., & Steele, D. M. (2002). Color blindness as a barrier to inclusion: Assimilation and nonimmigrant minorities. In R. A. Shweder, M. Minow, & H. R. Marcus (Eds.), *Engaging cultural differences*. New York: Russell Sage Foundation.

McGuire, W. J., McGuire, C. V., Child, P., & Fujioka, T. (1978). Salience of ethnicity in the spontaneous self-concept as a function of one's ethnic distinctiveness in the social environment. *Journal of Personality and Social Psychology, 36*(5), 511–520.

McIntosh, P. (2008). White privilege: Unpacking the invisible knapsack. In P. Rothenberg (Ed.), *White privilege: Essential readings on the other side of racism* (3rd ed., pp. 123–128). New York: Worth.

Mendoza-Denton, R., Page-Gould, E., & Pietrak, J. (2006). Mechanisms for coping with status-based rejection expectations. In S. Levin & C. van Laar (Eds.), *Stigma and group inequality* (pp. 151–170). Mahwah, NJ: Erlbaum.

Merton, R. K. (1988). The Matthew Effect in science, II. *ISIS, 79*, 606–623.

Minnich, E. K. (2005). *Transforming knowledge* (2nd ed.). Philadelphia: Temple University Press.

Monroe, K. R., Hankin, J., & Van Vechten, R. B. (2000). The psychological foundations of identity politics. *Annual Review of Political Science, 3*, 419–447.

Mukhopadhyay, C. C., Henze, R., & Moses, Y. T. (2013). *Race, culture, and biology: An educator's sourcebook* (2nd ed.). New York: Rowman & Littlefield.

Nosek, B. A., Greenwald, A. G., & Banaji, M. R. (2005). Understanding and using the Implicit Association Test: II. Method variables and construct validity. *Personality and Social Psychology Bulletin, 31*(2), 166–180.

Omi, M. A. (2001). The changing meaning of race. In N. J. Smelser, W. J. Wilson, & F. Mitchell (Eds.), *America becoming: Racial trends and their consequences*, Vol. I (National Research Council, Commission on Behavioral and Social Sciences and Education, pp. 243–263). Washington, DC: National Academy Press.

Omi, M., & Winant, H. (1994). *Racial formation in the United States*. New York: Routledge.

Padilla, R. V. (2004). *Unity and diversity in an ethnomorphic society*. San Antonio: University of Texas.

Parekh, B. (2008). *A new politics of identity: Political principles for an interdependent world*. New York: Palgrave Macmillan.

Phinney, J. S. (1990). Ethnic identity in adolescents and adults: Review of research. *Psychological Bulletin, 10*, 499–514.

Phinney, J. S. (1996). When we talk about American ethnic groups, what do we mean? *American Psychologist, 51*(9), 918–927.

Preves, S. E. (2005). *Intersex and identity*. New Brunswick, NJ: Rutgers University Press.

Putnam, R. D. (2007). *E pluribus unum*: Diversity and community in the twenty-first century. *Scandinavian Political Studies, 30*(2), 137–174.

Quinn, D. M. (2006). Concealable versus conspicuous identities. In S. Levin & C. van Laar (Eds.), *Stigma and group inequality* (pp. 83–104). Mahwah, NJ: Erlbaum.

Ragins, B. R. (1995). Diversity, power, and mentorship in organizations: A cultural, structural, and behavioral perspective. In M. Chemers, S. Oskamp, & M. Costanza (Eds.), *Diversity in organizations* (pp. 91–132). Newbury Park, CA: Sage.

Ramirez, M., & Castañeda, A. (1991). Toward a cultural democracy. In B. Murchand (Ed.), *Higher education and the practice of democratic politics: A political education reader* (pp. 115–121). Dayton, OH: Kettering Foundation.

Raskin, P. M. (2002). Identity in adulthood: Reflections on recent theory and research. *Identity, 2*(1), 101–108.

Rauscher, L., & McClintock, M. (1997). Ableism and curriculum design. In M. Adams, L. A. Bell, & P. Griffen (Eds.), *Teaching for diversity and social justice* (pp. 198–231). New York: Routledge.

Richard, O. C. (2000). Racial diversity, business strategy, and firm performance: A resource-based review. *Academy of Management Journal, 43*(2), 164–177.

Richard, O. C., Kochan, T. C., & McMillan-Capehart, A. (2002). The impact of visible diversity on organizational effectiveness: Disclosing the contents in Pandora's black box. *Journal of Business and Management*, 8(3), 1–26.

Riordan, C. M., & Shore, L. M. (1997). Demographic diversity and employee attitudes: An empirical examination of relational demography within work units. *Journal of Applied Psychology*, 82, 342–358.

Rosunee, N. B. (2013). Is it myth or dilemma to construct and negotiate identities in an increasingly changing and diverse global context. *International Journal of Diversity in Organizations, Communities and Nations: Annual Review*. Retrieved from http:ondiversity.com, ISSN 1447-9532.

Rouhana, N. (2004). Identity and power in the reconciliation of national conflict. In A. H. Eagly, R. M. Baron, & V. L. Hamilton (Eds.), *The social psychology of group identity and social conflict: Theory, application, and practice* (pp. 173–187). Washington, DC: American Psychological Association.

Rowe, M. P. (1990). Barrier to equality: The power of subtle discrimination to maintain unequal opportunity. *Employee Responsibility and Rights Journal*, 3(2), 153–163.

Sachs, A. (1999). Foreword to M. Cross, N. Cloete, E. F. Beckham, A. Harper, J. Indiresan, & C. M. Musil (Eds.), *Diversity and unity: The role of higher education in building democracy* (p. v). Cape Town, South Africa: Maskew Miller Longman.

Sagaria, M. D. (Ed.). (2007). *Women, universities and change*. New York: Palgrave.

Sanchez, G. (2004). *Crossing Figueroa: The tangled web of diversity and democracy* (Position paper no. 4, Imagining America). Ann Arbor: University of Michigan.

Sanjek, R. (1994). The enduring inequalities of race. In S. Gregory & R. Sanjek (Eds.), *Race* (pp. 1–17). New Brunswick, NJ: Rutgers University Press.

Schein, E. H. (1999). *The corporate culture survival guide*. San Francisco: Jossey-Bass.

Schiebinger, L. (2006). *Nature's body: Gender in the making of modern science*. New Brunswick, NJ: Rutgers University Press.

Schiebinger, L. (Ed.). (2008a). *Gendered innovations in science and engineering*. Stanford, CA: Stanford University Press.

Schiebinger, L. (2008b). Getting more women into science and engineering—knowledge issues. In L. Schiebinger (Ed.), *Gendered innovations in science and engineering* (pp. 1–21). Stanford, CA: Stanford University Press.

Sen, A. F. (2006). *Identity and violence: The illusion of destiny*. New York: Norton. Senge, R. M. (2000). The academy as learning community: Contradiction in terms or realizable goal? In A. F. Lucas & associates, *Leading academic change* (pp. 275–300). San Francisco: Jossey-Bass.

Shimahara, N. K., Holowinsky, I. Z., & Tomlinson-Clarke, S. (Eds.). (2001). *Ethnicity, race and nationality in education: A global perspective*. Mahwah, NJ: Erlbaum.

Sidanius, J., & Pratto, F. (1999). *Social dominance*. Cambridge: Cambridge University Press.

Sleeter, C. E., & Grant, C. A. (1988). A rationale for integrating race, gender, and social class. In L. Weis (Ed.), *Class, race, and gender in American education* (pp. 126–143). Albany: State University of New York.

Smedley, A., & Smedley, B. (2005). Race as biology is fiction: Racism as social problem is real. *American Psychologist*, 60(1), 16–26.

Smith, D. G. (Ed). (2014). *Diversity and inclusion in higher education: Emerging perspectives on institutional transformation*. London: Routledge.

Smith, P. (2004). *The quiet crisis: How higher education is failing America*. Boston: Anker.

Solórzano, D. G., Ceja, M., & Yosso, T. (2000). Critical race theory, racial microaggressions, and campus racial climate. *Journal of Negro Education*, 69(1), 60–73.

Steele, C. M. (1997). A threat in the air: How stereotypes shape intellectual identity and performance. *American Psychologist*, 52, 613–629.

Steele, C. M. (2010). *Whistling Vivaldi and other clues to how stereotypes affect us*. New York: Norton.

Sue, D. W., Capodilupo, C. M., Torino, G. C., Bucceri, J. M., Holder, A. M. B., & Nadal, K. L., et al. (2007). Racial microaggressions in everyday life. *American Psychologist*, 62(4), 271–286.

Symington, A. (2004, August). Intersectionality: A tool for gender and economic justice. *Women's rights and economic change* (Association for Women in Development), No. 9.

Takagi, D. (1998). *The retreat from race: Asian Americans and racial politics*. New Brunswick, NJ: Rutgers University Press.

Takaki, R. (1993). *A different mirror: A history of multicultural America*. New York: Little, Brown.

Taylor, C., & associates. (1994). *Multiculturalism: Examining the politics of recognition*. Princeton, NJ: Princeton University Press.

Thompson, G. L., & Louque, A. C. (2005). *Exposing the "culture of arrogance" in the academy*. Sterling, VA: Stylus.

Thompson, M., Sekaquaptewa, P. (2002). When being different is detrimental: Solo status and the performance of women and racial minorities. *Analysis of Social Issues and Public Policy*, 2, 183–203.

Tobias, S. (1990). *They're not dumb, they're different*. Tucson, AZ: Research Corp.

Tobin, K., & Roth, W. M. (Eds.). (2007). *The culture of science education*. New Directions in Mathematics and Science Education. Rotterdam, Netherlands: Sense Publishers.

Torres, V., Howard-Hamilton, M. F., & Cooper, D. L. (2003). Identity development of diverse populations: Implications for teaching and administration in higher education. *ASHE Higher Education Report*, 29(6).

Towers, S. (2008). *A case study of gender bias at the postdoctoral level in physics, and its resulting impact on the academic career and advancement of females*. Retrieved April 19, 2008, from http://export.arxiv.org/abs/0804.2026.

Tuan, M. (2005). *Forever foreigners or honorary whites? The Asian ethnic experience today* (Rev. ed.). New Brunswick, NJ: Rutgers University Press.

Wharton, A. S. (1992). The social construction of gender and race in organizations: A social identity and group mobilization perspective. *Research in Sociology of Organizations*, 10, 55–84.

Williams, K. C. (1994). Mapping the margins: Intersectionality, identity politics, and violence against women of color. In M. A. Fineman & R. Mylitiuk (Eds.), *The public nature of private violence* (pp. 93–118). New York: Routledge.

Williams, K. Y., & O'Reilly, A. (1998). Demography and diversity in organizations: A review of 40 years of research. In B. W. Shaw & L. L. Cummings (Eds.), *Research in Organizational Behavior*, 20, 77–140. Greenwich, CT: JAI Press.

Wilson, A. (1996). How we find ourselves: Identity development and Two-Spirit people. *Harvard Educational Review*, 66(2), 303–317.

Wise, T. (2006). Whites swim in racial preferences. In C. Hartman (Ed.), *Poverty and race in America* (pp. 3–6). Oxford: Lexington Books.

Woodward, K. (Ed.). (2000). *Questioning identity: Gender, class, nation*. London: Routledge.

Yoder, J. D. (2002). Context matters: Understanding tokenism processes and their impact on women's work. *Psychology of Women Quarterly*, 26, 1–8.

Yoder, J. D., Adams, J., Grove, S., & Priest, R. F. (1985). To teach is to learn: Overcoming tokenism with mentors. *Psychology of Women Quarterly*, 9, 119–131.

Yoder, J. D., & Schleicher, T. L. (1996). Undergraduates regard deviation from occupational gender stereotypes as costly for women. *Sex Roles*, 35, 389–400.

Yoshino, K. (2006). *Covering: The hidden assault on our civil rights*. New York: Random House.

Zandy, J. (1996). Decloaking class: Why class identity and consciousness count. *Race, Gender, & Class*, 5(1), 7–23.

Zandy, J. (Ed.). (2001). *What we hold in common: An introduction to working-class studies*. New York: Feminist Press.

Zavella, P. (1994). Reflections on diversity among Chicanas. In S. Gregory & R. Sanjek, *Race* (pp. 199–212). New Brunswick, NJ: Rutgers University Press.

Post-Reading Activities

1   Which of the definitions discussed in the introduction (Wagley & Harris (1967) and van Amersfoort (1978)) include a component of identity? How is identity important to the definition of a minority?

2   Which articles of the Universal Declaration of Human Rights address the importance of an identity?

3   Think about the first time you walked into a college classroom with other students. How did you identify others prior to selecting a seat?

4   How did you identify yourself in your introductions to those around you? If you identify yourself by identifying your majority statuses first, how might you view the world? Or, if you identify yourself by identifying your minority statuses first, how might you view the world?

5   Think of a particular minority group of interest, how does a member of the minority group learn to act like a minority member of the group? For example, how does a female learn to "act like a lady"?

6   How does an individual in society learn how to treat a member of your minority group (minorities fair) based on the behavior of the member of the minority group? For example, how does a male learn how to treat a female "like a lady"?

7   What role, if any, do you think the media plays in creating the minority identity?

Basic Race and Ethnic Lives, Minority and Majority

Race and ethnicity permeate the discussions of stratification, inequality, and minority. Despite the perceived conclusion of the Civil Rights Movement, many recent social events highlight that race and ethnicity remain a pervasive identity in the United States. In August 2016, the *New York Times* published an article discussing the emphasis that Americans were placing on race in social media commentary. This article, of course, discusses the many cases of violence that appear to be racially motivated (some of these cases have not been definitively classified as hate crimes, despite common belief), such as the Charleston Emanuel A. M. E. Church shooting, the shooting death of Freddie Gray, and the hanging of Sandra Bland, but it also highlights the awards shows such as the Grammys and Academy Awards (Chokshi, 2016).

The readings in this unit highlight that race and ethnicity affect more than violence and popular culture. Oliver and Shapiro (2006) compare the wealth inequality trends in the first writing. Wealth is different than income. Research consistently shows that inequality is greater in wealth (ownership) when compared to income (money earned in a given time period). Many college students (and some professors) have negative wealth, despite having an income. Wealth is calculated by adding up the value of all possessions that are owned and subtracting the amount of debt owed (i.e., student loans, mortgages, car loans, credit card debt). With wealth comes power. This article highlights racial and ethnic differences within wealth and income.

In the Rivera, Campon, and Herbert (2016) article, we are introduced to the idea of micro-aggressions and the application or experiences of Hispanics. Microaggressions are difficult to define, but recognizable. Outside of racial groups, microaggressions have been studied in relationship to religion. Dupper, Forest-Bank, and Lowry-Carusillo (2015) research the experiences of religious minorities in the education system in the United States. They highlight that the majority of school breaks coincide with Christian religious holidays (i.e., winter break coincides with the Christmas holiday). With this understanding, many Jewish and Muslim students must miss education instruction time to observe religious holidays. Although many of these students receive an excused absence, this does not account for the instruction lost and make-up work the student must do.

Chou and Feagin (2014) discuss the concept of a "model minority" with Asians. This idea of relative Whiteness allows some Asians to experience a freedom from inequality that other minority groups do not encounter. But, as Chou and Feagin stress, this experience is not always a positive opportunity for many Asian groups. Black (2008), on the other hand, reports on the often-overlooked minority of Native Americans and Alaska Natives. She introduces the idea of structural racism. Structural racism incorporates the historical relationships between the Native American and Alaska Native minority and the majority. Because of the long history of relocation, genocide, and war, many elements of racism became embedded in social policy were introduced to address these atrocities. Concluding this unit, Pedraza (2006) discusses the experience of the immigrant in the United States. Providing a historical approach to explaining immigration, Pedraza explains two theories of immigrant and majority interacting behavior by introducing the concepts of assimilation and transnationalism.

References

Black, S. S. (2008). Native Americans and Alaska Natives: The forgotten minority: American Indian Tribes and structural racism. *Poverty & Race Research Action Council, 17*(6), 1, 6.

Chokshi, N. (2016, August 15). The top news events that got America talking about race. *New York Times*. Retrieved from https://www.nytimes.com/2016/08/16/us/pew-study-race-twitter-news-events.html

Chou, R.S. & Feagin, J.R. (2014). Struggle and conformity: The white racial frame. In *The Myth of the Model Minority: Asian Americans facing racism*. London: Paradigm Publishers.

Dupper, D. R., Forrest-Bank, S., & Lowry-Carusillo, A. (2015). Experiences of religious minorities in public school settings: Findings from focus groups involving Muslim, Jewish, Catholic, and Unitarian Universalist youths. *Children & Schools, 37*(1), 37–45.

Oliver, M. L. & Shapiro, T. M. (2006). Black Wealth/White Wealth: Wealth Inequality Trends. In *Black wealth, white wealth: A new perspective on racial inequality*. (2nd Ed). London: Routledge.

Pedraza, S. (2006). Assimilation or transnationalism? Conceptual models of the immigrant experience in America. In *Cultural Psychology of Immigrants*. London: Psychology Press.

Rivera, D.P., Campon, R.R., & Herbert, K. (2016). The impact of microaggressions and structural inequalities on the well-being of Latina/o American communities. In *Talking about structural inequalities in everyday live: New politics of race in groups, organizations, and social systems*. Charlotte: Information Age Publishing.

Black Wealth/White Wealth

Wealth Inequality Trends

Melvin L. Oliver and Thomas M. Shapiro

The growth and dispersion of wealth continues a trend anchored in the economic prosperity of post-World War II America. Between 1995 and 2001, the median net worth of all American families increased 39 percent, and median net financial assets grew by 60 percent. The growth of pension accounts (IRAs, Keogh plans, 401(k) plans, the accumulated value of defined contribution pension plans, and other retirement accounts) and stock holdings seems to account for much of this wealth accumulation.

While wealth grew and spread to many American families, there was little action at the bottom of the wealth spectrum as the percent of families with zero or negative net worth only dropped from 18.5 to 17.6, and those with no financial assets fell from 28.7 to 25.5.

Wealth remains highly concentrated, especially financial wealth, which excludes home equity. In 2001, the richest 5 percent of American households controlled over 67 percent of the country's financial wealth; the bottom 60 percent had 8.8 percent; and the bottom 40 percent just 1 percent.[1]

The context of wealth growth and inequality in the last decade situates our concern about racial inequality and the progress of American families, as indeed, the rich have gotten richer. The number of families with net worth of $10 million or more in 2001 quadrupled since 1980. A *New York Times* article even bemoaned how the super rich are leaving the mere rich far behind.[2] These 338,400 hyper-rich families emerged as the biggest winners in the new global economy, as new technologies spurred by tax incentives evolved, as the stock market soared, and as top executives in the corporate world received astronomical pay.

The wealthy were the biggest beneficiaries of tax policy during President George W. Bush's first term. In fact, the bulk of the 2001 tax cuts—53 percent—will go to the top 10 percent of taxpayers.[3] The tax cut share of the top 0.1 percent will amount to a 15 percent slice of the total value of the tax cut pie. Another reason that the wealthiest fare much better is that the tax cuts over the past decade have sharply lowered tax rates on income from investments, such as capital gains, interest, and dividends. While there are many reasons for the continuing wealth inequality trend, government policy has clearly abetted, encouraged, and privileged the property, capital, and income of America's wealthiest families.

What Facts Have Changed?

In 1995 when *Black Wealth/White Wealth* was published, we presented data that were in many re-spects a new way of gauging the economic progress of black Americans visà-vis white Americans. Most commentators and analysts were familiar and comfortable with income comparisons that provided a window on whether there was growing or declining racial economic inequality. But the focus on wealth, "the net value of assets (e.g., ownership of stocks, money in the bank, real estate, business ownership, etc.) less debts," created a different gestalt or perspective on racial inequality.

This gestalt had two dimensions.[4] The first is the conceptual distinction between income and assets. While income represents the flow of resources earned in a particular period, say a week, month, or year, assets are a stock of resources that are saved or invested. Income is mainly used for day-to-day necessities, while assets are special monies not normally used for food or clothing but are rather a "surplus resource available for improving life chances, providing further opportunities, securing prestige, passing status along to one's family," and securing economic security for present and future generations.[5] The second dimension is the quantitative; to what extent is there parity between blacks and whites on assets? Do blacks have access to resources that they can use to plan for their future, to enable their children to obtain a quality education, to provide for the next generation's head start, and to secure their place in the political com-munity? For these reasons, we focused on inequality in wealth as the sine qua non indicator of material well-being. Without sufficient assets, it is difficult to lay claim to economic security in American society.

[handwritten margin notes: BLACK/ WHITE — ① DISTINCTION BETWEEN INCOME & ASSETS — ② WHAT EXTENT OF EQUALITY ON ASSETS — "ABSOLUTELY NECESSARY"]

The baseline indicator of racial wealth inequality is the black-white ratio of median net worth. To what degree are blacks approaching parity with whites in terms of net worth? The change in gestalt is amply demonstrated in comparisons of black-white median income ratios to black-white median net worth ratios. For example, the 1988 data reported on in *Black Wealth/ White Wealth* showed that black families earned sixty-two cents for every dollar of median income that white families earned. However, when the comparisons shift to wealth, the figure showed a remarkably deeper and disturbing level of racial inequality. For every dollar of median net worth that whites controlled, African Americans controlled only eight cents![6]

How has this landmark indicator of racial inequality changed since then? Using the most recent data available, it appears, not unsurprisingly, that the level of racial wealth inequality has not changed but has shown a stubborn persistence that makes the data presented in 1995 more relevant than ever because the pattern we discerned suggests a firmly embedded racial stratification. The most optimistic analyses suggest that the black-white median net worth ratio is 0.10, that is, blacks have control of ten cents for every dollar of net worth that whites possess.[7] However, the most pessimistic estimate indicates that the ratio is closer to seven cents on the dollar.[8] This slim range demonstrates that the level of wealth inequality has not changed appreciably since the publication of *Black Wealth/White Wealth*.[9] However, the story is far more complex.

Using 1988 data, we tabulated the racial wealth gap at $60,980.[10] By 2002 the racial wealth gap increased to $82,663, meaning the wealth of the average African American family fell further behind whites by more than $20,000 over this period. Isolating the period and dynamics of the past decade a little more closely, the racial wealth gap grew by $14,316 between 1996 and 2002. In the decade since *Black Wealth/White Wealth*, then, white wealth grew and then leveled off; black wealth grew and then declined. As a result, the overall racial wealth gap ratio persists at a dime on the dollar, and the dollar amount of the racial wealth gap grew.

Some contradictory facts and new dimensions of financial life in America have affected the persistence of the black-white racial wealth gap. They include a strong economy of the 1990s that enabled greater savings, especially in employer-based savings programs, but which has petered out recently; a stock market bust that punished some of the newest entrants into the market most severely; increasing credit card debt; a growing trend of black home ownership complemented by growing sub-prime and predatory lending directed at minority communities; and growth in the working poor due to the influx of the Temporary Assistance for Needy Families program population into the labor market. This mix of factors weaves the mosaic underlying the story of the continuing racial wealth gap in the first decade of the twenty-first century.

The Story of the Persistence of the Racial Wealth Gap

Traditionally, economists assume that wealth accumulation is the consequence of a "combination of inheritance, earnings, and savings and is enhanced by prudent consumption and investment patterns over a person's life course."[11] How these individual variables interact with the human capital attributes of family members, their education, their occupation, and their ability to begin asset accumulation at an early stage in their life course (the earlier one begins to accumulate assets, the more wealth one can accrue) moves us forward in explaining how differential accumulation occurs. But these individual factors are not the whole story.

As *Black Wealth/White Wealth* convincingly demonstrated, wealth accumulation occurs in a context where these individual attributes unfold to produce varying levels of wealth for different families and social groupings. It has been the different "opportunity structure" for savings and investment that African Americans have faced when compared with whites that has helped to structure racial inequality in wealth holding.

We developed a sociology of wealth and racial inequality in *Black Wealth/White Wealth*, which situated the study of wealth among concerns with race, class, and social inequality. This theoretical framework elucidated the social context in which wealth generation occurs and demonstrated the unique and diverse social circumstances that blacks and whites face. Three concepts we developed provided a sociologically grounded approach to understand the racial wealth gap and highlighted how the opportunity structure disadvantages blacks and contributes to massive wealth inequalities between the races. The first concept, racialization of state policy, explores how state policy has impaired the ability of most black Americans to accumulate wealth from slavery throughout American history to contemporary institutional discrimination. The "economic detour" helps us understand the relatively low level of entrepreneurship among the small scale and segmentally niched businesses of black Americans, leading to an emphasis on consumer spending as the route to economic assimilation. The third concept—the sedimentation of racial inequality—explores how the cumulative effects of the past have seemingly cemented blacks to the bottom of America's economic hierarchy in regards to wealth.

These concepts do much to show how this differential opportunity structure developed and worked to produce black wealth disadvantages. It also builds a strong case that layering wealth deprivation generation after generation has been central in not only blacks' lack of wealth but also whites' privileged position in accumulating wealth. As we noted:

> What is often not acknowledged is that the accumulation of wealth for some whites is intimately tied to the poverty of wealth for most blacks. Just as blacks have had "cumulative disadvantages," whites have had "cumulative advantages." Practically every circumstance of bias and discrimination against blacks has produced a circumstance and opportunity of positive gain for whites.[12]

The past opportunity structure that denied blacks access or full participation in wealth-building activities serves as a powerful deterrent to current black ambitions for wealth. Without an inheritance that is built on generations of steady economic success, blacks, even when they have similar human capital and class position, lag far behind their white counterparts in their quest to accumulate a healthy nest egg of assets. In *Black Wealth/White Wealth* we examined those current institutional and structural constraints that African Americans faced in the 1980s and early 1990s that curtailed and limited the ability of many African Americans to build assets. One area we focused upon was housing, the largest single element of most American's portfolio of assets, and a major part of the wealth in most African American's asset portfolio. We identified a number of institutional constraints ranging from differential access to mortgages, higher costs of mortgages, and differential levels of equity accumulation in homes owing to persistent residential segregation.

We want to extend this mode of theorizing and analysis to the period of the 1990s and into the first decade of the twenty-first century. We attempt to formulate a compelling picture of why African Americans continue to lag so far behind whites in asset holding. Here we focus on the social context of the labor market, the stock and housing market, and growing debt.

The Rise and Decline of a Tight Labor Market and a Bull Stock Market

Black Wealth/White Wealth documented wealth data that reflected a period in the American economy characterized by relatively high unemployment rates and a stagnant economy. However, this period was followed by one of the largest and longest economic expansions in the history of the United States. From its beginning in March 1991 to its ending in November 2001, the United States endured a record expansion. Positive economic indicators that were in sharp contrast to the previous period characterized this expansion. For example, family incomes went from stagnation during the 1979 to 1993 period, where they grew only 0.7 percent over the entire time frame to an increase of 17 percent, or more than $7,000 per family, from 1993 to 2000. In terms of job growth, during the 1992 to 2000 period, the nation created more jobs than at any similar period in American history: 22.6 million, 92 percent of which were in the private sector. Moreover, in contrast to the previous period, where 1.9 million manufacturing jobs were lost, the 1992 to 2000 period saw manufacturing job growth increase by 303,000. Finally, the unemployment rate fell by 42 percent, reaching below 5 percent from July 1997 through January 2001. The 4 percent unemployment rate in 2000—the lowest in over 30 years—stands in striking contrast to an average unemployment rate of 7.1 percent for the 1980 to 1992 period.[13]

For African Americans this was a period of tight labor markets that led to greater levels of labor force participation owing to the existence of greater demand for their participation in the economy. Employers made "extra efforts ... to overcome the barriers created by skill and spatial mismatch" to reach out to African American workers to fill their growing labor needs.[14] Moreover, "employers may find discrimination more costly when the economy is strong and their usually preferred type of job candidate is fully employed elsewhere."[15] In the throes of a heated and tight labor market, *Business Week* proclaimed, "With the economy continuing to expand and unemployment at its lowest point in 30 years, companies are snapping up minorities, women, seniors, and anyone else willing to work for a day's pay."[16]

African Americans, however, did not wholly benefit from this extraordinary period in American history. Black joblessness continued to be a problem. The historical ratio of two-to-one black-to-white unemployment rates persisted with black men averaging 7.1 percent compared with 3 percent for white men, while black women averaged 6.8 compared with 3.2 percent for white women in the latter half of 1999.[17] Nevertheless, those African Americans who were employed during this period saw real wage gains that could be translated into savings, investments, and an increase in net worth.

Another aspect of the expansion of the economy during the 1990s was the rapid rise in the stock market. Fueled by technology stocks and the growth of key stocks like Microsoft, Sun, Yahoo, and other new stock offerings in the technology sector, the stock market started to attract investments not only from high-income and high-wealth individuals, but also from an increasing number of middle-class families and even working-class families. This investment was facilitated by growing participation in employer-sponsored savings programs that enabled employees to make tax-deferred and/or matched contributions through payroll deductions. The ease of the transaction and the constant media and public interest in the high-flying stock market encouraged mass participation. The market rose steadily and rapidly. Beginning from a monthly average in 1992 in the low 400s, the Standard and Poor's 500 tripled in size by 1999.[18] If one were lucky enough to purchase Microsoft or Yahoo early then his or her gains would have been astronomical. For example, when Yahoo was first available as a public offering shares were sold for $1.24. By December 1999 Yahoo listed for $108.17.[19] It was the desire for these kinds of returns that fueled an overheated market and led to the description of "irrational exuberance" concerning the frenzy for the "market."[20]

African Americans, while constrained by resources, also entered into this frenzy. The decade of the 1990s was the breakthrough era for African American involvement in the stock market. Facilitated by employer savings plans and, for the first time, sought after by stock and brokerage firms, African Americans invested readily into the market. In 1996 blacks had a median value of $4,626 invested in stocks and mutual funds. At the height of the market, that value had almost doubled to $8,669. During this period African American stock market investors had closed the black-white ratio of stock market value from twenty-eight cents on the dollar to forty cents on the dollar. However, the market's plunge after 1999 sent African American portfolio values down to a median average of $3,050. This brought the black-white ratio of stock market value back in line with the 1996 level, eroding all the gains that the bull market had bestowed.[21]

African Americans did better in 401(k) and thrift savings plans, which were more likely to be diversified holdings. In 1996 African American investors held a median average of $6,939 in these instruments. With the market surging and regular savings deposits facilitated by payroll deductions, African Americans increased their value in savings or thrift plans to a median average of $10,166 in 2002. The comparison to whites is quite interesting in regard to thrift plans. Between 1996 and 2002 African Americans closed the black-white ratio slightly from 0.43 to 0.50. This is in striking contrast to the data on stock ownership.[22]

Home Ownership, New Mortgage, and Credit Markets

Over the past several years more families than ever across the United States have been able to buy homes. Home ownership rates reached 69 percent in 2004, a historic high. The main reasons for the high level of home ownership include the new mortgage market, where capital is readily available to both families and economic sectors where home ownership was always part of the

American Dream—but in dream only. With home ownership comes the opportunity to accumulate wealth because the value of homes appreciates over time. Indeed, approximately two-thirds of all the wealth of America's middle class families is not in stocks, bonds, investments, or savings accounts but in the form of home equity.

Home equity is the most important wealth component for average American families, and even though home ownership rates are lower, it is even more prominent in the wealth profiles of African American families. Although housing appreciation is very sensitive to many characteristics relating to a community's demographics and profile (which realtors euphemistically call "location, location, location"), overall home ownership has been a prime source of wealth accumulation for black families. For example, for the average black home owner, homes created $6,000 more wealth between 1996 and 2002.[23] However, fundamentally racialized dynamics create and distribute housing wealth unevenly. The Federal Reserve Board kept interest rates at historically low levels for much of this period, and this fueled both demand and hastened converting home equity wealth into cash.

Black Wealth/White Wealth demonstrated the color coding of home equity, and Shapiro's 2004 book, *The Hidden Cost of Being African American*, updates the data and extends our understanding of how residential segregation affects home equity. The typical home owned by white families increased in value by $28,000 more than homes owned by blacks. Persistent residential segregation, especially in cities where most blacks live, explains this equity difference as a compelling index of bias that costs blacks dearly. This data point corroborates other recent research demonstrating that rising housing wealth depends upon a community's demographic characteristics, especially racial composition. One study concludes that homes lost at least 16 percent of their value when located in neighborhoods that are more than 10 percent black. Thus, a "segregation tax" visits black home owners by depressing home values and reducing home equity in highly segregated neighborhoods.[24] Shapiro summarizes the case: "The only prudent conclusion from these studies is that residential segregation costs African American home owners enormous amounts of money by suppressing their home equity in comparison to that of white home owners. The inescapable corollary is that residential segregation benefits white home owners with greater home equity wealth accumulation."[25] Furthermore, most African American families rent housing and thus are not positioned to accumulate housing wealth, mainly because of affordability, credit, and access issues.

The home mortgage marketplace has evolved considerably since 1990, when mortgage packages were offered at a unitary price reflecting the terms of the loan, targeting prospective home owners who met stringent credit history rules and financial criteria. As housing wealth grew and the United States mortgage market became integrated into the global market system, mortgage products proliferated and thus have changed the way American families buy homes. Underwriting standards have become more relaxed, both as financial institutions ease rules to compete in this evolving market and as federal regulations and oversight have become less stringent.[26]

Minorities are making significant inroads into all segments of the housing market. Indeed, important components feeding the general trends of increasing rates of new home construction and home value appreciation include the demographic push from new immigrants, the accomplishments of second-generation immigrants, and the success of a segment of African American families. In 2004, home ownership reached historic highs as 69 percent of American families live in a home they own. In 1995, 42.2 percent of African American families owned homes, increasing to a historic high, 49.5 percent, in 2004. This 17.3 percent increase in African American home ownership is quite remarkable, indicating striving, accomplishment, and success. The black-white home ownership gap in 1995 stood at 28.5 percent and narrowed to 26.2 percent in 2004.[27] We might expect the home ownership gap to continue closing as black home ownership starts from a considerably lower base while the higher white rate may be close to exhausting the potential of those who want to become home owners.

In 1995, access to credit for minorities was a major issue. Financial institutions responded both to criticisms regarding credit discrimination and to the newly discovered buying capacity of minorities. Increasing numbers of African American and Hispanic families gained access to credit cards throughout the 1990s: 45 percent of African American and 43 percent of Hispanic families held credit cards in 1992 and by 2001 nearly 60 percent of African American and 53 percent of Hispanic families held credit cards.[28] The irony here is that as access to credit broadened under terms highly favorable to lenders, debt became rampant and millions of families became ensnared in a debt vice.

Credit card debt nearly tripled from $238 billion in 1989 to $692 billion in 2001.[29] These figures represent family reliance on financing consumption through debt, especially expensive credit in the form of credit cards and department store charge cards. During the 1990s, the average American family experienced a 53 percent increase in credit card debt—the average family's card debt rising from $2,697 to $4,126. Credit card debt among low-income families increased 184 percent. Even high-income families became more dependent on credit cards: There was 28 percent more debt in 2001 than in 1989. The main sources of credit card debt include spiraling health care costs, lower employer coverage of health insurance, and rising housing costs amid stagnating or declining wages after 2000 and increasingly unsteady employment for many. This suggests strongly that the increasing debt is not the result of frivolous or conspicuous spending or lack of budgetary discipline; instead, deferring payment to make ends meet is becoming the American way for many to finance daily life in the new economy.

Given that a period of rising income did not lift the African American standard of living, and given the context of overall rising family debt, an examination of the racial component of credit card debt furthers our understanding of the contemporary processes associated with the continuation of the economic detour and the further sedimentation of inequality. The average credit card debt of African Americans increased 22 percent between 1992 and 2001, when it reached an average of nearly $3,000.[30] Hispanic credit card debt mirrored blacks by rising 20 percent in the same period to $3,691. As we know, the average white credit card debt was higher, reaching $4,381 in 2001. One of the most salient facts involves the magnitude and depth of African American reliance on debt. Among those holding credit cards with balances, nearly one in five African Americans earning less than $50,000 spend at least 40 percent of their income paying debt service. In other words, in every 8-hour working day these families labor 3.2 hours to pay off consumer debt. Even though black families carry smaller monthly balances, a higher percentage of their financial resources goes toward servicing debt.

The median net worth of African American families at the end of 2002 was $5,988, essentially the same as it was in 1988.[31] Again, it is not as if nothing happened since we wrote *Black Wealth/White Wealth*; indeed, African American fortunes expanded with good times and contracted with recessions and the bursting of the stock market bubble. In the last decade, the high point of African American (and Hispanic) wealth accumulation was 1999, when it registered $8,774, just before the bursting of the stock market bubble in early 2000. Between 1999 and 2002, African American wealth declined from $8,774 to $5,988, wiping out more than a decade's worth of financial gains.

Median wealth and racial wealth gap data tell us about absolute wealth accumulation and the relative positioning of African American families. Another sense of the dynamics of the last ten years concerns the dispersion of assets among African American families. In 1996, 31.9 percent of African American families owned zero net worth or—worse still—had bottom lines that put them in the red. By 1999, this figure declined to 28.2 percent but deteriorated again after the stock market burst and the beginning of the recession, by increasing to 32.3 percent in 2002. This has left more African American families in absolute asset poverty than at the time of the book's initial publication.

New Dynamics of Markets and Institutions

As we have indicated, the decade between 1995 and 2006 really is marked off by two distinct periods: African American family wealth accumulates considerably and more families move into positive wealth positions until early 2000. From 2000 through 2005, however, the financial wealth of African American families made a U-turn, both losing actual wealth and increasing the number of families with zero or negative wealth once more. Throughout the entire period, home ownership and home equity continued to rise for all segments of American families, including African Americans. An important narrative, then, involves this great expansion of financial wealth, home ownership, and housing wealth; understanding what happened to this wealth; examining the opportunities this new wealth created, especially for financial institutions looking for new markets; and importantly, the impact of these developments and new dynamics on African Americans.

Housing Wealth and Its Uses

Households cashed out $407 billion worth of equity from homes in just three years, 2002 through 2004, in the refinancing boom that began in 2001. Although such data have not been collected for very long, American families were refinancing homes at record levels, three times higher than any other period.[32] Nearly half of all mortgage debt was refinanced between 2002 and 2003, averaging $27,000 in equity per home in the early stages of the refinancing wave.[33]

As mortgage interest rates fell to record low levels during the refinance boom, and as housing continued to appreciate and result in wealth accumulation, many Americans cashed out home equity to pay down debt and finance living expenses, trading off wealth to pay off past consumption and fund new purchases.

Refinancing at lower interest rates and hence lower monthly payments is certainly a good deal for families paying off mortgages because it leaves more money in the family budget for living expenses, discretionary purchases, or savings. We need to ask the important question of how families used this bonanza. Investing in human capital through continued education or career retooling, investing in other financial instruments, building a business, home improvements, and similar choices expand opportunities, improve living standards, and may launch further social mobility. On the other hand, paying down high-interest debt may slow down temporarily the debt-driven consumption treadmill but most likely does not improve the long-term standard of living or life chances of a family, and certainly does not improve the future wealth accumulation picture. Slightly over one-half used housing wealth to cover living expenses and to pay down store and credit cards. Another 25 percent used funds for consumer expenditures such as vehicle purchases and medical expenses. Thus it appears that a majority of households used these new home equity loans to convert credit card debt and current living expenses into long-term mortgage debt.

One result is that between 1973 and 2004, home owners' equity actually fell—from 68.3 percent to 55 percent so that Americans own less of their homes today than they did in the 1970s and early 1980s. And, it is worth remembering that home equity is by far the largest source of wealth for the vast majority of American families. The intersection of wealth and race illustrates the magnified importance of home equity for African Americans and Hispanics. Among whites, home equity represented 38.5 percent of their entire wealth portfolio in 2002. In sharp contrast, home equity accounted for 63 percent of wealth among African Americans and 61 percent for Hispanics.[34]

The Dark Side of Home Ownership

Subprime lending is targeted to prospective homebuyers with blemished credit histories or with high levels of debt who otherwise would not qualify for conventional mortgage loans. A legitimate niche for these kinds of loans brings home ownership within the grasp of millions of families. These loan products are essential in expanding home ownership rates. In return for these riskier investments, financial institutions charge borrowers higher interest rates, often requiring higher processing and closing fees, and often containing special loan conditions like prepayment penalties, balloon payments, and adjustable interest rates.

The subprime market expanded greatly in the last decade as part of new, aggressive marketing strategies among financial institutions hungrily eyeing rising home ownership and seeing promising new markets. Moreover, the mortgage finance system in the United States became well integrated into global capital markets, which offer an ever-growing array of financial products, including subprime loans. Subprime loan originations grew fifteen-fold, from $35 billion to $530 billion between 1994 and 2004. Reflecting the increasing importance of subprime loans to the financial industry, the subprime share of mortgage loans has seen a parallel meteoric rise from less than 4 percent in 1995 to representing about 17 percent of mortgage loans in 2004.[35]

Loan terms like prepayment penalties and balloon payments increase the risk of mortgage foreclosure in subprime home loans, even after controlling for the borrower's credit score, loan terms, and varying economic conditions.[36] One study from the Center for Community Capitalism demonstrates that subprime prepayment penalties and balloon payments place Americans at substantially greater risk of losing their homes.

Delinquency (falling behind in mortgage payments) and losing one's home through foreclosure are hitting vulnerable neighborhoods hardest. Concentrated foreclosures can negatively affect the surrounding neighborhoods, threatening to undo community building and revitalization efforts achieved through decades of collaborative public-private partnerships, community organizing, and local policy efforts.

Los Angeles is a case in point.[37] In a short three-year period, 2001 to 2004, over 14,000 Los Angeles families lost their homes through foreclosure. The foreclosure rate is highest in the most vulnerable neighborhoods. In predominately minority neighborhoods (80 percent or more minority) of Los Angeles County the foreclosure rate is almost four times the rate that it is in neighborhoods where minorities are less than 20 percent of the population. In the City of Los Angeles, foreclosures occur nearly twelve times more often in predominately minority communities compared with areas that have fewer than 20 percent minorities. Los Angeles is not alone; data from Atlanta, Baltimore, Boston, Chicago, and others show that Los Angeles is part of the larger, national pattern.

A study examining pricing disparities in the mortgage market provides more context, placing the Los Angeles story in a broader pattern. Of all conventional loans to blacks, nearly 30 percent were subprime compared with only 10 percent for whites.[38] These ratios would be in closer alignment in lending markets operating with maximum efficiency and equity. Creditworthy criteria, like debt-to-income ratios, do not explain the greater propensity for African Americans to receive subprime loans. The report also discovered that subprime loans in minority communities increased with levels of racial segregation. This finding suggests an alarming new form of modern redlining that targets minority neighborhoods for subprime loans.

Using a testing methodology adapted from those that explored job discrimination, the National Community Reinvestment Coalition was able to explore how pricing disparities resulting from intensified subprime lending in minority areas occurred. Essentially, white and black testers with similar credit records and qualifications applied for preapproval for mortgages. Given similar scripts and profiles (with African Americans actually presenting better qualifications), the testing uncovered a 45 percent rate of disparate treatment based on race. The testing revealed practices that may have destructive effects on African American families and communities. These include: differences in interest rates quoted; differences in information about fees, rates, loan programs, and loan terms; and whites more often referred up to the lender's prime lending division. In *Black Wealth/White Wealth* we wrote that differences in loan rejection rates and interest rates did not result from discriminatory lending practices but from blacks bringing fewer financial assets to the mortgage table; as a result, they paid higher loan terms. Racial pricing disparities and the targeted spread of subprime lending to minority communities, however, now persuades us that minority America is experiencing a new form of redlining organized by race and geographic space.

Black Wealth/White Wealth demonstrated the power of policy, government, institutions, and history to order and maintain racial inequality. The previous sections show further the significance of financial institutions in granting access to credit and the terms of credit, and the increasing dependence on credit and debt. The basis for excluding African Americans from opportunities and creating different rules in the competition for success is no longer just who is a capable worker. Now we must add who is a worthy credit risk and on what terms. Job discrimination against individual blacks based on perceived characteristics is not the only major arena in the struggle against inequality; exclusion in terms of creditworthiness is as well.

Discussion Questions

1   What are the three sociological concepts that help us understand the racial wealth gap and highlight how opportunity structure disadvantages blacks and contributes to massive wealth inequalities between the races?

2   African Americans continue to lag behind whites in asset holdings. Discuss the effects of the social context of the labor market, the stock and housing market, and growing debt.

3   To what degree are blacks approaching parity with whites in terms of net worth?

4   How did the subprime mortgage crisis affect minority communities differently than non-minority communities? Looking ahead, discuss what long-term impact this may have on wealth accumulation among African Americans.

Notes

1 Wolff, 2004.

2 Johnson, 2005.

3 Johnson, 2005.

4 Oliver and Shapiro, p. 30

5 Oliver and Shapiro, p. 32.

6 Oliver and Shapiro, pp. 85–86.

7 Shapiro, 2004a.

8 Kochhar.

9 Federation of Consumer Services data yield a more narrowed ratio. These data are inconsistent with virtually all other data measuring wealth inequality. We are not confident with its methodology or operational definitions of wealth. See Consumer Federation of America and BET.com, 2003.

10 We adjusted the 1988 figure originally reported in the book to reflect 2002 dollars.

11 Oliver and Shapiro, p. 36.

12 Oliver and Shapiro, p. 51.

13 The National Bureau of Economic Research's Business Cycle Committee keeps track of business expansions and recessions; see http://www.nber.org/cycles/recessions.html. For a general overview of the Clinton expansion's impact on the poor, see Blank and Ellwood.

14 Bradbury, p. 14, and Holzer, Raphael, and Stoll.

15 Bradbury, p. 14.

16 Bradbury, p. 15.

17 Bradbury, p. 4.

18 Shiller. Also see http://www.irrationalexuberance.com/index.htm for historical data on the stock market.

19 See quarterly stock prices for Yahoo at http://finance.yahoo.com/q/hp?s=Y HOO&a=03&b=12&c=1 996&d=07&e=14&f=2005&g=m&z=66&y=66.

20 The origin of the descriptor "irrational exuberance" is found in a speech by Federal Reserve Board Chairman Alan Greenspan, 1996.

21 These data are from a survey of high-income blacks (yearly incomes of $50,000 or more) sponsored by Ariel Mutual Funds/Charles Schwab & Co., Inc. This very valuable survey examines the financial behavior, asset value, and composition of this group of African Americans. See Black Investor Survey.

22 Black Investor Survey.

23 Kochhar, p. 18.

24 Rusk.

25 Shapiro, 2004a.

26 The exemplar for "easing" regulatory oversight and financial institution accountability was the repeal of the Glass-Steagall Act of 1933. This act was designed to protect the public from between commercial banks, insurance companies, and brokerage firms, which contributed to the stock market crash of 1929. The Financial Services Modernization Act of 1999 does away with restrictions on the integration of banking, insurance, and stock trading, which has encouraged a rash of mergers

leading to greater concentration in the financial sector. As a result, banks were looking for new markets and were anxious to provide new products. As part of the 1999 Act, regular oversight opportunities provided to community organizations through the Community Reinvestment Act were relaxed considerably. Consequently, the frequency of CRA examinations was limited. See Berton and Futterman.

27 Joint Center for Housing Studies, 2005.

28 Silva and Epstein.

29 Draut and Silva.

30 Silva and Epstein.

31 This section uses SIPP data from 2002 as reported in the Pew Hispanic Center report.

32 Joint Center for Housing Studies, 2004.

33 Silva.

34 These are based on distribution of mean worth, so the figure for whites, in particular, because of the skewed distribution, looks low and vastly understates the importance of home equity in the wealth portfolios of middle-class white families (Kochhar).

35 Joint Center for Housing Studies, 2005.

36 Quercia, Stegman, and Davis.

37 Duda and Apgar.

38 National Community Reinvestment Coalition; Adams.

References

Adams, John. 1988. "Growth of U.S. Cities and Recent Trends in Urban Real Estate Values." In *Cities and Their Vital Systems*, ed., J. H. Ausubel and R. Herman. Washington, DC: National Academy Press. 108–45.

Berton, Brad, and Susan Futterman. 2003. "Community Groups see Continuing Chill on CRA, Affordable Housing Finance." http://www.housingfinance.com/ahf/articles/2002/02OctCommunityLeanding/BET.com.

Black Investor Survey. "Saving and Investing Among Higher Income African-American and White Americans," July 2005. http://www.arielmutuafunds.com//funds/2004-survey/2004%20AAIS%20FULL%20EXTERNAL.ppt.

Blank, Rebecca, and David T. Ellwood. 2002. "The Clinton Legacy for America's Poor." in *American Economic Policy in the 1990s*, Jeffrey A. Frankel and Peter R. Orszag. Cambridge, MA: MIT Press.

Bradbury, Katharine L. 2000. "Rising Tide in the Labor Market: To What Degree do Expansions Benefit the Disadvantaged?" *New England Economic Review* 4 (May/June): 3–33.

Consumer Federation of America. 2003. "More African-Americans Save and Begin to Close Wealth Gap." http://www.consumerfed.org/102903blackamsaves.pdf.

Duda, Mark, and William Apgar. 2004. Mortgage Foreclosure Trends in Los Angeles: Patterns and Policy Issues. A report prepared for the Los Angeles Neighborhood Housing Services.

Greenspan, Alan. 1996. The Challenge of Central Banking in a Democratic Society. Address to the American Enterprise Institute at the Washington Hilton Hotel, December 5, 1996.

Holzer, Harry, Steven Raphael, and Michael A. Stoll. 2003. "Employers in the Boom: How Did the hiring of Unskilled Workers Change During the 1990s?" http://www.urban.org/UploadedPDF/410780_BoomPaper.pdf.

Johnson, David Cay. 2005. "Richest are Leaving Even the Rich Far Behind," *New York Times*, June 5.

Joint Center for Housing Studies of Harvard University. 2004. The State of the Nation's Housing. Cambridge, MA.

Joint Center for Housing Studies of Harvard University. 2005. The State of the Nation's Housing. Cambridge, MA.

Kochhar, Rakesh. 2004. *The Wealth of Hispanic Households: 1996 to 2002*. Washington, DC: Pew Hispanic Center.

National Community Reinvestment Coalition. 2005. Preapprovals and Pricing Disparities in the Mortgage Marketplace, June 2005. http://ncrc.org/pressandpubs/press_releases/documents/Preapproval_Report_June05.pdf.

Oliver, Melvin L., and Thomas M. Shapiro. 1995. *Black Wealth/White Wealth: A New Perspective on Racial Inequality*. New York and London: Routledge.

Quercia, Roberto G., Michael A. Stegman, and Walter R. Davis. 2005. "The Impact of Predatory Loan Terms on Subprime Foreclosures." Center for Community Capitalism. http://www.kenan-flagler.unc.edu/assets/documents/foreclosurepaper.pdf.

Rusk, David. 2001. *The 'Segregation Tax': The Cost of Racial Segregation of Black Homeowners*. Washington, DC: Brookings Institution Center on Urban and Metropolitan Policy.

Shapiro, Thomas M. 2004a. *The Hidden Cost of Being African American: How Wealth Perpetuates Inequality*. New York: Oxford University Press.

Shiller, Robert J. 2005. *Irrational Exuberance*. Princeton, NJ: Princeton University Press.

Silva, Javier. 2005. *A House of Cards: Financing the American Dream*. New York: Demos.

Silva, Javier, and Rebecca Epstein. 2005. *Costly Credit: African Americans and Latinos in Debt*. New York: Demos.

Wolff, Edward N. 2004. "Changes in Household Wealth in the 1980s and 1990s." In the U.S. Economics Working Paper Archive, Number 47. Annandale-on-Hudson, NY: The Levy Economics Institute.

The Impact of Microaggressions and Structural Inequalities on the Well-Being of Latina/o American Communities

David P. Rivera, Rebecca Rangel Campón, and Krista Herbert

Introduction

Latina/o Americans are one of the fastest growing and largest ethnic groups in the United States (US) (U.S. Census Bureau, 2011). Roughly 53 million people living in the US are Hispanic or Latina/o, which constitutes 17% of the nation's population (Brown & Patten, 2014). Of this number, 35.5% are first-generation (i.e., born outside of the US). Among the 40 million documented immigrants living in the US, about 28% immigrate from Mexico, 7.8% from Central American, and 6.7% from South America. More specifically, large numbers of Latinas/os are immigrating to the US from Mexico, followed by El Salvador, Cuba, Dominican Republic, Guatemala, Columbia, Honduras, Ecuador, Peru, Nicaragua, Venezuela, Argentina, Panama, Chile, Cost Rica, Bolivia, Uruguay, and Paraguay. These figures do not include Puerto Ricans, who are considered US citizens and comprise roughly 9% of the US population (U.S. Census Bureau, 2011).

Despite Latina/o Americans comprising a significant proportion of the US population, their story is nuanced, complicated, and contradictory at best. For example, older generations of Latinas/os tout themselves as being among the first non-indigenous citizens of the present day US and are likely to identify as culturally American, while newer generations are likely to identify as being bicultural or more culturally aligned with their country of origin (Marotta & Garcia, 2003). The contributions of Latina/o Americans are honored and celebrated, such as through the appointment of Justice

Sonia Sotomayor to the US Supreme Court. Conversely, the seemingly never-ending contentious debate over immigration reform has put a spotlight on Latinas/os, whether documented or undocumented, and contributes to the numerous ways this group is adversely treated on a daily basis (Rivera, Forquer, & Rangel, 2010). For example, Arizona sheriff Joe Arpaio was prosecuted due to a violation of civil and constitutional rights against Latinas/os (Wian & Martinez, 2012). Determined to rid the US of undocumented immigrants, Arpaio's tactics appeared to target all Latinas/os and included pulling over drivers and passengers during county traffic stops. Not only did Arpaio harass Latinas/os for proof of immigration documentation, but even when individuals possessed a valid documentation they were still arrested.

While Latina/o Americans are on the verge of reaching a critical mass population wise, there continues to exist a relatively consistent degree of inequalities and disparities in access to and participation in the vast majority of social institutions in the US. Despite being the largest growing ethnic minority group in the US, Latinas/os are still considered second-class citizens and are overrepresented among the unemployed and poor (Sue & Sue, 2012). Latinas/os also experience a significant discrepancy in income and housing when compared to White Americans. These experiences of social inequalities not only impact their education and work, but also significantly affect their ability to receive adequate and appropriate medical and mental health services. Furthermore, the lack of cultural understanding of Latinas/os among professional and laypersons further contributes to these disparities. Latinas/os' cultural beliefs, such as their strong ties and responsibility towards their families, strong Catholic religious affiliations, and traditional sex role beliefs can conflict with the individualistic and independent society of the US (Sue & Sue, 2012). For many Latinas/os, discrimination in their everyday lives has been considered to be the most important issue that they face (Sue & Sue, 2012). Not only does discrimination affect Latinas/os role in society, but it also affects their ability to succeed and achieve optimum quality of life. In order to help make sense of the various social inequalities that are experienced by Latina/o Americans, this chapter will focus on interpersonal and structural barriers that influence the well-being of Latina/o Americans.

Microaggressions & Interpersonal Barriers

Interpersonal barriers that Latinas/os report experiencing on a daily basis come in the form of microaggressions (Nadal, Mazzula, Rivera, & Fujii-Doe, 2014; Rivera et al., 2010). Microaggressions, originally conceptualized in the context of interracial interactions, are defined as "brief and commonplace daily verbal, behavioral, and environmental indignities, whether intentional or unintentional, that communicate hostile, derogatory, or negative racial slights and insults to the target person or group" (Sue et al., 2007, p. 273). Latinas/os report experiencing a variety of microaggressions on the interpersonal level that include having their intelligence questioned, being ignored or denied services in social settings, having their cultural values pathologized, receiving adverse treatment for speaking Spanish, and being treated like perpetual foreigners to name a few (Rivera et al., 2010). An example of a microaggression is found in the seemingly innocuous question "Where are you from?" This question seems harmless because it is a question that is frequently asked upon first meeting someone. However, it becomes microaggressive when the inquirer is not satisfied with the first answer and proceeds to question the individual further about their geographic origin. The implicit message conveyed from this line of inquiry is that the individual in question is not originally from the US. Furthermore, the microaggressive encounter is typically inspired by a stereotype internalized by the enactor that is informed by prejudicial beliefs about where people with physical (e.g., darker skin) and verbal characteristics (e.g., Spanish language, accent, etc.) similar to the aggressed individual are from. Microaggressions also manifest environmentally via the draconian legal measures proposed and taken in regards to immigration reform, as well as the underrepresentation of Latinas/os in managerial and professional occupations and overrepresentation in service related occupations (U.S. Department of Labor, 2008).

These interpersonal and environmental microaggressions (i.e., subtle, covert insults and invalidations embedded in public and private spaces, such as in the media) are correlated with compromises in well-being for Latinas/os (Nadal, Griffin, Wong, Hamit, & Rasmus, 2014; Rivera, 2012). For example, microaggressions were significantly correlated with compromised mental health such that Latinas/os who reported higher levels of microaggressions also reported compromises in mental health indicators, such as higher levels of anxiety and depression and poorer behavioral control and positive affect (Nadal et al., 2014; Rivera, 2012). Additionally, microaggressions have been linked with poorer general physical health as assessed by a global self-rating of physical health (Rivera, Molina, & Watkins, 2012). It has been suggested that a global self-rating of physical health can provide accurate information about mortality and health status (Idler & Benyamini, 1997). Although still in a nascent stage of development, microaggression and health-related outcomes research is beginning to provide support for the detrimental impact of these interactions.

In addition to this individual-level impact, microaggressions are also believed to play a role in creating and maintaining institutional- and societal-level inequalities (Sue, 2010). People of Color, including Latinas/os, describe the workplace as hostile and unwelcoming (Rivera et al., 2010; Sue, Lin, & Rivera, 2009). This hostility manifests in the form of interpersonal and environmental microaggressions that influence the movement of people through the social institutions we as citizens navigate on a daily basis. In effect, these hostile interactions help to maintain two vastly different pathways used to navigate daily life; one pathway that supports, validates, and encourages movement of the social majority through institutions (e.g., healthcare, education, workplace, etc.), and one pathway that opposes, invalidates, and discourages movement of the socially marginalized through these same institutions. Healthcare is one such institution where these different pathways operate to benefit some and harm others. The following sections will discuss the issues and structural inequalities that impact the healthcare of Latina/o Americans.

The following example illustrates the complexity of how microaggressions in the context of a racist system contribute to the above-mentioned structural inequalities. There is a long history of individuals being discrimination against until they have been forced out, to live with others "like themselves." The location of where one resides impacts many aspects of one's social life (Massey, 2004; Williams & Collins, 2001). For instance, the location of an individual's residence is a large determinant of which school they attend, what jobs are accessible to them, the type and quality of public benefits accessible to them, and what stores and other commercial resources are accessible near their residence. These social, educational and health resources, influenced by where the individual lives, in turn impact their quality of education, future careers, health and quality of life, as well as defining their lifestyle (Marger, 2006).

Taking accessibility to schools as an example, the results from the Education Trust Study demonstrate that clear inequities exist in state and local distribution of education dollars to districts with the highest student of color enrollments (Orlofsky, 2002). According to data collected between 1999–2000, 22 of the 47 states studied sent substantially less money per student to school districts that have the greatest number of student of color enrollment. One example is that of New York State which provides an additional $1,339 per student in state revenue to districts with the *fewest* student of color enrollments when compared to districts with the highest number of minority students. Thus, for New York, its districts with the highest populations of color have significantly *less* money allocated per student then its districts with the fewest students of color. Nationally, districts with the greatest number of poor students receive $966 less per student than districts with lower poverty rates. Hence, these statistics demonstrate the reality for individuals of color who statistically are more likely to live in poverty (U.S. Department of Health and Human Services, 2001) will have less access to quality education. Their districts (determined by where they live) have less funding to obtain the most qualified teachers and provide additional instructional time, resources and equipment that has shown to make a difference in education (Orlofsky, 2002). These overwhelming statistics represent the serious consequences of oppression that render people powerless and dependent. In this way, people of color may find themselves at a disadvantage and targets for daily microaggressions, thus feeling the weight of their social status in their everyday lives.

Structural Inequalities for Latinas/OS in Everyday Life

Access to Quality Healthcare

According to the National Healthcare Disparities Report (U.S. Department of Health & Human Services, 2013), disparities related to race, ethnicity, and socioeconomic status still pervade the American healthcare system and are observed across a number of dimensions including, effectiveness of care for common clinical conditions, effectiveness of care across the lifespan, patient safety, timeliness, patient centeredness, efficiency, health system infrastructure, and access to health-care. Analyses of these dimensions reveal significant disparities in healthcare for Blacks, Asians, American Indians, Alaska Natives, Native Hawaiians/Pacific Islanders, and Latinas/os when compared to their White counterparts. For example, Latinas/os experienced no significant change in the majority of indicators used to assess these dimensions, and experienced an increase in disparities for three of the indicators. In sum, these statistics demonstrate limited progress in the elimination of healthcare disparities and that significant gaps in quality and access persist.

Additionally, factors such as cost of care, lack of sufficient insurance for mental health services, social stigma, fragmented organization of services, and mistrust all present significant barriers to treatment. Economic and geographic factors also significantly influence mental health. Poverty is a risk factor for poor mental health as well as a result of poor mental health. Additionally, many people who reside in rural and remote areas with mental illnesses have less adequate access to care, more limited availability of skilled care providers, lower family incomes, and greater societal stigma for seeking mental health treatment than those residing in urban areas (NHDR, 2013).

In terms of access to healthcare, a logical issue to explore is that of insurance. Latinas/os are more likely to suffer from chronic conditions such as high blood pressure, arthritis, neck and back pain, diabetes, obesity, hypertension, heart disease, and comorbid substance abuse and other mental health disorders (Ai, Appel, Huang, & Lee, 2012; U.S. Department of Health & Human Services, 2009). Despite this obvious need for access to quality healthcare, Latinas/os are overrepresented among the uninsured (Betancourt, Green, Carrillo, & Ananeh-Firempong, 2003). As a result, Latinas/os are more likely to delay care for their chronic conditions and less likely to seek mental healthcare than any other ethnic group (Ai et al., 2012). Questions remain as to why Latinas/os lack health insurance, in addition to their underutilization of medical and mental health services.

There are several issues that may account for the lack health insurance coverage for Latinas/os, including quality of employment opportunities and access to public resources. For many Americans, health insurance coverage benefits comes with full-time employment opportunities; however, Latina/o Americans are less likely to be offered these healthcare benefits from employers (Weinick, Jacobs, Cacari Stone, Ortega, & Burstin, 2004). Although Latinas/os constitute a large portion of the labor force a disproportionate number have little or no access to public or private health insurance. Even those who qualify for public assistance coverage, such as Medicaid, find it extremely difficult to find quality providers who are willing to accept this type of insurance (Valdez, Giachello, Rodriguez-Trias, Gomez, & de la Rocha, 1993).

Additionally, many Latinas/os are employed at low-wage salaries and are less likely to be offered health insurance or be able to afford insurance on their own. Research has shown that regardless of the type of work, amount of hours worked, or size of the employer, Latinas/os are less likely to have employer-sponsored health insurance compared to White Americans (Weinick et al., 2004). For example, in every type of industry, from small firms and public administration to agricultural work, Latinas/os are significantly less likely to receive healthcare benefits from the employer (Brown, Ojeda, Wyn, & Levan, 2000). This inequality of health insurance for Latina/o Americans serves as a structural barrier to their access and utilization of healthcare, and also affects access to preventative care, high usage of emergency departments, and difficulty obtaining prescription medications (Betancourt et al., 2003).

Despite the fact that the high-uninsured rates hinder Latinas/os from receiving physical and mental healthcare, even the insured have significant barriers that prevent them from receiving adequate care. Racial and ethnic disparities in the access and utilization of healthcare, and in the diagnosing and treatment of various conditions exist even when researchers control for factors such as insurance status, income, age, condition, socioeconomic status and site of care (Betancourt et al., 2003). Microaggressions, bias, discrimination, and prejudice on the part of healthcare providers can significantly contribute to the variation in healthcare for Latinas/os. For example, many Latinas/os may experience maltreatment, be neglected or ignored, or not provided quality treatment from one or more providers that hinders their trust and desire to go back.

Many Latina/o Americans have reported that they feel racism and discrimination exists within the healthcare system, which impacts their willingness to go to a facility, the quality of care they receive, and satisfaction with their care (Chen, Fryer, Philips, Wilson, & Pathman, 2005). Latinas/os report that they receive substandard quality of care that often occurs when the healthcare provider is not Latina/o. Research has found that when Latinas/os perceive racism to exist in the healthcare system, they not only prefer a physician and mental health provider who is also Latina/o, but have also reported higher levels of satisfaction with the care, higher quality of care, and feel more comfortable and confident in a physician who is Latina/o because of factors such as shared cultural beliefs, social experiences, language, and how they treat the patient (Betancourt et al., 2003; Chen et al., 2005).

For example, patients' of color and low to middle socioeconomic status were associated with physicians' perception of patient intelligence, their perception of their ability to connect to and relate to the patient, and their beliefs about the patient's engagement in risky behaviors and adherence to medical advice (van Ryn & Burke, 2000). In addition to these perceptions, the race, ethnicity, and socioeconomic status of the patient are related to the physician's perception of the patient's personality, role demands, and abilities. The physician's perceptions of the patient directly impacts how they treat the patient, on both a personal and professional level, in addition to the decreased likelihood of patients of color continuing to get quality medical care.

Latinas/os without health insurance are often required to utilize public health services, which are often underfunded, understaffed, and antiquated in their design. These facilities rarely reflect the cultural or social concerns of the communities where they are located and too few providers locate their facilities in Latina/o communities (Valdez, et al., 1993). Some of the justified criticisms of healthcare provision Latinas/os consistently report include language problems/lack of interpreter services, long waits at the physician' office and to make appointments, limited clinical office hours, and the lack of culturally (and linguistically) appropriate physical and mental health resources (Betancourt et al., 2003; Flores, Abreu, Olivar, & Kastner, 1998; Valdez et al., 1993). For many Latinas/os, these factors are associated with dissatisfaction of care, and lower quality of care. When these cultural and linguistic barriers exist, they negatively impact communication and trust between patient and physician, thus causing poorer health outcomes and less comprehension and compliance with medical advice.

The structural inequalities that exist in the medical and mental health community go beyond that of the healthcare provider's bias and discrimination of Latinas/os, but are also reflected on a societal level. The nation's leaders in health-care and the healthcare workforce do not reflect the racial and ethnic composition of the general population, which affects the utilization and availability of healthcare for Latinas/os (Betancourt et al., 2003). African Americans, Latinas/os, and Native Americans are substantially underrepresented in the health professions. The absence of diversity in the healthcare system causes structural policies, procedures, and delivery systems to be poorly designed to serve diverse patient populations. Furthermore, the lack of culturally competent medical and mental health professions not only discourages Latinas/os and people of color from utilizing various services, but also significantly impacts the quality of services they receive. People of color in the healthcare professions are more likely to organize policies, procedures and healthcare delivery systems that meet the needs of people of color (Betancourt et al., 2003). Additionally, the lack of community outreach programs for Latinas/os creates significant barriers to receiving adequate care. This failure to provide education and target programs and services for Latinos significantly limits the services available for them, in addition to quality service available (Valdez et al., 1993). Without culturally competent physicians, mental health professionals, policies, and procedures, the healthcare of Latina/o Americans is severely compromised, thus preventing many Latinas/os from receiving necessary healthcare.

Interpersonal and Institutionalized Discrimination

According to the American Psychiatric Association (2006), "racism and racial discrimination are two of the factors leading to mental healthcare disparities" and encourages that those in the mental health field "should be mindful of the existence and impact of racism and racial discrimination in the lives of patients and their families, in clinical encounters, and in the development of mental health services" (Resolution Against Racism and Racial Discrimination and Their Adverse Impacts on Mental Health). For many Latinas/or, instances of racism and racial discrimination are daily occurrences (Pérez, Fortuna, & Alegría, 2008). Understanding the occurrences and impact of racism and racial discrimination among Latinas/os is vital to assessment, diagnosis, and treatment for Latinas/os, as these factors may significantly influence their worldview, symptoms, self-esteem, and ethnic identity. Evidence has found a significant relationship between racial discrimination and mental health disorders (e.g., Bhui, Stansfeld, McKenzie, Karlsen, Nazroo, & Weich, 2005; Gee, Spencer, Chen, Yip, & Takeuchi, 2007; Karlsen, Nazroo, McKenzie, Bhui, & Weich, 2005). For example, evidence suggests a relationship between perceived discrimination and psychopathology for Latina/o Americans (Chou, Asnaani, & Hofmann, 2012). More specifically, Latina/o participants who reported instances of perceived discrimination were more likely to report symptoms of panic disorder, agoraphobia, and depression. Other researchers have found that instances of racial discrimination have been association with poor self-assessed mental health for Latina/o Americans (see Araújo, & Borrell, 2006, for a literature review).

Despite the mounting evidence suggesting the negative implications of racism and racial discrimination on mental health for Latinas/os, few researchers have attempted to understand why these relationships exist. Gaining an understanding of the causal nature of these experiences could be vital when developing interventions for Latinas/os to help them cope with and respond to instances of discrimination. In their attempt to explore the causal relationship between discrimination and mental health problems, Pascoe and Smart Richman (2009) conducted a meta-analysis of over 134 articles and proposed a perceived discrimination-stress response model based on the results. The proposed model conceptualizes discrimination as a social stressor that could have a direct impact on the physical and mental health of Latinas/os and people of color. This study suggested that this relationship could be partially mediated by the individual's response to stress, such as negative emotions and psychological responses. The more occurrences of discrimination an individual perceives, the more likely this negative stress response becomes activated, potentially leading to a constant negative emotional state. Furthermore, the authors propose that health risk behaviors (such as drinking and substance use) could manifest as possible coping mechanisms, which could further impact mental health. In fact, Carter and Forsyth (2010) asked participants to describe significant moments of racial discrimination throughout their lifetime and found that about half of the participants reported feeling stressed 2 months to 1 year or long after the discriminatory event. They also found that more than half of the participants described events that occurred between 5 and 10 years prior to the study, suggesting that the memory and stress of those events are carried with the individual for a significant portion of their lives.

These racial disparities in healthcare are compounded by a lack of culturally and linguistically competent providers. In fact, lack of culturally competent healthcare providers and stereotypes perpetuated by healthcare providers may lead to underutilization of services. In 2009, the federally designated mental health professional shortage areas were estimated to be 3,291, an increase from 1,669. An analysis of data from the National Institute of Mental Health's (NIMH) Collaborative Psychiatric Epidemiology Surveys Initiative (CPES) investigated what types of care were used, to assess the extent the care used was consistent with the American Psychiatric Association (APA) *Guidelines for the Treatments of Patients with Major Depressive Disorder,* and how insurance, education and household income influenced rates of care (González, Vega, Williams, Tarraf, West, & Neighbors, 2010). Findings indicated that overall 51 percent of those individuals meeting criteria for major depression during the prior year received some kind of treatment with only 21 percent receiving care that was consistent with APA *Guidelines.* Noteworthy was the finding that prevalence and severity of major depression was similar among the five studied racial/ethnic groups- Mexican Americans, Puerto Ricans, Caribbean Blacks, African Americans and non-Latina/o Whites. Moreover, when compared to non-Latina/o Whites (54% received care), African Americans (40% received care) and Mexican Americans (34% received care) with major depression were least likely to receive any care or care consistent with the *Guidelines.* The authors concluded that there were distinctive differences in mental healthcare usage between Mexican Americans and other Latina/o subgroups that had not been previously reported and indicated that future research exploring the extent to which patients' perceived experiences of discrimination might affect their access and utilization of mental healthcare.

If such a need for mental health services is present, why is there such an underutilization of services rate and high early termination rates? In addressing this question, researchers utilized a grounded theory method to understand the dynamics of the early termination from the Latina/o client's perspective (Bein, Torres, & Kurilla, 2000). The sample consisted of twenty Latina/o clients who attended no more than four sessions in a Latina/o focused or non-Latina/o focused outpatient settings. From the data, the authors developed the central concept of the "repelled Latina/o client" in which it was determined that the clients presented themselves as motivated to receive counseling, but some adverse condition, behavior, or demand from the service provider caused them to react by staying away from the service provider. This study found that there were four distinct overarching reasons for early termination from the Latina/o client's perspective: service denial, institutional demands, cultural dissonance, and incompetence. It is possible that the Latina/o clients experienced their treatment provider as culturally biased in overt and covert ways, which created cultural impasses that encouraged the clients to prematurely terminate services.

Many studies have examined racial and ethnic discrimination and how it impacts quality of care. Equally as important to study is how microaggressions on a daily basis impact Latinas/os ability to receive quality healthcare. For example, Latinas/os spirituality and religiosity at times is not respected, as indicated by a roll of the eyes or slight joke from the healthcare provider or staff. Studies have shown that Latinas/os in particular tend to somaticize their symptoms that may stem from mental illness, among other distinct differences on how symptomology is manifested (Falicov, 1998). When providers fail to take into consideration the various ways that psychopathology manifests, they might write off the somatic pain as something "in their head" without doing further physical studies that they may have done on a non-Latina/o. This type of "health" stereotype is dangerous and can lead to improper care and diagnosis. Further, it consistently dismisses and treats the Latina/o individual as a second-class citizen. Understanding the cultural needs of Latinas/os in the US will help address the issues of engaging Latinas/os in treatment, early termination, and underutilization of services as well as educating providers in acknowledging their own biases.

Mental health services for marginalized populations usually lack sensitivity to cross-cultural issues, particularly in assessment and treatment. The cultural values for people of color may be ignored by mental health professionals who are not familiar with the cultural worldviews, lifestyles, values, norms, and histories of various racial and ethnic groups (Sue & Sue, 2012). This lack of culturally sensitive therapy not only can lead to mistrust of mental health services, but also misunderstandings in cultural values and beliefs, misinterpretation of experiences of people of color, and mental health needs being left unmet. Traditional individualistic methods of Western psychotherapy treatment based on verbal therapy and introspection may not match the needs and cultural values of clients of Latina/o descent.

For instance, the traditional Western views of psychotherapy place value and emphasis on the individual and independence, while many Latinas/os highly value the family unit (*familismo*) and have a strong identification, attachment, loyalty and respect for their family (Ayón, Marsiglia, & Bermudez-Parsai, 2010; Sue & Sue, 2012). Numerous studies have indicated that Latinas/os rely on family members for their main source of help when experiencing problems and mental health issues and often do not seek help until familial resources have been exhausted (Griner & Smith, 2006; Sue & Sue, 2012). The family provides such strong support, comfort, trust, empathy, and feelings of safety for many Latinas/os. In addition, many Latino families feel that it is a sign of weakness to experience mental illness and some Latinas/os have reported that their family may be stigmatized and feel ashamed and fear social criticism (Rastogi, Massey-Hastings, & Wieling, 2012). In fact, stigma from one's family and fears that their family will be stigmatized has been found to be a significant barrier to mental health treatment for many Latinas/os (Ayón et al., 2010). Thus, Latinas/os may be reluctant to share their problems and mental health issues with people outside of their family, especially mental health professionals. Many mental health professionals may try to encourage therapeutic techniques that promote the well-being and success of the individual, while neglecting take into account the client's cultural values and consider the consequences these techniques may cause for a Latina/o client. Furthermore, the Latina/o population may not respond well to this Westernized style of linear language and more elaborated verbal expression.

Additionally, some Latinas/os tend to explain psychological symptoms as being caused by supernatural phenomena and tend to somaticize psychological symptoms (Marquez & Ramierz Garcia, 2013; Ruiz, 2002). These alternative views of mental illness may actually be perceived as psychological symptoms rather than cultural views and beliefs. Furthermore, Latinas/os have traditionally used song, dance, rituals, theatre, poetry, and art as a means of emotional expression (Ciornai, 1983). As such, community healers such as a pastors, priests, curanderos, espiritistas, santerios, and shamans have been utilized by Latinas/os for spiritual and mental healing whom in turn use expressive modes of healing. Understanding Latinas/os cultural beliefs and norms is not only vital for therapeutic success, but also important in minimizing the barriers for mental health service utilization among the Latina/o community. Research has found that targeting and altering interventions that match clients' cultural, especially for Latinas/os, has been found to be four times more effective than traditional Western interventions (Griner & Smith, 2006).

Immigration Issues

Many immigrants encounter structural barriers during the process of entering and acculturating to the US. Specifically, Latina/o immigrants face significant challenges when seeking medical and mental healthcare. For many, they not only have to learn and become familiar with the US healthcare system, but they also face language barriers, stigma and bias, and acculturation issues (Weinick et al., 2004). For many immigrant Latinas/os, language barriers have the greatest impact on receiving healthcare. Due to the lack of Spanish speaking medical and mental health professionals, many immigrants have extreme difficulty in comprehending the education and treatment plans provided by healthcare professionals (Timmins, 2002). This can lead to poor patient satisfaction, as Latinas/os may feel judged for not speaking the native language, misunderstood, and even misdiagnosed, and also leads to poor treatment compliance (Timmins, 2002). Latina/o immigrants who experience stigma are less likely to want to be in treatment for medical and mental health disorders and underuse services in the future (Nadeem, Lange, Edge, Fongwa, Belin, & Miranda, 2007).

It can be very difficult to navigate a new culture, especially when the individual does not know the primary language. Ramos-Sanchez, Atkinson, and Fraga (1999) note that the "preoccupation of English subordinate clients on producing grammatically correct speech may interfere with the clients' emotional expression" (p. 126). This is an example of the client not only struggling to try to figure out how they are feeling, but also having to search for words in a second language to express and explain how they feel. This can be very taxing for any individual and can cause the healthcare provider to inaccurately interpret a language barrier as a sign of an uncooperative, negative, or repressed relational style (Sue & Sue, 2012). Thus, what may be expressed in body language as stress from the psychological and sometimes physical exertion of speaking in a second language might be perceived as symptoms of anxiety or other forms of psychopathology. Sue and Sue (2012) caution the practitioner that the problem may be linguistic and not psychological when working with people of color: "Euro-American society places such high premium of one's use of English, it is a short step to conclude that minorities are inferior, lack of awareness, or lack conceptual thinking powers" (p. 119). As such, bilingual clients not only have to worry about being understood verbally, they may also encounter misdiagnosis.

The language barrier causes feelings of discomfort in many Latina/o immigrants and instills a feeling of mistrust in the healthcare professions due to the stigma and bias they perceive. Most healthcare facilities are not adequately prepared to address language barriers, forcing family members or friends to stand in as the interpreter (Timmins, 2002). This is not only unethical, but also can impact the accuracy of information being transferred (Timmins, 2002). This lack of culturally competent care for Latina/o immigrants directly impacts their satisfaction with care, the quality of care they receive, and negatively affects the patient/healthcare provider relationship (Documet & Sharma, 2004). Many Latina/o immigrants have reported receiving substandard care due to their race, ethnicity, and because of language barriers. These negative experiences can cause Latinas/os to avoid using medical and mental health facilities in the future. When attempting to receive mental healthcare, many Latina/o immigrants were unaware of the mental health services available to them (Shattell, Hamilton, Starr, Jenkins, & Hinderliter, 2008). When they did seek services, many Latina/os felt misunderstood and as if they could not trust the mental health professional. Additionally, many felt that the mental health practitioner misdiagnosed them and misunderstood their needs.

Unfortunately, political and economic barriers exist in healthcare systems and inhibit the provision of culturally appropriate bilingual or interpretation services for monolingual Latinas/os. Most hospitals have protocols that interpretation services are required to be offered, but many times this is overlooked or the patient responds to English "enough" that the staff person believes that they are fluent and do not offer services. Other times providers are in a rush, are not familiar with the protocol, or do not feel it is important and do not provide an interpreter when it is appropriate and necessary for the provision of quality healthcare services.

Nonetheless, studies have shown that a therapist's ability to converse in the clients' preferred language may demonstrate a greater cultural sensitivity and thus affords them higher credibility (Ramos-Sanchez et al., 1999). Only 1% of US psychologist practitioners identify as Latina/o (Dingfelder, 2005), and obviously such a small number cannot keep up with the amount of individuals who prefer services with bicultural, bilingual psychologists. Nevertheless, these bilingual psychologists require the assistance of the field in order to preserve an ethical standard in their services. Very little is offered in terms of assistance for bilingual practitioners in providing services in Spanish. Biever et al. (2002) comment that "psychologists with conversational proficiency in Spanish have very few resources or guidance in making the transition from social to professional levels of Spanish proficiency" (p. 330). Furthermore, there is a lack of adequate training for bilingual therapists in the realm of psychology courses taught in Spanish in U.S. institutions. This lack of training opportunities presents an additional structural barrier to Spanish-speaking Latinas/os receiving culturally competent care.

In addition to language barriers, many Latina/o immigrants face employment and health insurance difficulties that impact their ability to seek healthcare. Many Latina/o immigrants are forced to work low-wage jobs due to their current legal status, skill level, or language barriers that exist (Shattell et al., 2008). Many governmental policies and changes in welfare reforms and Medicaid eligibility have impacted Latinas/os ability to receive public welfare funds or even employer benefits (Brown et al., 2000). For example, legal immigrants who came to the US after 1996 are not eligible for Medicaid for five years, and are reluctant to apply for it when they are eligible because they fear it will impact their citizenship or they will be forced to repay medical costs in the future (Brown et al., 2000). This is an example of how governmental policies can serve as structural barriers to healthcare.

Recommendations

Specific awareness surrounding the needs of Latinas/os in the US must be studied in order to become more multiculturally competent in the healthcare fields. When discussing treatment plans with Latina/o clients there are several cultural factors to consider. However, one must keep in mind that each individual may experience these factors differently. The Latina/o population is a very large, diverse group of individuals that represent a wide variety of ethnic, racial, political, socioeconomic, and religious backgrounds, for example. It is for this reason that we must be cognizant of these differences and be careful not to over generalize without first seeing the individual in their specific context. Nevertheless, there are some cultural beliefs, values, and practices that generally speak to the Latina/o population at large. Factors like level of acculturation, socioeconomic status, and ethnic background must be considered in determining applicability to Latina/o individuals. There are various culture-specific values that potentially impact a Latina/o individual's beliefs, thoughts, and behaviors.

The Latina/o culture is generally collectivistic and values interdependence. It is focused on the community and society at large and values group goals versus individual goals. It is seen as quite different from the American individualistic culture of independence, autonomy, and valuing the individual's goal over the group's goals. Latina/o clients may have familial or community responsibilities and/or obligations that precede their individual mental health that can potentially be misconstrued by a non-culturally sensitive clinician as reluctance or resistance to treatment. Therefore, when working with a Latina/o client it is important to assess the level that they adhere to collectivistic versus individualistic worldviews and consider how this might impact the therapeutic alliance. All these factors must be considered when treating Latinas/os/as. Again, it is in this area that microaggressions arise due to cultural misunderstandings, lack of knowledge, or insufficient multicultural training.

Understanding the various ways that Latina/o clients may conceptualize their illness is another vital aspect of the culture that is helpful in preventing microaggressions or in the very least informing a provider. The extent to which cultural differences are prevalent in today's society is made obvious throughout the *Diagnostic and Statistical Manual of Mental Disorders* (DSM–5; American Psychiatric Association, 2013) concerning culture's influence on the manifestation of mental issues. The DSM–5 describes several culture-bound syndromes that may be more familiar to clients more so than the conventional psychotherapy disorders. More specifically, these syndromes help the clinician differentiate between folk illnesses (from the client's perspective) versus mainstream psychotherapy labels such as anxiety or mood disorders. This assists in the clinician's attempt to be more culturally sensitive to the Latina/o client's experiences.

Religious and spiritual beliefs have also been found to be pertinent in the lives of Latinas/os in terms of intersecting with how they cope with physical and mental illness. The uses of natural healers who use herbs, oils, incense, massages, and 'homework' assignments as well as practice divination are common in some Latina/o communities. For example, *curanderismo* is an indigenous method that Latina/o individuals may go to heal folk illnesses such as *susto* or *mal de ojo*. *Curanderos, brujos,* and *espiritistas* (all known as folk healers) are reassuring and confident in their ability to diagnose and cure whatever ails the individual. Similarly, *santeros* (usually found in Cuba, Puerto Rico and other Caribbean countries) are very practical and try to solve the concrete problems presented to them. They too act as healers, diviners, and carry out rituals using special herbs, candles, potions, incense, and other ritual objects.

One last area of consideration is another form of coping with stress and aversive experiences through that of somatization (medically unexplained physical symptoms). These symptoms commonly point to emotional distress and seem to be observed more frequently in women and older individuals, those in developing nations, in lower socioeconomic statuses and lower education (Falicov, 1998). The presence of somatization may represent the integration of mind and body within the Latina/o culture. By asking Latina/o clients if they can speculate or guess about the emotional reasons for their physical ailments, they might ultimately uncover the meaning behind the somatizations. Moreover, as previously stated it is important to also honor and respect the Latina/o clients' beliefs and traditional theories regarding their health and healing practices.

The aforementioned underscore the value of understanding the Latina/o culture's concepts surrounding illness and healing in being able to be more effective in treating this population. Moreover, different clients within different cultures have preferred ways of expressing themselves. Healthcare providers are therefore challenged in helping clients and patients discover what works best for them at a particular time and place in their lives. By tapping into the various nuances of their culture, clinicians and researchers alike can promote a better understanding of their Latina/o clients' cultural backgrounds and thus a better understanding of the client as an individual. It is important to note that the creative arts works as a universal language, one that has found itself in almost every culture, in song, dance, visual art, storytelling, or poetry, and can be a powerful intervention.

Conclusion

Latina/o Americans represent a diverse culture that is more heterogeneous than homogenous. As such, one chapter can only speak to a handful of the significant issues and experiences that influence the well-being of this group. Despite the heterogeneity that exists within this group, Latinas/os consistently report that they experience microaggressions and other structural barriers in their daily lives. These microaggressions come in the form of individual and environmental interactions that insult and invalidate the lived experiences of Latinas/os, as well as help maintain the structural barriers that prevent Latinas/os from accessing and participating in social institutions. As discussed in this chapter, an area salient to the well-being of all Latinas/os is access to adequate and culturally responsive healthcare. It is difficult to negate the existence of a connection between the lack of access to healthcare and the health-related disparities that exist for Latina/o Americans. In order to foster a healthier sense of well-being within Latina/o American communities, the interpersonal and structural barriers that maintain a healthcare system that neglects the needs of Latina/o Americans must be addressed at the individual, institutional, and societal levels.

References

Ai, A. L., Appel, H. B., Huang, B., & Lee, K. (2012). Overall health and healthcare utilization among Latino American women in the United States. *Journal of Women's Health, 21*(8), 878–885.

American Psychiatric Association. (2006). *Position statement: Resolution against racism and racial discrimination and their adverse impacts on mental health.* Retrieved March 25, 2014 from http://www.socialwork-gatherings.com/Resolution%20Against%20Racism%20APA.pdf

American Psychiatric Association. (2013). *Diagnostic and Statistical manual of mental disorders: DSM 5.* Arlington, VA: American Psychiatric Association.

Araújo, B. Y., & Borrell, L. N. (2006). Understanding the link between discrimination, mental health outcomes, and life chances among Latinos. *Hispanic Journal of Behavioral Science, 28*(2), 245–266.

Ayón, C., Marsiglia, F. F., & Bermudez-Parsai, M. (2010). Latino family mental health: Exploring the role of discrimination and familismo. *Journal of Community Psychology, 38*(6), 742–756

Bein, A., Torres, S., & Kurilla, V. (2000). Service delivery issues in early termination of Latino clients. *Journal of Human Behavior in the Social Environment, 3,* 43–59.

Betancourt, J. R., Green, A. R., Carrillo, J. E., & Ananeh-Firempong, O. A. (2003). Defining cultural competence: A practical framework for addressing racial/ethnic disparities in health and healthcare. *Public Health Reports, 188,* 293–302

Biever, J. L., Castano, M. T., de las Fuentes, C., Gonzalez, C., Servin-Lopez, S., Sprowls, C., et al. (2002). The role of language in training psychologists to work with His-panic clients. *Professional Psychology: Research and Practice, 33,* 330–336.

Bhui, K., Stansfeld, S., McKenzie, K., Karlsen, S., Nazroo, J., & Weich, S. (2005). Racial/ethnic discrimination and common mental disorders among workers: Findings from the Empiric Study of Ethnic Minority Groups in the United Kingdom. *American Journal of Public Health, 95*(3), 496–501.

Brown, R. E., Ojeda, V. D., Wyn, R., & Levan, R. (2000). *Racial and ethnic disparities in access to health insurance and healthcare.* UCLA: UCLA Center for Health Policy Research. Retrieved from: https://escholarship.org/uc/item/4sf0p1st

Brown, A., & Patten, E. (2014). *Statistical portrait of the foreign-born population in the United States, 2012.* Pew Research Center, Washington, D.C. Retrieved from http://www.pewhispanic.org/2014/04/29/statistical-portrait-of-the-foreign-born-population-in-the-united-states-2012/#population-by-nativi-ty-and-citizenship-status-2000-and-2012.

Carter, R. T., & Forsyth, J. (2010). Reactions to racial discrimination: emotional stress & help-seeking behaviors. *Psychological Trauma: Theory, Research, Practice, and Policy, 2*(3), 183–191.

Chen, F. M., Fryer Jr., G. E., Philips Jr., R. L., Wilson, E., & Pathman, D. E. (2005). Patients' beliefs about racism, preferences for physician race, and satisfaction with care. *Annals of Family Medicine, 3*(2), 138–43.

Chou, T., Asnaani, A., & Hofmann, S. G. (2012). Perception of racial discrimination and psychopathology across three U.S. ethnic minority groups. *Cultural Diversity and Ethnic Minority Psychology, 18*(1), 74–81.

Ciornai, S. (1983). Art therapy with working class Latino women. *The Arts in Psychotherapy, 10*(2), 63–76.

Dingfelder, S. F. (2005). Closing the gap for Latino patients. *Monitor on Psychology, 36,* 56–61.

Documet, P. L., & Sharma, R. K. (2004). Latinos' healthcare access: Financial and cultural barriers. *Journal of Immigrant Health, 6*(1), 5–13.

Falicov, C. J. (1998). *Latino families in therapy: A guide to multicultural practice.* New York, NY: Guilford.

Flores, G., Abreu, M., Olivar, M. A., & Kastner, B. (1998). Access barriers to health care for Latino children. *Archives of Pediatric and Adolescent Medicine, 152,* 1119–1125.

Gee, G. C., Spencer, M., Chen, J., Yip, T., & Takeuchi, D. T. (2007). The association between self-reported racial discrimination and 12-month DSM-IV mental disorders among Asian Americans. *Social Science & Medicine, 64*(10), 1984–1996.

González, H. M., Vega, W. A., Williams, D. R., Tarraf, W., West, B. T., & Neighbors, H. W. (2010). Depression care in the United States: Too little for too few. *Archives of General Psychiatry, 67*(1), 37–46.

Griner, D., & Smith, T. B. (2006). Culturally adapted mental health interventions: A meta-analytic review. *Psychotherapy: Theory, Research, Practice, and Training, 43*(4), 531–548.

Idler, E. L., & Benyamini, Y. (1997). Self-rated health and mortality: A review of twenty-seven community studies. *Journal of Health and Social Behavior, 38,* 21–37.

Karlsen, S., Nazroo, J. Y., Mckenzie, K., Bhui, K., & Weich, S. (2005). Racism, psychosis and common mental disorder among ethnic minority groups in England. *Psychological Medicine, 35*(12), 1795–1803.

Marger, M. N. (2006). *Race and ethnic relations: American and global perspectives.* Belmont, CA: Thompson Learning, Inc.

Marotta, S. A., & Garcia, J. A. (2003). Latinos in the United States in 2000. *Hispanic Journal of Behavioral Sciences, 25*, 13–34.

Marquez, J. A., & Ramíerz García, J. I. (2013). Family caregivers' narratives of mental health treatment usage processes by their Latino adult relatives with serious and persistent mental illness. *Journal of Family Psychology, 27*(3), 398–408.

Massey, D. (2004). Geographies of responsibility. *Geografiska Annaler: Series B, Human Geography, 86*(1), 5–18.

Nadal, K. L., Griffin, K. E., Wong, Y., Hamit, S., & Rasmus, M. (2014). The impact of racial microaggressions on mental health: Counseling implications for clients of color. *Journal of Counseling & Development, 92*(1), 57–66.

Nadal, K. L., Mazzula, S. L., Rivera, D. P., & Fujii-Doe, W. (2014). Microaggressions and Latina/o Americans: An analysis of nativity, gender, and ethnicity. *Journal of Latina/o Psychology, 2*(2), 67–78.

Nadeem, E., Lange, J. M., Edge, D., Fongwa, M., Belin, T., & Miranda, J. (2007). Does stigma keep poor young immigrant and U.S.-born Black and Latina women from seeking mental healthcare? *Psychiatric Services, 58*(12), 1547–1554.

Page, D., & Shepherd, H. (2008). The sociology of discrimination: Racial discrimination in employment, housing, credit, and consumer markets. *Annual Review in Sociology, 34*, 181–209.

Orlofsky, G. F. (2002). *The funding gap: Low-income and minority students receive fewer dollars.* Washington, DC: The Education Trust.

Pascoe, E. A., & Smart Richman, L. (2009). Perceived discrimination and health: A meta-analytic review. *Psychological Bulletin, 135*(4), 531–554.

Pérez, D. J., Fortuna, L., & Alegría, M. (2008). Prevalence and correlates of everyday discrimination among U.S. Latinos. *Journal of Community Psychology, 36*(4), 421–433.

Ramos-Sánchez, L., Atkinson, D. R., & Fraga, E. (1999). Mexican Americans' bilingual ability, counselor bilingualism cues, counselor ethnicity, and perceive counselor credibility. *Journal of Counseling Psychology, 46*, 125–131.

Rastogi, M., Massey-Hastings, N., & Wieling, E. (2012). Barriers to seeking mental health services in the Latino/a community: A qualitative analysis. *Journal of Systemic Therapies, 31*(3), 1–17.

Rivera, D. P. (2012). *Microaggressions and health outcomes for Latina/o Americans: Understanding the influences of external characteristics and psychological resources* (Doctoral dissertation, Columbia University, New York, NY).

Rivera, D.P., Forquer, E. E., & Rangel, R. (2010). Microaggressions and the life experience of Latina/o Americans. In D. W. Sue (Ed.), *Microaggressions and marginality: Manifestations, dynamics, and impact* (pp. 59–84). New York, NY: Wiley & Sons.

Rivera, D. P., Molina, K., & Watkins, N. L. (2012, February). Microaggressions, generational status, and health outcomes for Latina/o Americans. Kevin L. Nadal (Chair) symposium entitled *The impact of racial microaggressions on physical and mental health: A review of quantitative research.* Paper presented at the 29th Annual Winter Roundtable on Cultural Psychology & Education, New York, NY.

Ruiz, P. (2002). Hispanic access to health/mental health services. *Psychiatric Quarterly, 73*(2), 85–19.

Shattell, M. M., Hamilton, D., Starr, S. S., Jenkins, C. J., & Hinderliter, N. A. (2008). Mental health service needs of a Latino population: A community-based participatory research project. *Issues in Mental Health Nursing, 29,* 351–370.

Sue, D. W. (2010). *Microaggressions in everyday life: Race, gender, and sexual orientation.* Hoboken, NJ: John Wiley & Sons.

Sue, D. W., Capodilupo, C. M., Torino, G. C., Bucceri, J. M., Holder, A. M. B., Nadal, K. L., & Esquilin, M. (2007). Racial microaggressions in everyday life: Implications for clinical practice. *American Psychologist, 62,* 271–286.

Sue, D. W., Lin, A. I., & Rivera, D. P. (2009). Racial microaggressions in the workplace. In J. L. Chin (Ed.), *Diversity in mind and in action, Volume 2: Disparities and competence* (pp. 157–172). Westport, CT: Greenwood.

Sue, D. W., & Sue, D. (2012). *Counseling the culturally diverse: Theory and practice* (6th ed.). New York, NY: John Wiley & Sons.

Timmins, C. (2002). The Impact of language barriers on the healthcare of Latinos in the United States: A review of the literature and guidelines. *Journal of Midwifery & Women's Health, 47*(2), 80–96.

U.S. Census Bureau. (2011). *Hispanic heritage month 2011.* Retrieved on March 25, 2014 from https://www.census.gov/newsroom/releases/archives/facts_for_features_special_editions/cb11-ff18.html

U.S. Department of Health and Human Services. (2001). *Mental health: culture, race, and ethnicity. A supplement to mental health: A report of the surgeon general.* Rockville, MD: U.S. Department of Health and Human Services, Substance Abuse and Mental Health Services Administration, Center for Mental Health Services.

U.S. Department of Health and Human Services. (2009). *Office of Minority Health.* Retrieved from http://www.omhrc.gov/templates/browse.aspx?lvl=1&lvlID=2

U.S. Department of Health and Human Services. (2013). *National healthcare disparities report.* Retrieved on February 9, 2015, from http://www.ahrq.gov/research/findings/nhqrdr/nhdr13/2013nhdr.pdf.

U.S. Department of Labor, Bureau of Labor Statistics. (2008). *Household data annual averages.* Retrieved on April 16, 2009, from ftp://ftp.bls.gov/pub/special.requests/lf/aat11.txt.

Valdez, R. B., Giachello, A., Rodriguez-Trias, H., Gomez, P., & de la Rocha, C. (1993). Improving access to healthcare in Latino communities. *Public Health Reports, 108*(5), 534–539.

van Ryn, M., & Burke, J. (2000). The effect of patient race and socioeconomic status on physicians' perceptions of patients. *Social Science & Medicine, 50,* 813–828.

Weinick, R. M., Jacobs, E. A., Cacari Stone, L., Ortega, A. N., & Burstin, H. (2004). His-panic healthcare disparities: Challenging the myth of a monolithic Hispanic population. *Medical Care, 42*(4), 313–320.

Wian, C., & Martinez, M. (2012, July 20). *Arizona sheriff faces civil trial in alleged targeting of Latinos.* CNN. Retrieved from http://www.cnn.com/2012/07/19/justice/arizona-arpaio-trial/

Williams, D. R., & Collins, C. (2001). Racial residential segregation: A fundamental cause of racial disparities in health. *Public Health Reports, 116*(5), 404.

Struggle and Conformity

The White Racial Frame

Rosalind S. Chou and Joe R. Feagin

A seventeen-year-old Chinese American male high school student was brutally beaten by seven other Chicago teens in February of 2012. The beating was captured on video and posted online. In early reports the news outlets were saying that it was likely to have been racially motivated because on the video it looked like the immigrant student's assailants were white, and as they punched, kicked, and robbed him, they shouted racist epithets, repeatedly calling the student the "N word" and making derogatory comments about his speaking Chinese. However, the media began to backtrack on their accent on racism when it was discovered that Asian Americans were among the attackers in the teenaged group.[1]

Nonetheless, we view this attack as racially motivated because it reveals the power of the white racial frame and its pervasive nature. People of color are not immune to adopting the racist stereotypes and ideologies of the white racial frame. As we will demonstrate in this chapter, our respondents often struggle to resist the anti-Asian framing of this white racial frame and, at times, conform to it. The Asian American teen attackers were using physical force to dominate someone they probably saw as "less American" because he was a recent immigrant to the United States. A follow-up video was posted on YouTube with a young Asian American woman saying that there were tensions with the attackers and a group near the school that call themselves the FOBs ("Fresh off the boat").[2] Systemic racism is powerful in creating many alienating relationships, and in this example it created alienated relationships among Asian Americans—and thus what was in part an Asian-on-Asian attack. Quite notable is the repeated use of the "N word" in this case. As these teens physically assaulted the Chinese immigrant, they utilized a potent racist slur used for hundreds of years by whites to demean and attack African Americans. Such white-racist framing is learned, and in this case the white framing was emulated and acted out in regard to a youth from the same racially constructed group as some of the attackers.

This country's omnipresent and systemic racism creates many social contexts in which individuals like our respondents are regularly ridiculed, humiliated, and excluded. As a result, they have developed important survival strategies and significant coping skills. One major strategy involves conforming aggressively to white norms and folkways, not only with the hope of achieving the American dream but also to reduce white hostility and discrimination. To protect themselves, many strive to be as "white" in their orientations and daily efforts as they can.

Everyone in U.S. society lives within the centuries-old white frame, and no subordinated racial group is exempt from its barrage of stereotyped views, images, and emotions. Buying aggressively into the dominant frame is not exclusive to whites, for people of color have often accepted and used numerous "bits" from this frame as well. As we have just observed, Asian Americans frequently embrace racial stereotypes created by whites about other groups, as well as the racist notions that whites have created for Asians themselves. Our interviewees have regularly conformed to white framing and folkways by attempting to change personal and family characteristics in their physical and social worlds—by giving up their Asian names, changing their style of dress, and trying to enter white networks, for example—and in the psychological realm, by adopting white ways of thinking, understanding, and acting.

Striving for Whiteness: A Nuanced Example

Many Asian Americans have gained some degree of acceptance into white social worlds because of their adoption of white framing and folkways. Because of this, an apparently privileged title is sometimes given by whites to Asian Americans: "model minority" or "honorary white," as we have previously underscored. This model imagery may appear to be a compliment, but such stereotyping is, as previous chapters demonstrate, oppressive and damaging. The damage is multilayered: (1) the model minority stereotype is used to insult other people of color, and as a measuring stick to accent their inferiority for not attaining high educational or career achievements; (2) the stereotype is another method by which whites reinforce racial othering and differentiate themselves from people of color; (3) on a personal level, the stereotyping creates stressful and unrealistic expectations, self- and externally imposed, that Asian Americans should succeed in fitting the stereotype or be deemed failures; and (4) the model stereotype creates unrealistic expectations within, and outside, Asian American communities that negatively impact all Asian Americans.

As we have shown in previous discussions, Asian Americans commonly feel like outsiders. To fit in, some make extensive efforts to be the all-American student, coworker, or citizen. As the scholar Frank Wu puts it, this aggressive assimilation "gratifies the ego of whites who are assimilated toward" and is seen as a ticket to the world of prosperity for Asian Americans.[3] To the latter, the image of success has a white face.

Take the example of Lara, a Chinese American who owns her own firm. She exemplifies the multidimensional character of dealing with everyday racism, including conforming to white folkways and to stereotyped images of the old white racial frame. Her life reveals great efforts to adapt to gain acceptance. Her academic and economic success has reinforced the white frame in her own mind. She thus adopts and uses it as a reference in her hiring practices, yet still faces discrimination by whites that she rationalizes as isolated incidents of individual ignorance or prejudice. Her experiences are not unique, for we could provide numerous similar accounts from other respondents.

In her revealing interview Lara notes that she was "quite lucky" to never have endured an overt act of racism. However, over the course of the interview she makes it clear that in fact white-generated discrimination has regularly been a threat. Instead of avoiding white spaces that were unwelcoming, Lara has made it a point to conform to white folkways as much as possible, believing that her conforming and hard work will be rewarded with acceptance. For example, she discusses her high school experience in this way:

> I was in the math club, and the Latin club, and the vocational club ... I was also a varsity cheerleader.... I was the only Asian; there were no African American cheerleaders in my group that I can recall. Um, so basically of a squad of, let's say, a squad of sixteen, it was all white and one Asian.... That would give me choices, and nobody would have anything on me, no one would say, "Well hey, well you know what, Asian Americans can't be cheerleaders because they are too geeky." Or I just figured there's never a disadvantage to joining everything. [She laughs.] I have tried so hard to assimilate.

Lara's attempt to be very involved in overwhelmingly white extracurricular activities was one important method she used to try to combat the Asian stereotype. Lara wanted access into high school spaces where young people commonly look down on those with academic prowess. She was motivated to prove that Asian Americans could do anything that a white person could do. She initially stated that her drive to assimilate was just part of her competitive nature to want to achieve and be "the best" in everything. Later, however, she admitted that her extensive involvement in school activities was also a protective measure against discrimination: "I mean, if nobody can say, 'Well, that person's less smart than me, or that person is less successful than me or less socially adept than me, or somehow nerdier than me,' then what can they say negative about the race? It was a *defense* tactic."

Lara tried to obtain the model minority status, where she was smarter and more successful than her peers, and yet at the same time to be socially integrated with whites. Asian Americans frequently find themselves criticized by whites no matter what they do. If they fail to achieve academically or economically, like some other people of color, they may be viewed by whites as inferior. If, however, they achieve more than average whites academically and economically, they may be treated as odd "grade grubbers," "nerds," and socially inferior. Lara puts forth much effort to meet the white stereotype of Asianness and the white standard for everyday whiteness. Shortly after making this statement about defensive tactics, Lara adds that if she had been raised in Asia, she might have done some of the same activities, except that the racial dimension would not have been there.

In reply to a question about what she has tried to defend herself against, Lara replies in this poignant fashion:

> A defense from the potential that there could be a race issue. It's not like I've never had a racial slur. And maybe I have a low tolerance for that type of aggravation or degradation and so I knew that that was a potential, and I tried to minimize it. I don't think it's that I didn't recognize the potential was there, I just wanted to make sure I was ready. Generally, I try not to be reactive. I try to say, let me get ready, I know what could happen, and so I am just going to prepare, so that life goes the way I want it and not how it is forced upon me by other people's actions or thoughts.

The threat of a racist incident is omnipresent in the lives of all Americans of color. Even though Lara has become exceptionally successful, she has often lived her life on "red alert," building her arsenal against racial attacks in the form of an impressive résumé and careful consideration of her defensive responses. Like numerous other respondents, Lara eventually shared with us her experiences with racial discrimination and how such experiences have motivated her to excel. She has overachieved in order to feel in control of her life. A top student in school and college, she later performed well for employers and got promoted, and then opened her firm. Her substantial accomplishments have often been used as defensive tactics in a racially harsh world.

Even when Americans of color attain socioeconomic success, they still pay a heavy toll. In this racist society whites have pressed them to think and act as whites would have them think and act, and thus often against their own individual and group interests. Whites have created social arrangements where those oppressed lose substantial control over lives and livelihoods. They are, to varying degrees, alienated from control over their ability to make decisions about many aspects of their lives. Lara's "choice" to prepare herself for everyday racism by being an overachiever is a survival technique. Although she clearly articulates the purpose of her "defense tactic," to protect her from discrimination, she still tries to convince us that she has not been significantly affected: "I just haven't been very traumatized by race differences. Again, part of it may just be me, the opposite side of me, you know, *ignoring* issues and always just trying to be *better* than the people around me so ... that they didn't have anything over me. There was nothing they could say: 'Oh well, she's Asian, so she's therefore less because of such and such.' I never gave anybody, or I tried not to give anybody, the opportunity to say anything like that." Her admirable accomplishments have required that she work much harder than comparable whites because of the embedded racial barriers. In her view, as long as she works hard enough, she will be accepted and achieve her American dream.

Lara believes her entrance into the white world has been awarded because of hard work, not because she adopted white ways. However, like many Asian Americans, Lara has worked so hard to assimilate to the model minority standard that she appears unaware of the fact that some of her important choices are not really her own. Previously, the second author has described this reality thus:

> Those who are not white, whether recent immigrants or long-term residents, are under great pressure, in the language of much social science and policy analysis, "to assimilate" to the white-determined folkways. The word "assimilate," however, does not capture the everyday reality of the pressure cooker–type demands on individuals to conform to that white environment and white folkways. There is often no choice for those who are not white but to more or less accept, mostly emulate, and even parrot the prevailing white folkways, including the white-generated negative images of racial outgroups, usually including one's own group. People of color constantly resist these pressures to conformity, but most have to accept and adapt to some extent just to survive in a white-controlled society.[4]

Lara's goal is to protect herself from discrimination by achieving a near-white position on the socioracial hierarchy. Yet, no matter how much they achieve, Asian Americans will still be viewed and treated as second-class citizens by many whites because the underlying racist structure of the society has not thereby changed. Like many others, Lara is apparently misled by the widespread rhetoric of the American dream to believe that someday she will be fully accepted into the white world. When she was in school, she attempted for several years to join a highly selective social club of white girls. These were the most popular girls, and the only stated qualification was a good academic record. As a top student, Lara should have been a shoe-in for the club. When asked about why she was never accepted, Lara cited personality differences and her inability to have a connection with club members, not intentional discrimination by the whites.

Lara has committed to the idea of assimilation to whiteness so fully that she admits that in hiring for her firm, she has a certain image of a new employee in mind. Even though her father had difficulty with English and was denied career opportunities because of that and whites' stereotyping of Asians, Lara asserts, "If you do not speak English well, which I was given the opportunity to do, if they don't speak English well, there is probably a *ton* of discrimination. Because even myself, when I am thinking about hiring someone, if they have an accent or if they don't speak English fluently, that affects my thought process as far as selecting them." To most Americans, discrimination on the basis of language, accent, or citizenship seems rational and acceptable.[5] White middle-class English is thought by many Americans to be "good English" and the desirable speaking norm.

When Lara was in elementary school, she used her grasp of the English language and her "excellent diction" aggressively to defend herself against racist slurs and whites' mocking comments, as she noted in her interview: "One time, I don't remember who it was. It was just some random kid, and he saw me and said something, you know pretending to speak Chinese, kind of mocking, and I just looked back at him in the eyes and said, 'Hey, I bet I read and speak English a lot better than you do. So you may as well just cut it out.'" In her mind, mastery of English elevates her status over the white child teasing her. Yet she in her interview does not seem to sympathize much with newer Americans who may have not yet mastered the language.

During her school years she reportedly did not befriend other Asian children and viewed herself as different from them. In her view they were not as involved with school social activities as she was and were, as she puts it, "loners." When asked why she called them that, she responds, "They may have felt more isolated. Again, I did my defensive tactic. Get involved with as many things as you can, just for the heck of it regardless of whether you know why you are doing it or not, and try to fit in as socially well as possible."

Even with all her work to get involved socially with whites, Lara has still faced recurring racist incidents. When she experiences such events, she says that she deals with the person head on. During her younger years she "just wrote it off as ignorance, you know. I think I just thought, well they may, they are clearly stupider than me if they are going to act like that, so therefore I'll just make it up by being their boss when we're both thirty. That's just how I wrote it off, as if 'you know what, they can continue to have those attitudes, and they are stupid enough to act like that then they are just not going to succeed.' And I will just let time tell the difference, I think." Lara has experienced racial discrimination but tends to attribute the events to individual ignorance, and her words reveal a little uncertainty as to whether her efforts will eventually pay off. She shared with us vivid memories of racist incidents, including one that occurred just a couple of years ago. White children at a grocery store mocked her Asian appearance like her white peers did in school. Systemic racism persists, and Lara's extraordinary achievements are not enough to destroy the anti-Asian notions and actions of whites she encounters. Once again, we see that the American dream is chimerical, hypothetical, and in reality for whites only.

The Psychological Impact of Discrimination: Strategies and Responses

Pressures to assimilate into the dominant U.S. culture and society, and specifically to conform to white framing and folkways, are intense for immigrants and their descendants. When Asian Americans become relatively successful, they are sometimes awarded certain privileges still inaccessible to other people of color. Because of this, they may appear to be, as some put it, the "darlings of whites."[6] However, it takes enormous work to be placed even in this "darlings" status, as analyst Vijay Prashad perceptively suggests:

> This puts enormous pressure on migrants, who seek to "assimilate" but find themselves confronted with a forbidding racism. This leads them in at least two directions, either into the shell of "national culture" (that is, retreating from an abandoned "outside society") or else into an intensified desire to "assimilate" and gain acceptance (that is, seeing the earlier attempt as insufficient, as having made mistakes that need to be remedied for a successful assimilation). Many of those born in the new land first try to assimilate in a one-dimensional way to become "American," discover the resilience of their own "pasts" as well as of racism's present, and then recover the resources within "national cultures" in a process that we may name "reverse assimilation."[7]

Such choices are open to Asian immigrants, and their children and grandchildren, as they attempt to move into the mainstream institutions of U.S. society and compete with white Americans. Here we examine aspects of the option of assimilating in a one-dimensional way; the countering option of reverse assimilation will be discussed in the next chapter.

Like other Americans of color, Asian Americans face additional, often high, levels of daily stress well beyond those normally faced by most whites. This added pressure creates or aggravates an array of significant psychological and physical problems.[8] It means the loss of much physical and psychological energy. Let us now examine life accounts of numerous respondents who have expended much energy to absorb a racist event and to strategize how to defend themselves from such racial threats. This psychological workout translates into a kind of psychological discrimination for Asian Americans, just as for other people of color. From a young age, our respondents have learned about the threats of white racism and put forth efforts to protect themselves, such as by changing their names, friends, and neighborhoods, all attempts to avoid discrimination or pass into a near-whiteness. Numerous respondents even spoke of wanting to significantly change their physical features, just as many Asians and Asian Americans now actually do with cosmetic surgery.

One of our respondents is a Vietnamese American professional who grew up on the East Coast, where she still lives. She recalls early attempts at social conformity:

> I remember when my dad took me to school, the first day of school ... the teacher asked, "Oh, what's your daughter's name?" And my dad was like "Fat" because it's the closest to my name in Vietnamese. I remember I was like five or something. I was like, "My name is Phan." I didn't want to be called Phat because I already knew what *fat* meant. I was like, "No, I don't want to be called 'Phat'" and they can make weight jokes and all that stuff, you

know? So I was like five years old, like "Don't call me Phat!" And then they called me "Fang" and all this stuff and made jokes about me being Chinese and Vietnamese.

At the tender age of five, "Phan" changed her name; she was already developing an understanding of and defensive reaction to racial ridicule by whites that she would endure because of her Vietnamese name. Conformity to white expectations as a protective adaptation strategy has been reported in at least one other study of younger Vietnamese Americans. Researcher Hung Cam Thai writes that his respondents have tried hard to be "American by acting and being white to fit in with peer groups."[9]

Indeed, children of all racial and ethnic backgrounds often pick up racial concepts and terms much earlier than in elementary school. Summarizing conclusions from an extensive ethnographic study of a multiracial child-care center, Debra Van Ausdale and Joe Feagin suggest that "many white adults still harbor deeply racist images and stereotypes and practice racial discrimination in settings they traverse in their daily lives. Not surprisingly, children are not protected from the reality and pain of this racist context, and their activities often reproduce and experiment with what they observe and understand about that racist society."[10]

In U.S. society, children usually do not live in a protective bubble that keeps them from learning about racial stereotypes and framing from parents, peers, and the mainstream media. If the framing of major social groups in the society in which they grow up is often racist, as it is in the United States, they will pick up and use some of that racial framing. Research such as that just cited shows that in preschool and school settings white children frequently exercise their racial power, and children of color soon learn their subordinate positions.

Phan changed her name early on because she had a better understanding of the racial hierarchy than her father did. She worked to save embarrassment for her younger sister as well, as she recounts at some length in her interview:

> I know I was six, because that's when my sister was about to be born ... and I remember telling my teacher, "Oh, I'm about to have a sister." And you know, the teacher was like, "Oh, that's great. You know, what's your sister's name going to be?" And you know, it's funny because looking back I don't like to embellish and come up with a story or anything about it, but I mean it was obvious that I told her that my sister's name was going to be Jennifer. I knew my sister's name was not going to be Jennifer. I knew my sister's name was going to be Tuyen. I remember telling—I don't remember why it came out of my mouth—I told my teacher, "No, her name's going to be Jennifer." So she wrote ... a congratulations or something like that ... and then she sent it to my parents. So my parents, of course, were highly upset about it, because they were like, "Why did you tell them your sister was going to be Jennifer?"

I was like, "I don't know, I want my new sister to be Jennifer. You don't call her an American name." I remember thinking it's going to be awful. They're going to name her Tuyen and [everyone will] make fun of her.

Again at a young age, Phan understood the painful nature of being different, but her parents did not appear to have understood. She was unable to articulate to her parents why she chose to change the name.

In contrast to Phan's parents, a great many Asian American parents see why a child like Phan might resist her Asian name. Many parents now give popular English names to their children. One New York City study, for example, found that the five most common names given by Asian American parents to their baby girls were Sophia, Emily, Michelle, Nicole, and Rachel, and the most common names given to boys were Justin, Ryan, Jason, Kevin, and Daniel. *Not one* of these is a typical name in Asian countries. Clearly, defensive conformity to important white folkways begins at birth.[11]

Jessica's parents emigrated from Vietnam, and she reports that they have had trouble understanding well how U.S. racism works, although over time they have become well acquainted with it. The learning process has been difficult for her to watch:

It's really hard that my parents *don't get it*. We're foreign. We're on welfare, and so, I guess for me my ethnicity has always been ridiculously intertwined with my class. And I can't separate the two because to me that's a specific experience, being from a Vietnamese immigrant family that's poor. I know it's hard for them. People gave my mom dirty looks because of the few things that she used, combined with the fact that she didn't know English. So it was like, "Oh, immigrants come in here, taking our money." That's exactly what that is. And it was really hard for her. It was embarrassing that she had to use her children to translate for her, and that's why she learned English. She became a citizen, and when she became a citizen she changed her name to "Christine." But the reason she did that is because they couldn't say her name, and they would never remember it. Right? If they can't say it, why bother to remember it. Yeah, and it's weird watching them assimilate.

Having been victims of substantial stereotyping and mistreatment, Jessica's parents have more or less been forced to conform to a white-controlled society that has psychologically assaulted them. In account after account we observe the constant and coercive pressures on immigrants and their children to adapt to U.S. society in a unidirectional way.

Many immigrants of color go through this process to protect themselves from white discriminators, and Jessica admits that it makes sense that her parents would choose to assimilate in these ways, but it is still unnerving. We ask Jessica what she means when she uses the word "weird" for the change in her parents. She replies,

> Because it's such a delayed reaction to their own children growing up and having success and seeing that success and wanting to be part of that. And, you know, dressing differently and buying different cars, and learning English and watching the shows that we watch and buying things that we buy. And ... I guess it just feels weird to me, because I'm in a stage of my life where I'm working through that internalized oppression. And working through who I am and what I think about myself, and watching my parents go through what I went through when I was younger and in school. And seeing them just try to fit in and having American friends and having white friends specifically, and it's weird! And my mom, she's been here for so long now.... It seems so long, and so even she doesn't feel that comfortable in her Vietnamese identity any more. She feels that she is a Vietnamese American. When people say that I'm first generation—and they count me as a first generation—they completely discount my mother, who's been here for [more than] twenty years. I think she counts as an American in this country. How do you discount that? ... So, come on, that's more than my life that she's been here. And so, I can't blame her for wanting to change and grow.

The way Jessica describes her success and that of her family revolves around how well they conform to certain conventional images of success in this consumer society. Acquiring the right kind of car and clothes and watching the right television shows are what she and her parents seem to view as rather necessary to become "true Americans." Jessica's parents hope to gain greater white acceptance by such conforming, but after nearly three decades in the United States, they are still treated by whites as foreigners.

Dealing candidly and perceptively with her internalized oppression, Jessica is aware of the pervasive psychological and other impacts of everyday racism. Yet, in regard to her mother she "can't blame her for wanting to change and grow." Describing this one-way adaptation to white folkways and framing as growth may signal some internalized racism at work, as it implies that the mother's mimicking of a certain whiteness is healthy. The discomfort her mother feels in her Vietnamese identity again demonstrates the powerful imposition of a stereotyped white framing on these relatively new Americans. It appears that Jessica realizes that her mother will never be accepted if she does not make these choices to conform to certain white folkways. The psychological discrimination that Asian Americans experience in a racist system is like an abusive interpersonal relationship: they must succumb to many norms and requests of whites, yet never be on a healthy equal footing with them.

Separating from other people of color, and perhaps from themselves, is a way some Asian Americans try to conform to white framing and folkways. Some respondents recalled that during their school years, they would yearn to look different physically and were often less than thrilled with having Asian American friends. Charlotte thus recounts a high school experience:

> I remember in high school, when we moved to a different part of town, meeting one girl who was Chinese. And her mother was giving me a ride home because it turned out she lived very close to me, and her mother said, "Oh, look, she's Chinese too. Maybe you could be friends." And she and I respectively rolled our eyes, I think, wherever we were sitting in the car, not at each other, and it was nothing personal, and we didn't take it personally. It was just annoying that—"Oh, somebody else is Chinese, maybe you can be friends with them." ... I think that it was just ... we were, I guess ... second generation, but we were the first ones that were born and raised in this country. And they [the parents] just didn't want to lose the cultural identity. I understand that a lot more now as an adult than I did as a kid growing up—where assimilation was the name of the game. I remember she [her friend] and I talked about it, and all she wanted to have was blonde hair and blue eyes and to be named, I don't know, Chris or something like that. And all I wanted to have was *regular* brown hair and *regular* brown eyes and be named Janet. And so, we would just talk about how all we wanted to do was be like everybody else.

Charlotte did not like the mother's assumption that because she and the daughter were both Chinese they should naturally want to be friends. In addition, she sought to be far removed from another Asian because that would draw further attention to the fact that she was Asian. Since "assimilation was the name of the game" in her youth, Charlotte often worked hard to be as far from being seen as Chinese as possible. In Charlotte's description, her desire to be like everybody else specifically means to be like a white person, with the desirable characteristics being "regular" (white-type) hair and eyes. Charlotte and her friend shared an understanding of what it means to be different from "everyone else." While other, usually older, respondents found comfort in common understandings and close relationships with other Asian Americans, initially the young Charlotte did not want to befriend the other Asian American.

When Charlotte was in school some time ago, cosmetic surgery was not readily available and affordable. Today, however, the most frequent Asian and Asian American cosmetic surgeries are procedures to Anglicize their facial and other body features. Recent reports show a sharp increase in cosmetic surgery for Asian Americans, to whom much aggressive advertising is directed now. The most common surgeries for Asian American women are eyelid surgery, nose reshaping, and breast augmentation. The nose surgery usually involves a nose bridge operation that changes a flatter-looking Asian nose into a protruding, more European-type nose. Thus, much cosmetic surgery is directed at making Asian women look more like a common white view of ideal female beauty.

In September 2013, Julie Chen, host of CBS's television show *The Talk,* revealed that early in her career she had cosmetic surgery to change her "Asian eyes." She chose to undergo the procedure because she had become deeply insecure after her boss told her that her "heritage" was "holding back her career."[12] Chen admitted that she was rewarded after getting the surgery and that was a decision she has to "live with," yet one that has helped her get where she is today. Chen admitted that her difficult decision was driven by white-imposed racism, and assimilation through permanently altering her body with a surgical procedure to be "less Asian" was what she had to do to "make it" in her media profession.[13] There is a white-standardized idea of beauty, and Asian American women do not fit that picture. Yet, with advances in cosmetic surgery, women of all racial groups can pay to try to match the white-normed images portrayed in the movies, on television, and in magazine spreads.

While Chen faced this workplace discrimination in the 1980s, this pressure to meet white beauty standards remains, if not growing stronger with globalized media images. In Japan, a woman who changed her name to Vanilla has undergone over thirty cosmetic surgeries, including double-eyelid and rhinoplasty, to look like the "perfect French doll." Vanilla is hoping to look "anything but Japanese" and believes "nobody would say a French doll is ugly."[14] She has internalized the racialized view that her Japanese features are unattractive and is going to great lengths to whiten her features.

Recently, one Chinese American teenager commented critically on countering the pressures from her own stereotyping and from female relatives to dramatically change her facial appearance: "After all these years of wanting to open up my eyes with tape and glue and surgery, I have opened up my eyes to a different definition of beauty, one that embraces differences and includes every girl … because being Asian is beautiful."[15]

Of course, many Asian American women cannot afford to surgically alter their appearances. Some, like Charlotte, seek to surround themselves with white friends, thereby downplaying their Asianness and hoping that whites may pay less negative attention to them. Amanda, a Filipina American, grew up in an area where there were many Asian Americans. She discusses some middle and high school choices: "For a while, I must have had this complex where I felt that I was whitewashed, and I didn't ever want, my choice of friends was never any other Asian Americans. I always hung out with people [who were] … not necessarily white but almost never Asian American." In reply to a question about her choice to be disassociated from Asians, she responds, "There was just a negative connotation with being FOB ["fresh off the boat"], and I remember that the few Asian American friends that I had, not necessarily from high school, but from church, I remember that we would always talk badly about immigrants. Or even people, like, traveling places or whatever and making fun of them, and how they talked so funny, and how they're giving the rest of the American-born Asians a bad look." In her youth Amanda poked fun at Asian and

Pacific Island immigrants, probably to differentiate herself as much as possible from those "fresh off the boat."

In her interview she indicates too that she has been very concerned for her parents when they are out in public, as they are not always treated well by those who do not understand their accents. Her parents have pushed her to conform as much as possible in order to access some privileges they had been denied. As she notes, "My parents wanted, really wanted me and my sister to identify as being American and not as a different kind of American." In this case being "American" means not being a hyphenated "Filipino-American."

Amanda explains that in school she hid her identity in interactions with white and other non-Asian friends, as she recalls in this reflective passage:

> We would talk about … music and clothes, and everything they would say, I would agree with them. And I would never, never mention anything that sounded even remotely Asian-ish. I would probably *never tell them* I was Filipino. The thing is that *secretly* I was really proud of … my racial identity. I really was. I'm almost fluent in Tagalog [language in Philippines], and my family is really important to me, and there was no doubt that I really loved my heritage and my culture. It's just, I guess, maybe I thought that my friends wouldn't understand…. One of my closest friends is black, and she is probably like twenty-fifth generation American, or something like that. And how can she possibly relate to immigrant parents? … I'm trying to think of problems my parents would have, but they assimilated very well.

Amanda did her best to "lay low" in the hope that her Asian identity would not be found out. Even with other people of color, she was worried that they would not be able to relate to her family's immigration experience, so she had to be proud of her national identity in secret. Clearly, numerous respondents have gone to significant lengths to lessen or hide their Asianness for defensive reasons.

Rejecting Asianness

Many respondents spoke of going through a process of rejecting some or many aspects of their Asian backgrounds and characteristics. Those who have chosen to make the effort to abandon their Asianness usually have done so to succeed in white-dominated institutions. They generally believe that this movement away from their backgrounds helps them achieve more and gain acceptance from whites.

Like some other respondents, Joel, a Hmong American, reports feeling a *double* burden from race and class. In his hometown, where there are many Asian Americans, the Hmong are commonly viewed by whites in much the same negative way that they view black Americans. In his poignant interview he points out the impact of this common framing:

> I guess because the fact the Hmong people were a new cohort of immigrants into the U.S. during that time period, there was a more negative perception of them.... There is the whole notion that the Hmong people are on welfare and that they're taking taxpayer money, etc. So I think from my perception, there's a negative perception of the Hmong people because they're new immigrants. And more likely that they weren't getting a junior high education. I chose to associate more with the white individuals so I can internalize their expectations and also go in the same route that they are going.... I got straight As, and then I was one of the valedictorians for our junior high. But then at the same time, I kind of like, I knew that I wouldn't associate with the Hmong people as much, because it was kind of like, they're not doing so well. And I was doing better because this is where my parents want me to go, and this is also where most of the individuals in my class are going. So I kind of turned my "Hmongness" off, and I kind of more associated with, like, white individuals or those individuals who were doing academically better.

Note the contrast here to the model minority stereotype. Joel himself bought into the negative stereotyping of his Hmong American group, which he associated with a lack of academic achievement. The recipient of racist actions from whites, he decided that academic achievement would shield him from further mistreatment. Just as other Asian Americans have chosen to do, Joel worked to distance himself from his Asian heritage because he thought that was necessary in order to succeed in U.S. society. Later on, Joel notes, he became aware of the impact of white racism on him and the larger Hmong community, as well as of the insidious nature of pressures to hyper-conform.

May Ia, a Hmong American from a heavily Asian area in the Midwest, has not reached Joel's level of critical awareness. She sums up her experiences with adopting white ways thus: "Because growing up, I chose to follow more of the prosperity of the Caucasian culture, the white culture. Therefore, a lot of my thoughts, my attitudes, are more of an American culture.... [The white mindset] pretty much means individualized, be independent." She associates her own people with economic and racial hardship, and white culture with success. In her interview, however, she never mentioned the role of discriminatory whites in creating severe political and economic problems for the Hmong people.

Indeed, the Hmong were exploited by U.S. government (especially CIA) officials in waging a secret war in Laos against Vietnamese communists during the Vietnam War. This Hmong involvement in helping the U.S. military and intelligence organizations made them targets for retaliation after the United States withdrew. The Laotian government retaliated against them, and those unable to flee or hide in the mountains were very destitute and placed in refugee or reeducation camps.[16] Beyond the U.S. borders, white political and military officials have long exploited various peoples of color to enrich or protect U.S. national interests. Nonetheless, May Ia only blames her own people, who typically immigrated as impoverished refugees, for their economic and social failures today, while she credits white folkways as the necessary route to Hmong success. Her views seem heavily shaped by an acceptance of much of the dominant white racial framing of the Hmong and other Asian Americans.

Frank, a Korean American, formerly a technical worker and now business owner, comes from a city with a large Asian American population. He too has adopted significant aspects of the white mind-set on various societal matters. [...] He initially said that he had faced no discrimination but later discussed at length the significant glass ceiling that prevents Asian American advancement. Let us now consider some of his thoughts about assimilation and conformity over the years:

> I didn't feel like I was a minority because they [whites] treated me just like one of them. And also, I assimilated to the U.S. very quickly. At that time, I had a younger brother who was six years old. And he got assimilated even faster. So we became just like they did. Even today, a lot, I have a lot of Korean friends who call me "banana" now. I look Oriental, Asian, in the face, but inside is pure white.... I look like all Asian outside. I am Asian. But inside, and the way I think, and the way I behave, [the] way I approach the problem, the way I approach the government, or whatever, I act exactly like white Americans. I do everything correctly, do step by step as the government requires, which causes far less problems.... I am a conservative and a Republican. And the way I look at it is, I know that most white people I know, I don't know the exact political affiliations, when I talk to them, we are talking the same thing, the same language, and the same subject. And we both agree on it, so I assume he and I are both [the] same.

Frank seems to relish his stereotyped "banana" identity. He articulates strong views and uses clear language to describe his actions as he conforms to and mimics whites. He argues that the white ways are the "correct" ways, and that contrasting Asian ways are usually "wrong." An interesting part of Frank's societal analysis is that in his view much important "white thinking" and political orientation are conservative and Republican, even though in fact a great many whites are moderates, liberals, Independents, and Democrats. The reason for his false impression may lie in his significant reliance on the mainstream media, such as television networks, several of which have become more conservative in their reporting on U.S. society over the decades of significant Asian immigration since the 1960s. One irony in Frank's views is that about the same time that some Asian Americans shifted their political allegiances to the Republican Party, that

READING 7 STRUGGLE AND CONFORMITY | 129

party shifted its political goals and efforts even more in the direction of white voters and their political interests. Indeed, white Republican leaders have periodically admitted that they have little interest in actively recruiting Americans of color, especially immigrants of color, into the party and instead prefer to rely heavily on white voters.[17]

At the root of these adaptations by numerous respondents to white thinking and folkways is the view that they are correct and normal, and that other ways of doing things are undesirable if not dangerous to life, family, or career. From this perspective, Americans of color must protect themselves by adopting the white framing and folkways. Recall Janice Tanaka's documentary on Japanese Americans who decided after the World War II concentration-camp experience to conform more aggressively to white ways to stave off a recurrence of that highly racist and destructive process.[18]

Brian, a Sansei administrator who grew up in a community heavily populated with Asian Americans, recounts this experience involving his father, who was put into one of those concentration camps during the war:

> It was passed down to us in regards to being raised in an assimilationist household. There's a piece of us [that] was reinforced from the rest of the [Japanese] culture, but there was also a strong push for us to assimilate, to [be] raised to conformist status, and to be as white in America as possible.... In essence, he's telling me implicitly that, when he was twenty, he didn't have that opportunity. There's too much racist policies, and mobs and attitudes, and so one of the only things available to him was gardening. So he did gardening. I have a lot more options. So that's what I chose. But going back to where I am, he would do anything to help me assimilate.... So, from not learning the [Japanese] language ... and then [to] being involved much like our current millennials, being involved in soccer Little League ... and then not learning the language. But [he still taught me to have] ... a little cultural pride by knowing some stuff, so it wasn't a total conformist upbringing. But I don't think it was really a childhood—by pushing the biracial in regards to knowing and honoring the Japanese side, and the white and American cultural side.

Brian uses the word biracial to describe the approach that his father used to raise him during formative years, yet he is *not* in fact half white and half Japanese, but of Japanese (and Okinawan) descent. Thus, biracial is an unusual term for his being socialized in many white ways and some Japanese ways, especially in what he describes as an "assimilationist household." Brian's father wanted him to have opportunities that he never had because of extreme racial oppression, and his father, like many of that generation, saw these opportunities as coming from an aggressive adoption of white framing and folkways.

In a probing interview, Lin, a Chinese American head of a community center, explains the phenomenon of Asian American conformity:

> So many people in the past have worked to make this a great nation, but we have to really ... , Asian Americans, have to really take that responsibility and go beyond just to have comfortable homes, two cars, have good children that grow to be knowledgeable. [We have] to really understand the struggle of single moms, the struggle of affordable housing, the struggle of affordable health care, all the basic needs for all people. I think there is not enough discussion in the Asian American community about all the other social issues. It could be because we don't think that we have the power to change it, because, after all, we are disempowered, and maybe it is because we are so consumed by the busy pace, the fast pace of life. And I think it's also because we are not being treated as American citizens [that] we don't think that we are allowed to contribute to the social issues.

By achieving economic stability and acquiring some consumer comforts, many Asian Americans seem to be lulled to sleep. In her interview Lin refers to middle-class comforts that many Asian Americans enjoy as "crumbs" that have been "tossed" to them from whites, crumbs that are often enough to keep them compliant and grateful. Asian Americans frequently conform, and whites are often idolized in this process. Yet, in a kind of odd Newtonian social law ("with every action there is an equal and opposite reaction"), even conforming people of color are often vilified by whites for not living up fully to various white standards.

While social "laws" are not directly comparable to the laws of physics, there are certainly recurring socioracial patterns in societies like the United States. One of these is seen in what happens when Americans of color adopt the white racial frame in their minds, which adoption binds them closely to the racist system. The latter, in turn, continues to oppress them. Often favored by whites among people of color, Asian Americans who substantially adopt the dominant racial frame seek to gain yet more favor from whites. In his interview, Josh, a Chinese American in a northern city, mentioned that his father taught him to assimilate and fit in with whites as much as possible to be successful. Reflecting on this, he comments thus: "My dad probably adjusted best to America because of assimilation. He just kind of accepted that to survive in America you have to become a little more Americanized. If you hear him talk to any of his brothers, he ends up talking more in English than Chinese. He definitely speaks more English than Chinese now."

When Josh's father reached a comfortable place economically and socially, he encouraged his family to play up limited aspects of their Chinese background, but mainly if it assists in societal advancement. Josh's father has recognized the significance of certain Asian stereotyping among whites and apparently hopes that by playing into that stereotyping he and his family can do better. Josh explains,

My dad always talks about if he's meeting up with someone who is Caucasian, [who] doesn't have any idea of Asian culture, he will always take them to a specific Chinese restaurant. He knows the entire menu and takes them there. He can just talk about how Chinese and how Oriental and how this has a certain value in the Chinese culture. Like potential patients or potential contacts that can help politically or, like, you know, just people of power. He tries to impress the right connections by *exploiting,* but not really exploiting, like really advertising Asian culture to like everything. Like, he might take up a teapot and be, like, this is a kind of duck [on the teapot], in this era of China. And, like, basically kind of bullshit them. And he would actually use the word *bullshit* when he was explaining it to me. He would just—well you know, people are like, "Aw, that's so interesting and fascinating of Asian culture." ... He also would encourage me to do similar things to my college application, back when I applied to schools.... So like, you know, to differentiate yourself from every other person, [not] just from everyone else but also from Asians. Maybe do a different kind of exploitation.

There is a fine line for Josh's father to walk between being substantially assimilated to white folkways and yet being proud of, and using his connections to, Chinese culture and history. Because a weak type of multiculturalism is fashionable in many organizations, Josh's father can sometimes accent or exaggerate aspects of Chinese culture in ways that he hopes may benefit him. Josh uses words like "bullshit" and "exploitation" to describe the technique that his father advocates for certain settings. What seems to be involved here is an attempt to play into white interest in Asians and Asian cultures as "exotic." There is a blending of a type of resistance strategy that involves conning whites ignorant of Asian culture with what is a submissiveness seeking to please powerful whites—so as to advance economically or socially, yet still mostly in white terms. Once again, we see the great power of the surrounding and systemic racism in shaping Asian American strategies of both adaptation and resistance.

Internalized Racism: Yet More Dimensions

Asian American conformity to white folkways and framing usually involves internalizing racism. We have already seen numerous examples of this process. In this section we seek to delve more deeply into understanding how this internalizing works and into some of its important effects. Americans of color are generally forced to adopt many white folkways and at least some white racist framing. This framing frequently creates much conflict with how people of color wish to regard themselves. There is a substantial literature on the negative self-concepts that groups like African Americans have developed in reaction to systemic racism.[19] This research reveals much about how certain groups of color have internalized negative stereotypes of their group from the omnipresent white racial framing surrounding them.

In similar ways many Asian Americans adopt some white stereotypes about Asian Americans. Anti-Asian stereotypes and related sentiments manifest themselves in some of the following ways: opposing the choice of Asian partners, purposely denying a job to an Asian American, discouraging Asian Americans who challenge the racial status quo, perpetuating negative Asian American stereotypes, seeking to change physical characteristics to appear white, and denying one's Asian heritage.

Searching for a White Partner

Before the large increase in Asian immigration facilitated by the 1965 immigration law, Asian American men outnumbered Asian American women, but since the late 1960s the population of Asian American women has grown, and they now outnumber Asian American men. Asian American women are more likely than Asian American men to marry outside of their group. They out-marry more than other women and men of color, and much more than Asian American men.[20]

In many cases, a white racial framing in the minds of Asian American women may intersect with the sexualization of Asian American women in white male minds. One study of Asian-white interracial relationships in the Southwest found that "contrary to popular utopian celebration of mixed-race marriage as a sign of multiracialization, interracial intimacy is still regulated by racial, gender, class, and national hierarchies." That is, the Asian American women interviewed "saw white men as sources of power through which they might transform their marginality" in their communities and the larger society.[21] Asian and Asian American women often see white men as avenues of liberation and mobility from the patriarchal or modest-income realities of their own backgrounds, even as white men are often attracted to them because of old stereotypes of Asian female docility or exotic sexuality.

Among our female respondents with partners, four had married Asians before they immigrated to the United States, and ten formed relationships in the United States after arrival here or as U.S.-born citizens. Of those ten, six partnered with white men, three with Asian Americans, and one with a Mexican American. Among our male respondents, those who immigrated were all single when they arrived. Of those who formed relationships in the United States, four are partnered with Asian or Asian American women, and one with an Iranian American woman. Not one has partnered with a white woman. Our sample thus reflects the higher out-marriage rate for Asian American women than for Asian American men found in other research studies.[22]

One Japanese American respondent, Alice, is distressed by the extent of this out-marriage. In her interview she discusses the resultant "whitening" of her Sansei generation:

> Why is it that Asian women are dating white men three to one over Asian men? And you know, for Japanese Americans, that out-marriage started in

the '60s where 50 percent were out-marriage, but now amongst all Asian American women, the statistic is three to one. Ironically, we have three couples that are very good friends, and they are all Asian women and white guys. And they are all having children this year. So it's like, Oh my God, it's true. But it's a strange phenomenon. And, like, I keep talking with the Asian men, and they get more and more mad as time goes on…. So it's a very strange racial thing that is happening. And now we have a lot of "Hapa" kids. And what are their lives going to be like? You know, there're going to be a lot of women with the half-Asian [children], like Tiger Woods. And in reality, mothers have much more influence over things like culture, over things like values because they spend more time naturally with their kids. But, who knows, I think it's really a dilemma that we're facing.

Younger Japanese Americans are among the most integrated of all non-European groups into numerous areas of various European American communities. What this integration means for the future of Japanese Americans is unclear, but Alice calls out this racial blending in her area as a "dilemma" in regard to the future. Some Japanese Americans view the children of mixed marriages, often called *Hapa* (from a Hawaiian word for half), as definitely Japanese American, with a goal in mind of somehow socializing them into the traditional culture. Analysts like Greg Mayeda have suggested that eventually the typical Japanese American family may be a Hapa family: "Community leaders must recognize this and encourage Hapas and their multicultural families to participate in Japanese American organizations and customs. If given the opportunity, Hapas can unify and reinvigorate the Japanese American community."[23] However, Alice does not seem so hopeful, as there is an undertone of fear that the Hapas will lose important connections to the traditional Japanese culture.

In the nineteenth century Asian American men were commonly stereotyped in an omnipresent white framing as oversexed and threatening to white women, but in recent decades they have been more likely to be stereotyped as feminized and emasculated, a shift that may link to the rise of model minority stereotyping.[24] However, this docility stereotype does not fit with Alice's experience. As she notes, many Asian American women, including herself, have an opposite view:

> You know, a lot of Asian women say from their point of view that Asian men raised by Asian mothers have a lot of macho expectations, especially if they are from China or from Korea or from India, wherever…. Asian men, well … some of them are really angry…. It's an interesting dilemma to me, because I see the seething Asian man. You have the angry Asian man, and they are so outspoken about why, and so enraged about why. But nobody ever comes to any conclusions except that it's just happening.

According to this interview, Alice and other Asian women commonly believe they will be treated better by a white man and be granted more freedom. Yet there is no empirical evidence to support their claims. Indeed, some research suggests the opposite is more likely—that the inequality characteristic of Asian American female relationships with white men makes these women very vulnerable to significant abuse and mistreatment by their white male partners.[25]

Accepting the dominant racial framing makes white men the desirable partners for some Asian women. The latter are frequently bombarded with messages of white superiority and of the desirability of white privilege, and it is hard for them to combat these powerful influences on their thinking. One respondent, Lee, emigrated from Thailand some years ago. Before she came, she was working in what she called a "secret American factory" in Thailand making "forty times" less money than she does now. Yet those she knew there loved Americans and wanted to move to the United States. Sponsored by a relative, she was able to find work at a U.S. factory, where she met a white man. In her interview she reports that "I married him, white guy, everybody just thinks I am so lucky for that too. Like I said, I always think I like American people. I think they look wonderful. I always like them. Thai love American people." Attempting to clarify what Lee means here by "Americans," we follow up with a question asking if she means all Americans including black Americans. She responds in an interesting way: "Yes. White and black. [long pause] Because [pause] I don't know. Uh, maybe white more than black. [another long pause] I don't know, but I think so. [pause] Yes. I think white, more white." Lee's initial answer was a clear "white and black," but as she thought about the question and began to answer further, she apparently realized that black Americans are not held in such high regard as white Americans. She transitioned from definite, to hesitant, to unsure, and finally to a different certainty about "white."

Lee has a daughter who is white and Asian American. Like numerous respondents, she claims early in her interview to have not experienced racial hostility and discrimination. However, she later mentions that she is "so worried" for her daughter. In reply to a question about this, she reveals that she had in fact been a target of racial discrimination frequently from her white coworkers at a previous job. In addition, she now owns a business, and white customers sometimes treat her badly, probably because of her racial identity. She reveals that she wants to go back to Thailand as soon as she can, and with her daughter. She indicates that she would rather work for the low-paying "secret American factory" than stay in the United States. Marrying a white man has not protected her from racial hostility and discrimination, but that marriage, she believes, will give her increased social status in Thailand. She comments further, "Thai people like American people. I don't know if they like us, but we like them.... My people love American people. That's why I want [my daughter] to go back home, and they're going to treat her wonderful.... Here, it makes me worry." Interestingly, Lee wants to move back to Thailand because she perceives that her biracial daughter will receive better treatment there. Asian American women may gain some white acceptance and respite from discrimination by forming relationships with white men. However, as here, some fear that they will not be able to protect their children from that same discrimination. We might note also that at no point in her interview does Lee actually put *herself* in the important category of the "American people."

If whites are the preferred partner choice for some Asian Americans, then partners of color become an unwanted and unattractive choice. In her interview Amanda (a Filipina American, discussed earlier) recalls her partner preferences while she was attending middle school and high school: "I remember growing up that I always thought the cutest guys were all white. They were all pretty much white." Amanda could not remember where her preference for white males came from but noted that it did change over time as she became much more comfortable with her Asian American identity.

Ann, a Vietnamese American, clearly recognizes the messages she has regularly received from her parents about their preferences of partners:

> I swear to God, if I ever brought, dated a black man and brought him home, I would be disowned by my father. [Regardless] of whether he went to an Ivy League, is a doctor, a lawyer or whatever, he could be the most gentle person, the greatest person on the face of this earth, my father would disown me—because he does, he thinks that every black person is on welfare and no good. Even if I went for a Cambodian guy, I think my dad would think the same way. He doesn't think highly of the Cambodians either. My dad has that idea of that "dirty Mexican," and kind of stereotypic and racist ideals against the blacks and the Latinos. Whites, of course, of course, are better than any Asian person I could ever be with. My mom thinks so too. That she'll be blatant about.

The racially framed stereotypes that Ann's father strongly articulates about black Americans and Mexican Americans are standard ones that whites have long used to describe these Americans of color. He did not invent this hostile white racial framing but has accepted it, probably influenced by the mainstream media and other mainstream sources. Our second- and later-generation respondents often spoke of how their relatives have pushed them to adopt and conform to white standards in regard to dating and partners. These pressures to prefer white partners are commonly coupled with significant pressures to distance themselves from certain people of color.

Some choices result from personal experiences. Josh, who is Chinese American, recalls this experience when he was in elementary school and middle school: "I definitely remember actually half of my girlfriends were minority ... at the time. They were all Asian, or ... , or yeah. I think they were all Asian. And like, maybe one was Indian, and definitely no one was Caucasian. I had friends that were Caucasians but all the girls ... I was in a relationship with were Asian." It is not clear if Josh dated Asian Americans because of his personal preferences or because white females did not consider him desirable.

As he grew older, however, Josh's preferences shifted away from Asian American females. He explains why:

> But I do have a problem, like, last year a lot of Asian American females I end up meeting and talking with, it's no offense to them, but … a lot of them actually end up like they're trying to be something else. I know this one girl, this Asian girl in my high school, and she would always talk about how popular she could have been. "I could have been so popular. I could've been so popular." She had an *image problem*. "I could be a cheerleader." She just really dreamt of being a popular girl in our class, but it was primarily an upper-class white population. I meet a lot of Asian American females, and not all of them, but some just end up really, not really wanting to be who they are. It's as if they … are trying to really push toward something really different or really trying to be something that they naturally aren't. And I do end up dating less Asians as a result.

Josh makes an important point about identity struggles that we have highlighted previously. Some Asian American females with whom he has interacted have struggled significantly with their personal identity and have a strong desire to be socially integrated into white-dominated spaces. To Josh, this is not what they should aspire to. Indeed, he describes his sister as being at risk of losing her cultural and family connections because of a partnering choice:

> One thing that's happening with the Asian American identity, I mean, for example, my sister, when she got married, she definitely became less Asian American and just American, definitely by far. Because when she became part of [her white husband's] family it became all about his family. So it's like her race is never anything at all. It doesn't seem to come up with her, or with anyone like the in-laws. But as a result, she also has kind of lost ties in our family. She is not as well connected. But basically, if you go to her house there is nothing Asian American about it. Nothing. Nothing.

A common report of Asian American women in such relationships is that they are not only distinctively dependent on their white husbands but usually rather subordinate to his white family. The Asian American relatives of the wife often have to take a distant second place in extended family interests and gatherings. Interpersonal connections are reduced, and personal isolation may well increase.

Notice several important issues in these last few accounts: (1) whites are the ideal partners for Asian Americans; (2) there is fear on the part of Asian Americans in interracial relationships that their half-Asian children will suffer discrimination from whites; and (3) out-marriages may disconnect Asian Americans from Asian American traditions, culture, and family connections.

Most importantly, whether conscious or unconscious, partner "choice" is affected by the larger societal structure. As an individual creates a checklist of traits they deem desirable in a partner, racial stereotypes and inequality in society play a role. Often there are racial politics involved in partner choice. That politics affects Asian American men and women in different ways. Asian American women are often exoticized and are constructed as sexually attractive, frequently giving them more diverse partnership opportunities, but Asian American men are not constructed in the same way and, at times, find their partner choices more limited.[26] A study of expressed dating preferences online confirmed that the odds favor white men and Asian American women the most, while Latino and Asian American men have the lowest response rates to their personal posts.[27]

Asian-on-Asian Stereotyping and Discrimination

We have already observed how numerous Asian Americans participate in at least some Asian-on-Asian stereotyping and discrimination. Some attribute negative characteristics to Asians or Asian Americans as "natural." Some articulate group-hating views. Some with the power to hire and promote consciously deny people of Asian heritage jobs or promotions. Yet others openly criticize Asian Americans who actively work against anti-Asian racism. Such Asian-on-Asian mistreatment substantially serves the interests of whites and the U.S. system of racism.

Blaming Asians and Asian Americans

Recall from a previous chapter that one respondent, Bari, was a victim of a hate crime while coming home from his college campus. He was the first victim of several street attacks on international students near this university, all of whom were Asian. Bari's incident came up when we interviewed another Asian international student, David, who has served as a leader in a campus association that represents many Chinese students. Asked by a campus student association to alert the students in his organization to the danger of further white attacks, he took no action because he believed, in fact erroneously, that the only students being attacked were South Asians.[28] In his interview he rationalizes the violent attacks on South Asians thus: "I know the people that got beat around that area. They are from India. Maybe for the Chinese, they don't really get into trouble. Maybe because they don't speak very good English, so they kind of get away from the trouble, get away, the Chinese students. But Indian students, they speak better English. They want to argue [he laughs]."

When we explain that the attacks were unprovoked and that the targets included East Asians, he replies, "Oh, really, that's really bad." In regard to informing students in his organization, at first he said that he had not received complaints of discrimination from students that he represented, but after further discussion he did cite numerous instances where Chinese and Chinese American students did report feeling unwelcome on campus. Later in the interview, he has this to say about how other students at the university feel about international students: "People say they don't really care or interact with international students. But still I can feel there is a barrier between international students and American students. They hang around American students, but I don't think many international students interact with that many American students. It depends; maybe it's our problem. We are probably too conservative."

When David refers to "American students" at this large historically white institution, he makes clear that he means *whites*. Other researchers have found too that "Americans" and "whites" are often interchangeable terms used by Asians and first-generation Asian Americans—and apparently for many people around the globe.[29] David's comments about the campus area hate crimes and other mistreatment of Asian students never mention or fault the violent white perpetrators. He specifically blames the divide between Asian and white students on certain tendencies of Asians, such as the latter being "too conservative" in certain styles of interaction. Yet in his interview, Bari, the target of a hate crime on that campus, says that when he first arrived on campus he felt an immediate chill from the white students that made it impossible to make friends with them.

Alex, who lives in a Pacific Coast area heavily populated with Asian Americans, says that he too believes that Asian Americans should take the blame for some of their problems. In his interview he notes that the government pays little attention to Asian issues:

> The government ... they don't care for Asians that much. But at the same time, the Asians aren't very good about coming forward with political issues, I think. So lots of times you watch TV, or listen to the radio. When they talk about minorities, they're usually talking about African Americans. They hardly mention Asian Americans. And that's because I think that we as Asians are not very good about putting up the issues in American government. Or maybe other Americans, they don't look at it being an issue, even when we actually do. So actually I think it goes both ways. For example, when I go to Costco, and sometimes there are people, they are collecting signatures to make [something] into law, or whatever they are doing. I would observe those people, and most of the time they won't bother to ask Asians. Because, I think, we have a poor voting rate.

Even in West Coast areas with many Asian Americans, some Asian American political organizations, and a few Asian American elected officials, Alex has noticed the lack of interest that activists have in soliciting Asian Americans to be involved in political petitions. Asian Americans do have a relatively low voter turnout rate, but that rate is steadily growing.[30] His statement also assigns responsibility to Asian Americans for not asserting their political interests and issues and for a low voting rate, but does not assess critically the possible reasons for this. In contrast, Asian American analyst Vijay Prashad explains this lack of political involvement as linked in part to historical exclusion and discrimination and thus to "being socially detached from U.S. life," which "justifies withdrawing even further from the social and political life of the United States."[31]

Taking Asian-on-Asian stereotyping and discrimination a step further, Frank, who lives in a city with large Asian American communities, reports often acting out of a perspective shaped by the white framing of Asian Americans:

> I have my own company. I use an American white female and I send her out to sell, and then I send the Oriental girl out there. I found that the white American females consistently have higher sales. So as a business owner, ... of course I'm going to lean toward the white American girl. She's bringing more money for me. It's a simple fact of life. And you know, I don't think you can force that issue. At the end of the day, who's writing a check to your company, right, and if I send the white girl out there, and she gets more money for me, I'll be using her. Not because of race, just as a fact of life. I wouldn't say that it's fair or not fair. Nothing in life is fair. I look at it this way: life is not fair from the beginning to end. If you try to make everything fair, it won't work. If I was born as Brad Pitt, it would be great, but I'm not. Brad Pitt may be making a couple movies, making a hundred million dollars, but since I'm not, I make less than $150,000. Am I unhappy? Of course I'm happy. I'm happy. It's a fact of life.

Note how Frank uses the negative word "Oriental," one that whites invented and have long used to categorize and denigrate Asians and Asian Americans. His unreflective use of the term suggests acceptance of a stereotyped white framing of Asians, one that he openly acknowledges in various parts of his detailed interview. In addition, although many of his customers are Asian American, he prefers whites as salespeople. Complicating an assessment of his perspective, we observe too that Frank is adamant that life in the United States is "not fair," so he must just accept that racially biased reality.

Attacking Asian Americans Who "Rock the Boat"

Most of our respondents have refrained from openly protesting racist incidents that they have seen or been involved in, even if they live in areas with many Asian Americans. One reason is fear of white retaliation. As we have shown, acquiescing has long been an individual and group survival technique. Parents pass down these strategic techniques to children, often conjoined with admonitions to individual conformity. This conventional adaptation to racial hostility poses serious problems for those who choose to challenge that racial reality. Asian American activists thus have often found themselves alone when standing up against discriminatory incidents. They have been accused of "rocking the boat" and have been targeted with negative criticism from the very communities that they are attempting to serve and protect.

Take the example of Jessica, a Vietnamese American whose family situation we described earlier. At a major university with a substantial Asian and Asian American student population (approaching one-fifth), Jessica's student group published a well-documented report about problems of Asian and Asian American students there, with the hope of securing significant institutional change. The group made modest demands, including more Asian American representation in student government and one Asian American mental health counselor. After the report was released, the university administration claimed to be responsive to its findings and planned meetings to discuss the issues. The most intense criticism of this rather moderate report came from an unexpected sector—from other Asians and Asian American students in the university community. When word got to those students, as Jessica puts it, "the shit really hit the fan." She continues with her account:

> But the students, that was the most hurtful because a lot of the criticism came from our own community. And I can see it. And it's like watching a video about the model minority being perpetuated. You know, it's like here it is. This is how the model minority is perpetuated, and then just look at it. I mean, people were saying, "Why do you have to rock the boat?" People saying, "Why are you looking for trouble? Why are you seeing things that aren't there? I've never experienced racism. It must not exist." It was ridiculous, and people were personally attacking the women of [the organization] ... and it was so hurtful for [the president], and it was really hard for me to see it. In Asian American Studies classes, people would say, "That's ridiculous," where I would think the most progressive Asian Americans would see. People saying that "this is crap" and like, "this doesn't exist."

Much criticism of the important report came from Asian American students, yet the intent was to provide better representation and support for that population. For these students fear of white backlash trumped even modest actions to bring campus change. Like the Japanese Issei and Nisei before and after World War II, Asian Americans today can work hard and become high-achieving citizens, yet still *greatly fear* losing everything at the whim of discriminatory whites. At Jessica's university, the Asian student population is the largest among the students of color, yet being critical of the university's often anti-Asian climate is still too difficult for many.

Fareena, a Bangladeshi American, was head of this bold student organization at the time. In her interview she discusses the backlash she received after the report was released:

> There was a lot of hate mail from Asian American males. A lot of them were Asian Studies majors saying, "Why are you causing a ruckus? You're making us look bad." I remember taking an Asian American Studies class at that time. The women in that class hated me. I would get nasty little notes on my desk, "You're just doing this for your résumé." I thought, "If I was doing this for my résumé, I would get better grades. I wouldn't be messing up my classes," because that's what I was doing. One of them had said that I just "needed to take a Midol and cool down. These issues aren't that big of

a deal." I thought the Midol reference was very interesting. I talked to her about it, and she just said, "It's a pain killer." These are all Asian American females, saying, "Why are you making Asian Americans look bad? Why are you saying that?" ... No group likes it when someone's rocking the boat. People think differently in terms of belonging to an imagined community or not. Some people are very defensive of it, and some are not.

Fareena bore the brunt of the criticism from the student community she was trying to serve. She was labeled an agitator, and many Asian Americans on campus worked to distance themselves from being associated with the "trouble seekers" in the Asian organization. She continues by describing some positive responses, as well as her personal costs:

I've had a lot of nice e-mails and messages from people, but they were primarily people of color that were not Asian American. Or Asian Americans would send it in, but they would remain anonymous. I thought that was weird. I remember that it was a really bad semester for me. For me in the beginning I was like, "I'm ready to take it! I'm ready to take it! I don't care. If I believe in these issues and I made this report, I have to be responsible for whatever consequences come. I will learn from it. It will be an opportunity." But I had to seek counseling. I really did.

Interestingly, Fareena received much support from other racial groups, especially African Americans and Latinos, that many whites label as "troublemakers" when they openly resist the serious manifestations of white discrimination. She explains more about the character of the backlash and the major impact of the events on her:

A lot of our members weren't expecting this big of a backlash from Asian Americans. One member quit because he felt like he was going to lose his friends and he felt like he shouldn't have to defend our organization to them.... Some of the members were questioning, "Did we go about this the right way? Should we have made this report? Should we have kept it quiet?" Which is what the person who quit had advocated for. Now that I think about it, I think we did do the right thing. But back then I felt silenced and I think I took it a little harder and I didn't tell people, and people didn't realize because I was quoted so much. I was also in Asian American Studies classes at the time, the other people were not.... I failed it. I never explained it to the professor, who was the adviser for Asian American Studies.... It was just hard and if it was hard to tell her, because the class would have discussions about it every day in the beginning. They would say things out loud very passive-aggressively to me or by even saying my name. Me being the person I am, I would want to say, "Actually, you have that wrong, because this is what happened." The professor would shut me down. I don't think she realized she was shutting *me* down, but she saw that it was becoming a back-and-forth argument.

Shortly after Fareena began being harshly criticized by other Asian students, she stepped down from the leadership of the organization.

Even with the Yellow Power movement near the end of the 1960s, successful pressures for reparations for imprisoned Japanese Americans, and the recent increase in Asian American Studies courses (some even being taken by her critics), the collective memory of racial oppression and resistance to it that is passed along to Asian Americans is relatively weak, indeed sometimes nonexistent. This greatly complicates the protest efforts of Asian American activists. Even later, fellow Asian students in Fareena's Asian American Studies courses still make similar remarks to her when there is news of a new racist incident in the campus area.

In her interview Jessica reasons in a sharp and probing way with regard to why many Asian American students reacted negatively to discussions of anti-Asian racism:

> It happens because we internalize that racism and that oppression. You know, it goes back to, you know, when you are little, and all you want to do is fit in. And if you feel like you fit in and someone else is making a racket.... I mean, like, *shut up,* you know, stop being such a [sore] thumb! You know, *stop*! I think that's part of what it is. And part of it is because the Asian American community is very diverse, and I mean some people may have not experienced that kind of discrimination. That doesn't mean it doesn't exist. I mean, it does, and maybe you just weren't aware of the discrimination that you experienced because it's everywhere. It's pervasive. It's the little things, and you can't deny the numbers when you talk about the professional world, and how many people you have—just look at the university—how many Asian Americans there are and how many of them are high ranking. So, I mean, it's undeniable it exists, but when we don't learn about our history, and we don't learn about our role here in this country and we're not even seen as Americans, I mean, we internalize all of that and we don't see it. A lot of times Asian Americans don't consider themselves people of color, and other people don't consider them people of color either. So they don't understand it, they don't get it. Or they say, well yeah, I guess you're right, but it's not as bad as, you know, the black community or the Latino community, so we should shut up.

When Jessica asserts that "we don't learn about our history," she is highlighting the lack of collective memory of historical oppression and resistance to it among most Asian Americans, an issue to which we will return later. Because many Asian Americans lack a substantial knowledge of the history of oppression, they sometimes do not even see themselves as people of color—or at least as people who need to organize and resist the racism they regularly face. This is highly problematical for those who not only understand that oppression but seek to organize and to change it.

At least one other study has found Asian Americans in similar situations. Thus, pioneering researcher Mia Tuan has concluded from her interviews with Asian Americans that

> some Asian Americans have embraced the model minority label, and see it as their ultimate ticket into gaining social acceptance.... Youth were convinced that with hard work, patience, and a little help from the model minority stereotype, they would someday gain the full approval of white Americans. They wrote off repeated incidents involving racism or discrimination as the acts of ignorant individuals, isolated experiences that they did not take seriously.[32]

Similarly, Fareena and Jessica's classmates are hoping that Fareena's brave actions do not "ruin it for the rest of them," as they too believe discriminators are just ignorant and they remain naively hopeful that whites will honor their hard work with success and real acceptance.

Stereotyping Other Americans of Color: Targets and Discriminators

In his pioneering analysis of Asian Americans, Frank Wu has argued that their in-between role in the U.S. racial hierarchy makes for a complexity of situations, which often shift and mutate significantly from one to the next: "When considering Asian Americans it is easier to realize that people can be both perpetrators and victims of racial discrimination. We can simultaneously play both roles, inferior to one, superior to the other. Asian Americans can feel ostracized by whites and terrorized by blacks. Asian Americans can even simultaneously play both roles in relation to the same group, regarding either blacks or whites with contempt only to have the favor returned."[33]

One point that Wu fails to address in his otherwise insightful analysis is that it is the centuries-old white racial frame that provides most major stereotypes that Asian Americans and other people of color adopt in regard to U.S. racial groups, including their own group. Like almost all critical analysts, Wu skirts around directly naming white discriminators as such even as he discusses the serious discrimination Americans of Asian descent face "in society" and assesses well how they often add to their somewhat favored position "by disparaging other people of color." Wu attributes this process to personal choices made by individual Asian Americans. However, these Asian Americans are making such choices within a societal context that is deeply and structurally racist, one where they are forced to collude to some degree with the existing racist system and where they often accept much of the white racial framing of society and the racial hierarchy that age-old frame buttresses.

The impact of U.S. racism is not confined to the borders of the United States. Indeed, U.S. economic, political, military, and mass media power makes the country very important, indeed often dominant, in many global settings. The United States not only exports commercial goods but also propagates important ideals and ideas as well. The U.S. media are very influential and perpetuate important aspects of the white racial frame to many countries around the world. Certain U.S.-oriented products and their advertising also spread a U.S. racial framing. One conspicuous example of the global perpetuation of this white racist framing can be seen even in brands of toothpaste used in some countries overseas. For example, in Taiwan the "Darkie" toothpaste brand still shows a man in "black face" with bright white teeth. Another toothpaste brand is not so subtly called "Whiteman"! The Darkie brand depicts a blatantly racist image of a white man mocking "blackness" in the fashion of the old white minstrels once commonplace in the United States, while the Whiteman brand overtly shows "whiteness" as the standard for beautiful and ideal oral hygiene. Other products, such as some candy packages in Europe, Asia, and Mexico, also carry extraordinarily racist representations. Moreover, U.S. movies and television shows, some from the 1930s–1950s era, are regularly shown around the globe, and they too often carry racist messages not only about white superiority and black inferiority but also about the inferiority of other Americans of color.

Thus, many new immigrants from overseas countries enter the United States with their heads already full of racist stereotypes and images—especially those targeting African, Latino, and Asian Americans—which they have picked up from their contacts with the U.S. mass media and other sources. Asians thus frequently receive racialized messages about Americans of color long before they step on U.S. soil. After immigrating, they and their children live under the aegis of the white frame and quickly learn many folkways of this still racialized society. Because of this, many learn and accept old racist stereotypes of themselves and other Americans of color long promoted by whites.

Sociologist Claire Jean Kim has studied conflict between Korean Americans and African Americans in New York City. She concludes from her research that "by celebrating Asian American 'success,' White opinion makers implicitly assert that nothing is standing in the way of other nonwhite groups except their own bad habits or cultural deficiencies."[34] This aspect of the white framing of the latter Americans of color is often adopted by Korean and other Asian Americans. For example, Alex, a Korean American professional from the West Coast, discusses such views held by his grandparents:

> It's interesting because my grandparents … just wouldn't like African Americans. For no particular reason…. They don't change their minds…. My grandpa, all the time he would like always, for whatever reason, he wouldn't like African Americans. And then they never really gave me any

clear reason when I [said], "What did they do to you?" "Nothing." So that's pretty disappointing. But that's the way things are, I guess.... I think that in L.A., those riots going on, and there's a big conflict between Koreans and blacks. And I think that has something to do with it. Their interaction with African Americans is almost nothing. They go to church; they're in the Korean community, because understandably they don't speak the language, so they just stay in the Korean community. And what they know is what they see in the newspaper.... They read the Korean newspaper, and I don't know what the content areas [are], but I would guess the only time [African Americans] get a mention is when some kind of crime happens.

Alex is able to pinpoint the likely source of his grandparents' views—a Korean American newspaper and its reporting on 1990s conflicts between Korean American merchants and African Americans in cities like Los Angeles. However, his grandparents' antiblack sentiments likely preceded these conflicts. As we suggested previously, Korean and other Asian immigrants to the United States frequently have preconceived stereotypes about African Americans even before they immigrate, to a substantial degree because of contact with U.S. media operating overseas.[35] In addition, Korean-black conflicts in the United States, and the way they are reported in mainstream and Korean news media, seem to have worsened the stereotyping that Korean Americans hold in regard to African Americans (and, likely, vice versa).

Such conflict between Asian Americans and African Americans is not new. Since the importation of Chinese workers onto the West Coast in the 1850s, and into the state of Mississippi during the 1870s Reconstruction era after the Civil War, Asian immigrants have periodically been used by whites to undercut other workers of color. In Mississippi, these Chinese immigrants were brought in as cheap workers to harvest crops on former slave plantations, thereby undercutting newly freed black laborers. However, this effort did not work out well for the Asian immigrants, and some then opened small stores catering to the black southerners. Chinese immigrants were then mostly shut out of doing business with white customers, and whites' racist beliefs often kept whites from catering to black customers, thereby leaving this modest business opportunity open for these Chinese Americans.[36]

Many Asian Americans, like these Chinese merchants long ago, have continued to find ways to prosper by providing economic services for African Americans. Thus, recent Korean immigrants, some of whom cannot find jobs in line with their educational credentials because of various types of discrimination by white employers, sometimes use their economic resources to start small businesses catering to low-income communities, especially those of African and Latino Americans in central cities. The U.S. racial hierarchy thereby creates the possibility of serious conflict, as Korean American scholar Kim argues:

Korean immigrants find themselves in a disadvantaged position relative to Whites but in an advantaged position relative to Blacks. It is in this way that the very economic opportunities that are closed to Blacks become the ticket to upward mobility for Korean immigrants. To the degree that Korean immigrants also buy into the racial constructions that underwrite the racial order—that is, to the degree that they accept that Blacks deserve their lowly status because they are lazy, unintelligent, undisciplined, etc.—they become further implicated in American racial dynamics.[37]

A number of our respondents articulated or discussed negative stereotypes of African Americans and other Americans of color. Frank, a Korean American, offers these comments about some people in his own ethnic group:

> I noticed that Koreans tend to discriminate a lot more than any other race. Yeah, they tend to make nasty comments about Mexican Americans and black Americans.... I think that the main damage of the movie media—every Mexican you see in the media is usually a drug dealer or crazed killer, or a sexual predator, or some very, very nasty role. Every movie you go and see, a drug dealer is usually a South American driving a Rolls Royce with a three-foot-long cigar in his mouth. But that's going [to] keep every Korean in their head that every Mexican must be like that. Then on the news, every news you hear, some Mexican group is killing people, you know, for no reason. But a lot of people think they *must* be like that. Every one of them. I told them, they are not. Believe me, they are not. You know. The African Americans too.

Like Alex above, Frank identifies the mainstream media as a major source for negative type-casting of Mexican and African Americans. He presents himself as someone who understands this mass media distortion, yet also articulates in his interview some strong stereotyped notions about Mexican Americans: "The main problem seems to be education. They do not have a con-cept of education, and one thing I noticed—I don't know whether this is true or not—they are truly much better at this element than Asians—but you know, I count the fifteen- or sixteen- or seventeen-[year-olds], they are fully grown, mature physically, but mentally they're not."

Here Frank seems to be accepting a negative image of Mexican American teenagers as too mature physically and perhaps as threatening, but not as mentally mature. We might note here the common framing of Latinos (and African Americans) as not being interested in education for themselves or their children. This too is a central stereotype in the old white racial framing of these groups, in part because it deflects attention from many years of white discrimination against these groups, including continuing discrimination in the provision of first-rate educa-tional facilities and opportunities. Yet, numerous research studies show that most Latino parents, like most African American parents, are *committed* to securing good educations for their children and others in their communities.[38]

Frank continues with a mixture of insight and stereotyping about Mexican Americans:

> So also another thing I noticed about Mexican Americans is that, when I didn't have a contact with them, I could have a bad news, bad things about them, you know what they do and all that stuff. But once I got to know them I found most of them are very hardworking, most of them are very honest. There's a very few—one in a hundred—which make every Mexican American look bad. They do some crazy things, you know, crazy, crazy things that I just cannot comprehend.

After discussing the fact that the media reality is contradicted in his own positive everyday experiences with most Mexican Americans, Frank returns to his strong notions about self-help:

> I saw them for about two years. I talked to them, and I did find out that [what] Mexican Americans need are good role models, and then someone to really get on the podium and tell them to get an education…. You know, if I was an African American and I was a leader, I would tell all African Americans … two things: one, it doesn't matter how much political pull you have if your group does not have economic power. And I'd tell the Mexican Americans too. The Mexican Americans are going to vote for, you know, people into the city hall and all that stuff, and I told them, "So what? So what?" Let's say, for instance, I go to Salinas, California. In that town 85 percent of the east side is Mexican American…. They all work for somebody. You know what I found out? One hundred percent of the land is owned by white Americans. And then they think they have political power. I told them, you got nothing. Political power means … you have to have a dollar sign behind there. You guys don't have it. And African Americans too.

Frank stereotypes Mexican Americans as not being interested in working for themselves and as not having good role models. He offers unsolicited advice to both Mexican Americans and African Americans that they need to aggressively get into business in order to have significant economic power. Here, of course, he overlooks the fact that these groups lack access to economic and political capital because of past and present racial discrimination, such as in the U.S. lending industry.

Then Frank provides yet more advice:

> And one thing I like to tell African Americans is they got to stop saying about the racism from now on. Because they've been here long time, almost 200 years. See, the Chinese and Koreans and Indians can come over here, and then they can become a multi-multi-millionaire within one

generation, why couldn't they do it? And then one thing that I'd like to tell them is they've got to have all those black kids into the school.... African Americans, I don't think they have a right now even to say racism is holding them back. I don't think so.... As a matter of fact, if you take a look at the government program, like ... all of those companies set aside over 15 percent of the proposition to the minority, specifically for African Americans, and they cannot fill it because there is not enough candidates. I just tell, would like to tell those African Americans, U.S. government is giving you every opportunity to get ahead, but you are not taking it. And if you go over to that [successful] school, everybody is busy, every student is busy because they are trying to catch up with homework, or whatever.... Most [black] kids are not doing anything inside the classroom. They're joking around, they're playing around. They're not reading. That's why they are not getting ahead. Also, it's a chance to improve. I don't think, from here on, I don't think anybody would say it's racism that is holding them back. That it's absolutely not true. Maybe 5 percent true, and 95 percent not.

Frank recites numerous stereotypes and related notions and thereby perpetuates the white framing long used to rationalize the subordination of both African Americans and Mexican Americans. Although he has personal experience with white discriminators in his own life, he embraces the white-generated "bootstraps" ideology, arguing that African Americans and Mexican Americans just need to get educations, work harder, and start businesses. His analysis does not recognize the role of institutional racism, and indeed he chides African Americans for asserting there is white racism, the longevity of which (approaching 400 years now) he seriously underestimates. Although he discusses in his interview the glass ceiling that prevents upward mobility for Asian Americans, he does not relate such institutional racial barriers to the job and educational problems faced by a great many workers of color.

In contrast to Frank's views, some Asian American scholars have critically analyzed white attempts to play off Asian Americans against African Americans. In his probing analysis, Wu puts it thus: "Telling African Americans they ought to be like Asian Americans ... only aggravates racial tensions among African Americans and Asian Americans. It is a paternalistic suggestion, as if whites were the elders telling the older siblings, African Americans, that they should be more like the younger ones, Asian Americans."[39] Similarly, Prashad underscores his role as an Asian American in the racial hierarchy: "I am to be the perpetual solution to what is seen as the crisis of black America.... Meanwhile, white America can take its seat, comfortable in its liberal principles, surrounded by state selected Asians, certain that the culpability for black poverty and oppression must be laid at the door of black America."[40]

Because Asian Americans are often used by the white-controlled media, politicians, and other analysts as exemplars and weapons against black Americans, it is unsurprising that respondents such as Mylene, a Filipina American, parrot stereotyped views of African Americans:

The thing in the news is there's racial profiling by the police, but I'm not really familiar with that. I don't see any correlation because if you are committing the crime, you are committing the crime. It doesn't matter what race you are. It's excuses, you know what I mean? If you are that race and you commit a crime, don't say you're targeted because they caught you…. You know what I mean? I don't know where that racial profiling, where they get that; [it] doesn't make sense…. Yeah, that they always study hard and what not. But also, African Americans, a lot of them [are] into sports, and they make millions of dollars, and they are more richer than lots of Asians. Sports figures, like Shaq and Kobe, all these sports figures, and family and friends. And there are some rap singers, they make millions more, lots of millions more than a lot of Asians…. So it can be equalized in that way, money-wise.

Mylene seems to misunderstand the serious problem of racial profiling, information on which she apparently has gotten from the news media. Many Americans of color, including Asian Americans, have faced frequent discriminatory racial profiling by police officers and other government officials, most of whom are white. Indeed, several state and local police departments have recently had to change their racial profiling policies because of community protests against this type of institutionalized discrimination.[41]

Mylene believes that the reality of a very small proportion of African Americans being well-off athletes and entertainers somehow equalizes the general economic situations of African Americans and Asian Americans as groups. However, government income statistics indicate that the median income of African American families lags well behind the median incomes of most major Asian American groups as well as the median income of white Americans.[42] As with other respondents, and a majority of whites, Mylene relies heavily on the mainstream media, yet these sources frequently offer much misinformation and a white framing of society's racial issues for many millions of viewers of all backgrounds.

Katherine, who is Chinese American, is retired but now does substitute teaching. In her efforts to improve the relationships among the racially diverse students at her school, she reports that she imparts to them some distinctive messages:

I substitute teach here, and I also take care of kids with broken families, and they are in middle-school age now, twelve, thirteen. And this little girl that I've been caring for ever since she was eight, she started telling me, she said, you know in the cafeteria they sit in groups now. [She's] Hispanic, she would play with just any kids, and now she said they kind of sit together now, the black kids together. I said … you and I both know that, especially the black kids, a lot of them are not black. They're half-black, half-white. It's just that the white kids don't want to claim them because their skin color is darker. And they think they are black. They're not black, you know. And there are some Hispanic kids that are not Hispanic, and there are some Asian kids that are not Asian. I mean, they are half-Asian and half-white, so I told my students that in class.

This respondent is concerned about what she views as self-segregation of black children in the cafeteria, a phenomenon commonly misinterpreted as involving just the unfortunate personal choices of black children—and not the recurring impacts of a racist society on them. Katherine also relates how she has tried to distance the biracial children from their non-European heritages. She is arguing that they are not truly children of color because they are partly white. She appears to be saying that if these biracial children accent their whiteness, they can be relieved of their lowly status as children of color and be in effect "white" children. Although she does note the biased preference of the white children, she seems to be under the impression that African, Latino, and Asian American children with some white ancestry can personally choose how they will be identified in society, neglecting the reality that their racial identities are usually imposed on them by those discriminatory white children and other whites.

One cautious respondent, Ginzi, argues in his responses to our questions that Asian Americans get mistreated by other groups of color: "Are we treated on the same level as everybody in this country? More or less. Like, I think—I think—let me not say anything stupid. Hmm, by the white population we're treated pretty fairly. From other minority groups we get more shit than from white people." Ginzi carefully chooses his words so that he does not say anything too offensive against others of color. This suggests that he may have deeper feelings about these racial issues that he does not wish to share. Significantly, in his interview at no point does he suggest a substantial role for white discriminators in creating problems for Americans of color.

One older Chinese American respondent from an urban area with a substantial Asian American population, Henry, has been ridiculed and even physically harmed by racist whites over nearly five decades. Recall his comments about whites in Chapter 3: "Why do they want to make fun of you? Because that's the way the culture is, because they want to make fun of Chinese culture because of the movies they see. Take the N-word, they banned that word, but they are still calling the Chinese 'Chinamen.'" In spite of this white discrimination, he still articulates images of African Americans from the dominant racial frame. For example, he discusses differences between Chinese Americans and African Americans in how they respond to white discrimination: "The Chinese don't complain about it. The Chinese culture is not like black. If [you] do something they don't like, they either attack you, or frighten you, or even kill you. How many Asians got the guts to do that? We should try to get them to ban the word 'Chinaman.' I think we need Chinese people to get together, just like the blacks do. I think a lot of things should change."

Over the course of his interview, however, Henry offers no evidence from his experiences for this strong stereotyping of African Americans as routinely violent, but rather seems to be drawing his images from distorted and stereotyped "news" presentations in the mainstream media. Wu has suggested that "many whites and Asian Americans do not have enough contact with African

Americans to have formed a sense of any individual African American as a human being."[43] Indeed, many of our respondents articulate racist stereotypes of African or Latino Americans with little reservation or qualifying, and probably with limited or no personal experience with them. In the U.S. case, systemic racism masterfully and routinely creates racial tensions and conflicts among Americans of color by making all who live within this society accept, at least to some degree, its powerfully invasive and white-imposed racial framing of Americans of color.

Conclusion

In 2007 *AsianWeek* published a controversial article by an Asian American author, Kenneth Eng, on "Why I Hate Blacks." In this opinion piece he listed reasons for his hatred. Among his stereotyped statements was this: "Contrary to media depictions, I would argue that blacks are weak-willed. They are the only race that has been enslaved for 300 years. It's unbelievable that it took them that long to fight back." Eng cited personal experience and historical reasons for his strained relationship with the black community, but his cursory analysis points to a much larger problem: a widespread lack of knowledge in the Asian American community about the historical background and development of nearly four centuries of racial oppression in this country.[44] In contrast to his view, the reality is that African Americans were enslaved for about 240 years in North America and did indeed fight back in many ways from the first days of enslavement. The harsh criticisms directed against African Americans and other Americans of color in his analysis—and indeed in other articles that he wrote for *AsianWeek*—underscore the extent to which an extensive white racist framing of society has penetrated the minds even of well-educated Asian Americans.

The interview responses showcased in this chapter demonstrate the depth of the penetration of the white racial frame and the racial hierarchy it rationalizes in the lives of these Asian Americans. All must struggle against these oppressive realities every day of their lives in the United States. They may resist, or they may conform. They all do both. Both strategies are defensive and imposed on them by the surrounding society.

As we have seen, substantial efforts are put forth by numerous respondents to copy, mimic, and extend the white framing and folkways, including in regard to the racial hierarchy. Many clearly take measures to protect themselves from future white discrimination by conforming and trying to enter once exclusively white economic and social spaces. The impact of systemic racism, including white discrimination of many kinds and at several levels, has forced these interviewees to take significant defensive measures to protect themselves, as several of them sagely analyzed. They have changed names and social networks, adopted what they deem as white values and political stances, and even chosen white partners. At rather young ages, many respondents reported feeling and understanding great pressures to conform to the white framing and folkways, and all have worked hard to be accepted into white social worlds. Indeed, some respondents no longer think of themselves, or choose not to openly identify, as Asian American.

The dominant racial frame is so powerful that numerous interviewees have adopted some negative stereotypes about Asian Americans, about themselves and their group, as well as about other Americans of color. Many observe the racially subordinate position of African Americans in society and respond in a rather distancing and protective way. As Wu sagely notes, they "benefit just by not being black.... It may be that the ability of Asian Americans to pass into whiteness depends on their ability to distance themselves from blackness."[45] As our interviews make evident, many people distance themselves from blackness and go to great lengths to cozy up to whiteness. Their own identities often seem to be muddled in their minds as they grapple with how the white framing of Asian Americans dictates who they should, and should not, be. These respondents have learned the racial stereotypes and images of Asian Americans that are central in that dominant framing, racialized lessons they have often internalized.

Significantly, all our respondents noted or recognized in some way during their interviews that they or their families do face significant racial hostility and discrimination at the hands of white Americans in various places. However, most do not seem to view this continuing problem as structural and systemic but rather as a matter of incidents generated by white individuals acting out of ignorance or various other nonracial reasons.

Notes

1 NewsOne staff, "Teens Brutally Beat Asian Boy While Calling Him N-Word," January 17, 2012, http://newsone.com/1801685/video-white-teens-brutally-beat-asian-boy-while-calling-him-n-word (retrieved January 19, 2014).

2 YouTube video: www.youtube.com/watch?v=Iseu8MpXhjQ.

3 Frank Wu, *Yellow: Race in America Beyond Black and White* (New Haven, CT: Yale University Press, 2003).

4 Joe R. Feagin, *Systemic Racism: A Theory of Oppression* (New York: Routledge, 2006), p. 47.

5 See Wu, *Yellow*.

6 Ibid.

7 Vijay Prashad, *The Karma of Brown Folk* (Minneapolis: University of Minnesota Press, 2003), p. 123.

8 Joe R. Feagin and Karyn D. McKinney, *The Many Costs of Racism* (Lanham, MD: Rowman and Littlefield, 2003), p. 32.

9 Hung Cam Thai, "Formation of Ethnic Identity among Second-Generation Vietnamese Americans," in *The Second Generation: Ethnic Identity among Asian Americans*, ed. Pyong Gap Min (Walnut Creek, CA: Altamira, 2002), p. 76.

10 Debra Van Ausdale and Joe R. Feagin, *The First R: How Children Learn Race and Racism* (Lanham, MD: Rowman and Littlefield, 2001), p. 127.

11 The research is cited in Stephen Steinberg, *Race Relations: A Critique* (Palo Alto, CA: Stanford University Press, 2007), p. 131.

12 Chiderah Monde, "Julie Chen Reveals Workplace Racism Led Her to Get Plastic Surgery for 'Asian Eyes," *New York Daily News*, September 12, 2013, www.nydailynews.com/entertainment/tv-movies/julie-chen-reveals-plastic-surgery-asian-eyes-article-1.1453535.

13 Ibid.

14 "Japanese Model Spends over $100k on Plastic Surgery to Look Like French Doll," *Your Health Asia One*, May 8, 2013, http://yourhealth.asiaone.com/content/japanese-model-spends-over-100k-plastic-surgery-look-french-doll.

15 C. N. Le, "Cosmetic and Plastic Surgery," *Asian-Nation*, www.asian-nation.org/cosmetic-surgery.shtml (retrieved December 21, 2006); the quote is from Olivia Chung, "Finding My Eye-Identity," in *YELL-Oh Girls,* ed. Vickie Nam (New York: Quill, 2001), p. 139 (italics omitted).

16 Jeff Lindsay, "Why the Hmong Are in America," *Future Hmong Magazine*, June 14–15, 2002.

17 Feagin, *Systemic Racism*, pp. 252–258. See also Joe R. Feagin, *White Party, White Government* (New York: Routledge, 2012).

18 Tanaka, *When You're Smiling*.

19 See Kenneth B. Clark and M. P. Clark, "Segregation as a Factor in the Racial Identification of Negro Preschool Children," *Journal of Experimental Education* 8 (1939): 161–163; William H. Grier and Price M. Cobbs, *Black Rage* (New York: Bantam, 1968); and Kiri Davis, *A Girl Like Me* (New York: Media Matters, 2005).

20 U.S. Census Bureau, *Current Population Survey,* November 2004; Joe R. Feagin and Clairece B. Feagin, *Racial and Ethnic Relations*, 8th ed. (Upper Saddle River, NJ: Prentice Hall, 2008), pp. 297 and 336–337.

21 Kumiko Nemoto, "Intimacy, Desire, and the Construction of Self in Relationships between Asian American Women and White American Men," *Journal of Asian American Studies* 9 (2006): 51.

22 Feagin and Feagin, *Racial and Ethnic Relations*, pp. 336–337.

23 Greg Mayeda, "Japanese Americans Don't Lose Identity," *New York Times*, December 28, 1995, p. A20; Feagin and Feagin, *Racial and Ethnic Relations*, chap. 10.

24 Ronald Takaki, *Strangers from a Different Shore* (Boston: Back Bay, 1998).

25 Karen D. Pyke and Denise L. Johnson, "Asian American Women and Racialized Femininities," *Gender and Society* 17 (2003): 33–53; Alexandra Suh, "Military Prostitution in Asia and the United States," in *States of Confinement*, ed. Joy James (New York: St. Martin's, 2000), p. 150.

26 Rosalind S. Chou, *Asian American Sexual Politics: The Construction of Race, Gender, and Sexuality* (Lanham, MD: Rowman and Littlefield, 2012).

27 Kat Chow and Elise Hu, "Odds Favor White Men, Asian Women on Dating App," NPR's Code Switch, November 30, 2013, www.npr.org/blogs/codeswitch/2013/11/30/247530095/are-you-interested-dating-odds-favor-white-men-asian-women.

28 Three were South Asian and two were East Asian.

29 Min Zhou, "Are Asian Americans Becoming White?" *Context* 3, no. 1 (2004): 29–37.

30 U.S. Census Bureau, *Current Population Survey*, November 2004.

31 Prashad, *The Karma of Brown Folk*.

32 Mia Tuan, *Forever Foreigners or Honorary Whites? The Asian Ethnic Experience* (New Brunswick, NJ: Rutgers University Press, 2003), p. 8.

33 Wu, *Yellow*, p. 30.

34 Claire Jean Kim, *Bitter Fruit: The Politics of Black-Korean Conflict in New York City* (New Haven, CT: Yale University Press, 2003), p. 45.

35 See also Feagin, *Systemic Racism*; and Feagin and Feagin, *Racial and Ethnic Relations*.

36 James Loewen, *The Mississippi Chinese: Between Black and White* (Longrove, IL: Waveland, 1988).

37 Kim, *Bitter Fruit*, p. 41.

38 See Feagin and Feagin, *Racial and Ethnic Relations*, chap. 8.

39 Wu, *Yellow*, p. 67.

40 Prashad, *The Karma of Brown Folk*, p. 6.

41 See Joe Feagin, *Racist America: Roots, Current Realities, and Future Reparations*, 3rd ed. (New York: Routledge, 2014), pp. 157–201.

42 See U.S. Census Bureau, *Current Population Survey*, November 2004; and Feagin and Feagin, *Racial and Ethnic Relations*, chaps. 10–11.

43 Wu, *Yellow*, p. 318.

44 Kenneth Eng, "Why I Hate Blacks," *AsianWeek*, February 25, 2007, www.asianweek.com (retrieved June 2007).

45 Wu, *Yellow*, p. 66.

Native Americans and Alaska Natives: The Forgotten Minority

American Indian Tribes and Structural Racism

Sherry Salway Black

A merican Indian tribes and people face circumstances unique to any other racial or ethnic group in the United States. No other racial or ethnic group has as the basis of its relationship with the U.S. a legal framework of treaties, executive orders, judicial rulings and laws spanning centuries. This legal framework, developed over the past 300 years, has resulted in a system that was supposed to protect the rights and trust assets of tribes and Indian people, but in reality has created structures and systems that thwart self-determination and diminish the value of Native assets. These constraints, coupled with social and economic inequities, are the root cause of the severe problems that tribal governments face in providing the infrastructure, services and conditions necessary for healthy community development.

Analysis of the socio-economic conditions confronting tribes and Indian people today typically focuses on this unique federal Indian history and relationship. It is not often described in terms of racially-based policies and inequities, but rather a direct "[federal] nation-to-[tribal] nation" relationship, from which the federal trust responsibility is derived. Yet, one cannot overlook or undermine the racial basis of many policies of colonialism and paternalism that are the hallmarks of federal-Indian relations—and are reflected in present-day policies.

Historically and continuing into the modem era, the Indian policies of the federal government have been aimed either at dismantling tribal governments and assimilating Native people or at paternalistically isolating tribes to misappropriate their assets. By all accounts, these mixed and often misguided efforts resulted in the devastating social conditions found on many reservation communities today. Moreover, these policies left tribal governments facing a host of structural impediments that hamper their ability to fulfill their governmental responsibilities to their citizens.

At various times, the federal government has forcibly removed Native people from their homelands to reservations; divested Native people of millions of acres of valuable land filled with natural resources; required generations of Indian children to attend residential boarding schools far from their homes; passed legislation authorizing the termination of more than 100 tribal governments; forced tribal governments to adopt unfamiliar and inappropriate governance structures; and initiated a large-scale effort to relocate Native people from their tribal communities to urban areas. These policies had, as their basis, a prevailing view of the inferiority and incapability of Indian people in managing their own affairs and economic assets, and a goal of assimilation into the dominant, or "white, Anglo-Christian" culture. The lasting impact of these federal policies on tribal communities cannot be overstated.

Given these structural barriers and the resultant devastating conditions, it would be easy to let a sense of hopelessness overwhelm efforts for positive change in Native communities. Yet starting in the new era of self-determination in the 1960s and growing to the present day, tribal leaders are forging a new path to break down the pillars of structural racism that diminish opportunities for their peoples. Building strong foundations of tribal governance through systemic reform, leadership development and citizen engagement is a growing movement in American Indian communities today. Overcoming centuries of colonialism and paternalism will not be easy or quick—but the alternative cannot be considered.

> One cannot overlook the racial basis of many policies of colonialism and paternalism that are the hallmarks of federal-Indian relations.

Assimilation or Transnationalism? Conceptual Models of the Immigrant Experience in America

Silvia Pedraza

mericans are immigrants—people whose origins are various but whose destinies made them American. Immigration—voluntary or involuntary—is what created all multiracial and multicultural nations. The United States is a prime example. Sometimes the migrants moved freely from the area of origin to the area of destination. Such was the experience of the European immigrants. Sometimes their movement was coerced and resulted from processes not of their own making. This was the experience of enslaved Africans, as well as of Mexicans, Native Americans, and Puerto Ricans, whose history began with conquest and annexation. Sometimes their movement was semicoerced and semifree—the experience of indentured servants (whether Japanese, Chinese, Irish, or German) in the 19th century and of refugees, such as Jews at the turn of the 20th century and Cubans, Cambodians, Guatemalans, and Salvadorans in the latter part of the 20th century.

The major questions in immigration research can be summarized briefly as follows: What led people to make the decision to move—what "push" and "pull" factors impelled them to displace and uproot themselves (see Lee, 1966)? What is the nature of the crossing—not only literally but also, more abstractly, the policies of two governments that can, in societies that have developed long histories of emigration and immigration, result in their developing systems of economic and political migration (see Burawoy, 1976; Pedraza-Bailey, 1985)? and, What can people attain afterward? A recurrent question in studies of immigration is: How do we best describe that process—as assimilation, adaptation, integration, incorporation, or transnationalism and diasporic citizenship? This chapter traces the development of these concepts overtime as social scientists struggled to explain these important social processes. Before doing so, we turn to a brief history of immigration to America.

History of Immigration

As Philip Martin and Elizabeth Midgley (2003, p. 11) underscored, European colonization of the New World entailed three processes—colonization, coercion, and immigration—that super-imposed a new population on the native peoples of the Americas. Colonization took place in the 17th and 18th centuries when English colonists established the cultural and institutional foundations of what became the United States. They also seized control of various Dutch, French, and Spanish settlements, and established English as the public language and English common law as the basis for the legal system. In addition, Martin and Midgley underscored, two types of coercion were involved in the peopling of America: the importation of slaves from Africa (19% of the population in 1790) and the incorporation of American Indians, French, Mexican, Puerto Ricans, and other populations "through political deals, war settlements, or purchase of territory as the United States expanded westward," such as the Louisiana Purchase (1803), the Treaty of Guadalupe Hidalgo at the end of the war between Mexico and the United States (1848), and the Spanish-American War (1898). The third source of Americans, and the largest, was immigration. Over the course of several centuries, immigrants to the United States came in waves—an image that denotes that the number of immigrants could be seen to start, rise, peak, decline, and eventually disappear onto our shores.

Four waves of migration transformed America over the course of history (Muller & Espenshade 1985). In the first wave, northwestern Europeans immigrated to the United States up until the mid-19th century; in the second, southern and eastern Europeans arrived at the end of the 19th and the beginning of the 20th centuries; in the third, precipitated by two world wars, African Americans, Mexicans, and Puerto Ricans moved from the South to the North; and in the fourth, immigrants mostly from Latin America and Asia arrived, from 1965 into the present. Each wave has been characterized by a different racial or ethnic composition and coincided with profound changes in the nature of American society. The immigrants of the first wave came to an essentially colonial, agrarian society; those of the second and third waves came to an urban society where they supplied the cheap labor essential to industrialization and expansion; and those of the fourth wave are coming to an increasingly postindustrial, service-oriented society. Because immigration is American history, yesterday as well as today, immigration is central to the identity of its people as hyphenated Americans; it is also central to America's identity as a nation of immigrants. This is what is distinctive about the American experience.

In 1890, 86% of the foreign-born in the United States came from European countries—Great Britain, Ireland, Germany, Scandinavia, and France being the lead countries—plus 11% came from Canada (U.S. Bureau of the Census, 2001). In 1910, at the peak of immigration from southern and eastern Europe, there were 13.5 million foreign-born residents, nearly 15% of the total population of the United States. In 2002, of the total population of over 281 million, the foreign-born population reached an all-time high of 32.5 million, according to the Current Population Survey (CPS), but they also constituted around 15%. Most notable was the shift in origins, as now most come from Latin America and Asia (Martin & Midgley, 2004). This large number of immigrants at the turn of both centuries mostly settled in California, New York, Florida, Illinois, and Texas. In the early 1900s, nativism was expressed in cartoons in leading magazines, such as *Life*, that depicted Irish men as brutes and drunkards and Jews as vulgar social climbers and also expressed anti-Catholic prejudice (see Higham, 1955). In 1994, the same nativism was expressed in California's Proposition 187, which sought to deny schooling and the use of social services to undocumented workers and their children. Faced with deteriorating economic conditions and natural disasters, such as earthquakes, the people of California attributed their social ills to the presence of a large number of illegal aliens.

High rates of immigration, coupled with the high birth rates of many minority groups, such as African Americans and Hispanic Americans, are also changing the composition of the United States. At the dawn of the 21st century, Hispanics surpassed African Americans as the largest minority population. Forecasts put the proportion of White Americans at less than half of the population by the middle of the century. At that point, the traditional "minorities" will, together, constitute the majority (Martin & Midgley, 2003). Hence, the United States is once again being transformed. Such profound demographic shifts can be expected to generate conflict and resistance, which will be most keenly felt in the areas where "minorities" are most concentrated: California, the southwestern states, Texas, Florida, Illinois, and New York.

The First Wave

The first wave of immigration consisted of those who arrived prior to 1880, when the nation was predominantly a colonial, agricultural society. In 1790, the English constituted 60% of the population. Entries began to be recorded only in 1820. Between 1820 and 1880, over 10 million immigrants arrived, mostly from northwestern European nations such as England, Scotland, Germany, the Netherlands, France, Spain, Norway, Sweden, and Ireland. In 1890, of the 7.3 million in the United States who were born in northern and western Europe, 1.25 million came from Great Britain (England, Scotland, and Wales), 1.87 million came from Ireland, 2.8 million came from Germany, and close to half a million came from Scandinavia (U.S. Bureau of the Census 2002). These immigrants were motivated by political, economic, and religious factors.

The involuntary migrations of Africans from West Africa as slaves, the subordination of the American Indians, and the annexation of a large part of Mexico's territory, what is today the American Southwest (California, Arizona, Texas, and parts of New Mexico, Colorado, and Utah), also shaped the people of the United States. In addition, the free movement of Mexicans to *"el Norte"* began as a seasonal labor trek (Corwin, 1978). Because travel was expensive and entailed a long, precarious voyage, many European immigrants indentured themselves to pay for the passage.

Few immigrants were as impelled to move as the Irish, who were "pushed" not only by the displacement of the peasantry that was the result of the transition from feudalism to capitalism taking place throughout western Europe then (cf. Bodnar, 1985), but also by the famine that resulted from the potato blight at midcentury. It is estimated that one-third of the total population of Ireland emigrated throughout the 19th century, about 4 million people. In 1914, the population of Ireland was half what it had been in 1840 (Diner, 1984).

Most of the early immigrants came looking for land—for security, for work, to support their way of life as farmers. The Homestead Act of 1862 that President Lincoln signed made it possible for them to obtain the deed to the land they had worked. It also promoted the settlement of the West, the frontier expansion that Frederick Jackson Turner (1893/1920) argued was what shaped the American experience of substantial upward mobility; it also forged the core American value of rugged individualism. Both constituted an American exceptionalism.

The Second Wave

Between 1880 and 1924, during the second major wave of immigration, over 27 million immigrants arrived in the United States; about 81% were from the southern and eastern European nations, such as Italy, Greece, Austria-Hungary, Poland, and Russia. In 1910, of the 4.5 million people who had been born in southern and eastern European countries, over 1.3 million came from Italy, 1.2 million from the Soviet Union (mostly Jews), nearly 1 million from Poland, and close to half a million from Hungary. Due to the severe restrictions imposed on Asian immigration—the Chinese Exclusion Act (1882) and the Japanese Gentleman's Agreement (1906)—only 124,500 came from China and Japan (U.S. Bureau of the Census 2002).

To this day, the peak number of immigrants to the United States arrived in the years 1907–1908. As these groups passed through the processing center that was largely a welcoming center at Ellis Island, New York, significant numbers of immigrants from China and Japan were arriving on the West Coast, where they were processed through the detention center at Angel Island, California. On both coasts, most of these migrants were rural, with very low levels of literacy, and unskilled—peasants whose identification was, first and foremost, with their village and their parish.

By the early 1900s, the frontier was closed, and most newcomers found jobs in Eastern and Midwestern cities. Many became the industrial working class that fueled the economic growth that attended industrialization and the growth of capitalism. Immigrants made up more than half of the operatives in the key industries of steel, mining, and meatpacking (Martin & Midgley, 2003).

Among the European immigrants were the Jews, who fled Europe because of the anti-Semitic violence they encountered in the *pogroms*—anti-Jewish riots—at the end of the 19th century. Contrary to most of the other immigrants at the time, the Jews were already urban and very often literate and skilled, particularly in the needle trades. It is estimated that approximately one-third of all Jews in Eastern Europe migrated to the United States between 1880 and 1924. Pushed by circumstances beyond their control, they fled violence and persecution and came searching for personal and religious liberty. Their story in the United States was clearly a story of success, particularly in comparison to the other immigrant groups who came at the same time (Gold & Phillips, 1996). Clearly, they were refugees, although immigration law at this time did not recognize refugees as a separate type of immigrant. The legal category of refugee did not begin to develop until after World War II, with the 1948 Displaced Persons Act and a series of Refugee Relief Acts and Refugee Assistance Acts in the 1950s and 1960s that were largely brought about by the Cuban exodus and under which the Vietnamese and other Indochinese refugees were admitted. Only in 1980 did the United States finally pass a Refugee Act, shortly before the arrival of 125,000 *Marielitos* from Cuba's Mariel harbor and 10,000 Haitians who washed ashore onto the beaches of Florida and its Keys (Pedraza, 1996b).

In the beginning, U.S. immigration law had barred the entry of only those persons considered unfit, such as prostitutes, convicts, lunatics, idiots, and the very ill. But partly because of World War I, nativism peaked in the 1920s. Nativism involves the fear many feel of the threat—cultural and economic both—that immigrants pose. This led to further restrictions. With the 1924 Immigration and Nationality Act, the door to further immigration was closed. National-origins quotas were set that favored immigration from northern and western European nations while curtailing immigration from southern and eastern European nations. At the same time, all immigration from Asia was banned. These quotas remained in place until they were abolished by the 1965 amendments to the 1952 Immigration and Nationality Act.

Yet even as immigration from southern and eastern Europe was being curtailed, an exception was made for Mexico. Agricultural growers successfully argued to Congress that they needed Mexican workers because World War I had caused a labor shortage. The Western Hemisphere Exemption constituted an enormous "pull" to Mexican immigrants. But although growers expected the Mexicans to return home, "like a homing pigeon," many did not go back but instead put down roots and created communities on this side of the border (Pedraza-Bailey, 1985).

The Third Wave

After the closing of the door to European immigration in 1924, the third major wave of migration was mostly internal. The migration of African Americans, Mexicans, Native Americans, and Puerto Ricans from the South to the North transformed rural people into urban dwellers. This entailed a dramatic social transformation, as large as the one of immigrants who crossed the oceans. For example, at the beginning of the 20th century most African Americans lived in the agricultural South; by 1960, about half were living in the industrial North. They were attracted by the employment opportunities generated by the industrialization of the North and by World War I. Between 1940 and 1960, when agriculture in the South declined further and World War II created yet more economic expansion, particularly in the Northeast and the Midwest, it is estimated that millions of African Americans, Mexicans, Native Americans, and Puerto Ricans left the rural areas of the South to look for work in cities and in factories. This urbanization set the stage for the Civil Rights Movement (Piven & Cloward, 1979). The Civil Rights Movement inspired other social movements, such as the Mexican American movement *La Causa*. These social movements broke down the systematic exclusion imposed by "Jim Crow" legal segregation.

World War II also gave rise to the Bracero Program (from the Spanish word *brazos*, arms), which was initiated through the influence of agricultural growers, who once again argued to Congress that instituting this contract-labor program was absolutely necessary, given the wartime shortage of labor in California's fields. During the course of more than 22 years, approximately 4.7 million *braceros* came to work in California, then the leading agricultural state. What was supposed to be an emergency, wartime measure lasted a full generation, until substantial labor displacement of American workers led to its termination (Galarza, 1964; Massey et al., 1987). The Bracero Program also gave rise to substantial illegality (cf. Samora, 1971). A renewal of this plan has now been proposed by President George W. Bush as a way of curbing excessive undocumented migration from Mexico and of providing for the orderly, administered importation of temporary help. In the 1940s and 1950s, approximately 30 to 40% of immigration came from the Western Hemisphere (Martin & Midgley, 2003), although a substantial number of Jewish refugees from the holocaust perpetrated by Nazi Germany also arrived.

The Fourth Wave

The fourth wave of migration began in the immediate post-World War II period. It gained particular impetus from the 1965 amendments to the McCarran–Walter Immigration and Nationality Act of 1952 that abolished the national origins quotas of 1924. In so doing, it reopened the door to immigration to the United States. The major criteria for legal admission to the United States in this period are still the ones in place at the beginning of the 21st century: occupational certification (giving preference to immigrants whose occupations were in a "relative shortage" in the United States) and family reunification (giving preference to immigrants whose immediate family had been divided by the migration). In 2002, more than half of the foreign-born residents were born in Latin America—30% from Mexico alone—whereas 26% were born in Asia, 14% in Europe, and 8% in Africa and other regions (Martin & Midgley, 2004). In 1990, of the 8.4 million immigrants who were born in Latin America, 4.3 million came from Mexico, 1.9 million from the Caribbean (Cuba and Haiti leading), 5.4 million from Central America (El Salvador and Nicaragua leading), and 1 million from South America (Colombia and Peru leading), with Canada contributing an additional three-fourths of a million. Among the 5 million immigrants who were born in Asia, China and India were the leading sources, each contributing close to half a million (U. S. Bureau of the Census, 2002). There have always been two immigrant Americas—a working-class immigrant America and a middle-class immigrant America (cf. Bodnar, 1985). Our present-day admissions criteria contribute to the development of both. In recent decades, occupational preference has been given both to very poor immigrants, such as Mexicans, Puerto Ricans, Dominicans, and Jamaicans, who were often contracted to work in the fields, in construction, and in other menial service jobs, and to very skilled immigrants, such as Colombians, Filipinos, Asian Indians, Koreans, Taiwanese, and Ecuadorians, who were often contracted to work as doctors, accountants, computer technicians, and nurses.

The European immigrant struggle at the turn of the 20th century was shaped by the transition from feudal, agrarian societies to industrial manufacturing capitalist societies in the Old World and the New. John Bodnar (1985) underscored that "transplanted by forces beyond their control," the immigrants were "indeed children of capitalism." At the turn of the 20th century, the artisans, craftsmen, and illiterate, unskilled peasants from the feudal societies of Germany, Ireland, Poland, Italy, and Mexico went on to become the American working class and to supply the cheap labor that made possible the enormous economic growth of this developing, industrial, capitalist society. At the turn of the 21st century, the immigrant struggle is not only the child of capitalism but also the child of communism, in the case of Cubans, Vietnamese, Cambodians, Chinese, and Soviet Jews. It is estimated that over the course of 45 years of Cuba's communist revolution, more than 12% of the Cuban population left the island, turning their backs on the land of their birth. Most of these emigrants went on to live in the United States.

To undocumented workers of working-class origin from Latin America, the 1986 Immigration Reform and Control Act (IRCA) brought a fresh start, as it both offered amnesty for illegal aliens who had lived and worked in the United States as upright contributors to this nation's economy, and placed the brunt of the problem on employers who knowingly hired illegal aliens. The Mexican community especially benefited from IRCA, as did many workers from Central and South America. Many of the new immigrants who come to the United States bring substantial social resources with them (of social class, capital, education, institutional know-how). As a result, these new immigrants can quickly insert themselves at rather high levels in this society—what Ivan Light (1983) called "leapfrog migration." At the same time, the prospects for working-class immigrants grow increasingly dim. These bear the brunt of the economic restructuring of America, of the declining number of good jobs in manufacturing industries, as well as of persistent and growing poverty. Clearly, there are two Americas. In fact, a more accurate image may be that of a third America, as Jorge Ramos (2004) recently argued. The third America encompasses the undocumented workers—not only Mexican but also Central and South American, Caribbean, Asian, at times even European—who are the most vulnerable and powerless inhabitants of our nation yet do much of the labor others do not want to do.

Assimilation

The study of immigrants was closely wedded with the beginnings of social science in America at the turn of the 20th century (Portes 1978). Immigrants and their plight were the focus of vivid studies from the early days of "the Chicago school," whose work on immigration, ethnic, and urban studies laid the very foundations of American sociology (e.g., Park & Burgess, 1921; Park, 1950, 1928; Thomas & Znaniecki, 1927). Despite varying emphases, they shared the expectation that the outcome to the process of integrating those who arrived at its shores would be a process of assimilation. Yet from the outset there was an ambiguity in the idea that Park himself (1913/1950) underscored. That ambiguity remained until Milton Gordon (1964) distinguished between types of assimilation: cultural versus structural. But the fundamental characteristic of assimilation theory was already evident: Assimilation was expected to be a one-way process that would also be natural and evolutionary, which as time passed would yield the inevitable outcome of the adaptation of minority ethnic groups to the mainstream culture. A very different concept—transculturation—arose in Cuba, the peopling of which through conquest and immigration resembled that of the United States. Fernando Ortiz (1963/1983), one of Cuba's leading social scientists, proposed the notion of transculturation to signify how one culture comes to express itself in another, as was the case of *Santería*, the popular religious expression in Cuba that blended West African beliefs with Spanish Catholicism. Even in the United States, another important text of the time, Nathan Glazer and Daniel Patrick Moynihan's (1963) *Beyond the Melting Pot*, examined the incorporation of Blacks, Puerto Ricans, Jews, Italians, and Irish in New York City and found substantial ethnic malleability and persistence. But the leading influence was that of the assimilation school, a major exponent of which was Glazer (1971), who argued that while Blacks did not seem to be assimilating to the mainstream, due to the Southern experience of slavery and "Jim Crow," in the North their experience more closely resembled that of other immigrants, and, in due time, they would also achieve assimilation.

As Gordon (1964) defined it, cultural assimilation entailed a process of acculturation on the part of the immigrants, of becoming "like" in cultural patterns, such as language, behavior, and values; while structural assimilation resulted only when the immigrants had been "taken up and incorporated" and entailed the full integration of the immigrants and their descendants into the major institutions of the society (educational, occupational, political) and into the social cliques, clubs, and institutions of the core society that lead to intimate primary relationships, including intermarriage. This distinction aimed to provide a more exact conceptual tool to gauge the reality of the assimilation of immigrants and racial minorities in America.

The Chicago school in the early part of the century also emphasized the "natural history" of ethnic relations, as best expressed in Park's race relations cycle. Park (1913/1950) evolved his theory of the race relations cycle as stages of interaction through which immigrant or racial groups progressed irreversibly: contact, competition, and accommodation, culminating in eventual assimilation (pp. 138–158). Because at the root of his thinking was the ecological emphasis on race relations as spatial relations that defined the Chicago school of urban sociology, Park expected that the notion of assimilation and the stages of the race relations cycle could be extended to immigrants and racial minorities alike. From his point of view, both European immigrants and American Blacks came from rural, peasant backgrounds and, on migration to the urban ghetto, confronted a similar clash of cultures. Thus, immigration and race and ethnic relations could both be viewed within the same frame of reference.

This perspective was clearly apparent in another of the classics of the Chicago school: W. I. Thomas and Florian Znaniecki's *The Polish Peasant in Europe and America* (1927). Drawing from the work of Thomas, Park also was responsible for disseminating the theory of the "marginal man." Park (1928) stressed that marginal human beings—those who, as a result of migration, ended up living simultaneously in two separate worlds—were not only marginal, never fully belonging to one world or the other, but also enormously creative and intelligent, as experiencing more than one social world had sharpened their vision and sensibilities. Again Park extended the concept of the marginal man from its origins in the notion of the human being caught between two cultures—the immigrant, the mixed-blood person (Eurasian, mestizo, or mulatto), the outcast and stranger (the Jew)—to encompass the experience of American Blacks who shared the same national culture but lived at the margins of society in social, rather than cultural or ethnic, marginality. Thus, it was left to E. Franklin Frazier (1957), student of the Chicago school and Black sociologist, to demarcate the difference between race relations and ethnic relations. He underscored that American Blacks had experienced successive forms of economic subordination (slavery, the plantation society, "Jim Crow") with the outcome of extensive cultural assimilation but, rather than final structural assimilation, complete social and institutional segregation. Sociologists, then, in the early part of the 20th century were concerned with what the experience of immigration had done to the immigrants' lives themselves and with the outcomes to the process of integrating those who arrived at its shores, outcomes that were usually conceptualized as acculturation and assimilation—becoming like the dominant population, which at the turn of the century clearly meant conformity to Anglo-Saxon ways (Gordon, 1964).

Research on immigrants and the eventual outcomes of the processes of immigration, therefore, was at the very foundations of American sociology. But that emphasis began to wane until, in the 1960s, it all but disappeared. Several different trends promoted its disappearance. First, the Immigration and Nationality Act of 1924 cut the massive waves of European immigration to the United States. Second, under the pressures of Anglo-conformity, the children of those European immigrants went on to assimilate in American society at a time when the price of success was often one's ethnicity and identity. Like Paul Cowan (1982), writer for *The Village Voice* whose real name should have been Saul Cohen, many successful Americans became orphans in history, having lost their ethnic legacies. This can be seen in how often the old immigrants had to change their names, to Anglicize them. Looking at the first generation of Hollywood movie stars, for example, Kirk Douglas (father or our Michael Douglas today) was really the Eastern European Jewish Issur Anielovitch; Rita Hayworth, the love goddess, was really Spanish—Margarita Carmen Cansino; and Dean Martin was really Dino Crocetti (Baltzell, 1964). And third, as Portes (1978) stressed, the research focus on immigrants and immigration was also lost as a result of the arrival of the racial demands and militancy of the Civil Rights Movement, so that the analytical focus shifted to that of racial and ethnic relations. In the process, what is really distinctive about immigrants was lost. What is distinctive about immigrants? At the micro level, it is that they have experienced another whole life in another country and culture, which they bring with them and which decisively continues to influence them; at the macro level, it is that the state in two societies permits the immigrants to exit and enter. As gatekeeper, the state regulates and directs migration through a body of law.

From the theoretical vantage point, immigrants are also distinct in that they bring with them a whole host of social resources (their social class, education, occupation, culture, values) from another society, and their outcomes in American society will be partly a function of those initial resources, partly a function of the nature of their migration (whether they are political or economic immigrants, victims of genocide, settlers or sojourners), and partly a function of the social context that greeted them, of the amount of opportunity available to them in their new society (in the particular cities and industries where they became concentrated, and in the nature of the discrimination or exclusion they afterward faced).

Internal Colonialism

In sociology the major challenge to assimilation theory came from the proponents of the internal colonialism model, the theoretical effort to delineate in what ways the experiences of the racial minorities (Blacks, Puerto Ricans, Mexicans, Native Americans—some of its oldest immigrants and most indigenous native sons and daughters) differed significantly from the experiences and eventual assimilation of the White European immigrants at the turn of the century. The internal colonialism model underscored that the experience of these groups was different in that they had suffered a process of internal colonization due to their place and role in the system of production, place and role they came to occupy because of their color, their race (Barrera, 1979; Blauner, 1969). Proponents of the internal colonialism model underscored that the European migration had been voluntary, the result of decisions the immigrants themselves had taken, whereas the migration of the racial minorities had been involuntary, the result of slavery, annexation, conquest—processes that involved substantial violence. Moreover, they stressed, the European immigrants had changed their cultural patterns at will, gradually over the course of generations, while cultural change had been imposed on the racial minorities. Even more, the ghetto had been only a one- or two-generation phenomenon for the European immigrants and their descendants, whereas for the racial minorities it had become a nearly permanent condition. Last, they stressed, the European immigrants had substantial control of their own communities, through teachers, police officers, small business owners, and social workers, whereas the racial minorities' communities had been manned and controlled by outsiders. Hence, the racial minorities had suffered from a process of colonization unlike anything experienced by the European immigrants.

An important corrective to the assimilation model, the internal colonialism model itself suffered from stretching the colonial analogy overly far, not recognizing the essential differences between the domestic situation of race relations in the United States and what happened in Africa and Asia. Thereafter, Joe Feagin (1978) sought to transcend the shortcomings of both the assimilation and internal colonialism models by focusing on the varying ways in which different ethnic groups were incorporated, became a part of the society, by paying attention to the initial and continuing placement and access of various groups within the economic, political, and educational institutions of the society.

Still, as a central concept that guided research, incorporation, like its predecessor, assimilation, assumed a one-way process, failing to take into account that immigrants not only become incorporated into a new society, they also transform it. Immigrants did not just become incorporated into American society; they made and remade America and are fashioning her still.

Despite the challenges the concept of assimilation and acculturation received from other concepts, such as internal colonialism, incorporation, and more recently transnationalism and diasporic citizenship, Richard Alba and Victor Nee (2003) argued in *Remaking the American Mainstream* that it is still a necessary concept. In their view, assimilation is a grand narrative that served to describe well the experience of the southern and eastern European immigrants, as well as the Asian immigrants who arrived at the turn of the 20th century and, over the course of several generations, went on to join the mainstream of American life in terms of their levels of educational attainment, patterns of suburbanization, and intermarriage. As Alba and Nee emphasized, the process by which they achieved parity in terms of their life chances was partly historically contingent—dependent on two World Wars, the GI Bill, and the like. It was also racialized—that is, exclusive to those who had become "White" in the process. Banks, other credit lenders, and real estate developers kept Blacks, Mexicans, Puerto Ricans, and Native Americans from joining the mainstream of life in suburbia due to their race. Still, even for those formerly excluded groups, there has been progress. Reynolds Farley and Richard Alba, in "The New Second Generation in the U.S." (2002), examined the pattern of occupational distribution for older immigrants and for the new second generation in the United States in 1998–2000. They showed that even for those groups dominated by low-wage labor immigrants in the first generation (such as Mexicans, Central Americans, and Afro-Caribbeans), there has been considerable improvement in the average occupational position in the second generation, although not to the point of parity with native-born whites, as is the case for Asians and South Americans, immigrants who arrived with high levels of human capital. Hence, it would seem that for all the challenges to the concepts of assimilation and acculturation over time, the concepts are still useful in exactly the way Gordon intended them to be: as a conceptual yardstick with which to measure the extent to which various groups have joined the American mainstream over the course of time.

Transnationalism

As a result of the fourth wave of American immigration that we are still living through, sociology refocused its research on immigrants as a social category distinct from racial and ethnic minorities and on immigration as an international process that reshuffles persons and cultures across nations, until we now find ourselves amid a veritable explosion of immigration research as well as a search for new concepts such as those of transnationalism and diasporic citizenship with which to describe the new realities.

The concept of transnationalism arose when social scientists noticed that under the impact of changes in the nature of modern communications at this century's end, many immigrants failed to shed their old identities and totally assimilate. Instead, they developed new bicultural identities and lived their lives and were quite involved in more than one nation, more than one world—in effect, making the home and adopted countries both one lived social world. In his study of Mexican working-class immigrants living in Redwood City, California, Roger Rouse (1992) found that "while they lived in Redwood City, they were also living deep in western Mexico" (p. 45) and were obliged to balance two quite different ways of life, which resulted in "cultural bifocality," as he expressed it.

Basch and colleagues (Basch, Schiller, & Blanc, 1994, p. 7) formalized the definition of transnationalism now in use: the process by which immigrants "forge and sustain multi-stranded social relations that link together their societies of origin and settlement." Thus, they underscored, immigrants "take actions, make decisions, and develop subjectivities and identities embedded in networks of relationships that connect them simultaneously to two or more nations" (Basch et al., 1994, p. 7). Like all social processes, this has economic, political, and social dimensions, both in its causes and consequences. However, soon thereafter the cry arose that transnationalism is not new, although much of the literature sounds as if it is (Foner, 1997; Moya, 2004; Waldinger, 2004). Comparing immigrants at the turn of the century with contemporary immigrants to New York—the quintessential immigrant city—Foner (1997) showed that many transnational patterns actually have a long history. At the turn of the last century, many immigrants were involved in what is now called transnationalism. For example, Italian and Russian immigrants also kept ties of sentiment and family alive with those back home by living in what today are called "transnational households" with members scattered across households; by sending remittances back home; and by making political contributions for particular causes, such as the Irish support for the nationalist cause back home. Moreover, with the exception of Russian Jews who fled from political and religious persecution, the return rates for many immigrant groups, like the Italians, were extremely high, around one-third, even higher than today's.

Although these critiques are valid, my own view is that, nonetheless, much is distinctive about our current transnationalism. In today's global economy, changes in the technologies of transportation and communication (jet air travel, faxes, electronic mail, the Internet, videos) have changed the qualitative experience of immigration. These modern communications (or are they post-modern?) have enabled immigrants to maintain more frequent and closer contact with their home country and to participate regularly—both actually and vicariously—in the life they once left behind. Based on substantial participant observation in various immigrant communities, as well as observing the changes over time in my own transnational relationship to my country of origin, I argue that although immigrants in the past also led transnational lives, there is a qualitative difference in the transnational experiences immigrants live today. Because the new technologies allow immediate communication, immigrants can experience the world they left behind as if they were still there. For example, today Costa Ricans can easily and rapidly travel between "home" and "host" societies, rather than spending many months at sea, as was the voyage that Italians took to return to Italy in the 19th century; likewise, cable television has brought Greece, with its colorful festivals and Olympics, right into the living room of Greek immigrants. Moreover, although in the past communication was not reliable and was painfully slow, today it is nearly certain and fast. For example, the "overseas Chinese" that lived scattered throughout the Southeast Asian nations in the early part of the 20th century often paid a "letter writer" to write the letter they could not, so as to send their messages back to their families in China. However, the letter often did not reach those in the rural areas, or it took a month or two to reach them, so that the news had grown old, whereas today a fax sent to a temple or a benevolent association will penetrate deep in China and arrive immediately. Even Cuban Americans, whose travel is so restricted by the perennial conflicts between the United States and Cuban governments, now communicate regularly with relatives and friends back in the island through electronic mail, since a friend who works for a state corporation with access to e-mail can invariably be found. Although Irish immigrants in the early part of the 19th century heard that a new baby had been baptized in Ireland long after the event, today Mexican immigrants can quickly see the baptism that just took place back in their village on video. Rather than being substantially cut off from the past, today's immigrants live—existentially speaking—both in the past and the present at once. A strong emotional thread now ties the two realities, as never before.

Immigrants today are there not just in their memories and imaginations, but vicariously, in that very moment; they are able to participate—economically, politically, socially, emotionally—in a regular, constant way, often creating two "homes" that rest on the pillar of an identity (or identities) that incorporate two or more nations, social worlds, at the same time. This is true even when, as Waldinger (2004) pointed out, dual loyalties can be conflicting. My point is not to emphasize a past/present divergence, as Waldinger put it, but to emphasize that we do now live in a brave new world that is both vastly more impersonal and personal at once. We know the ways in which our new world is more impersonal—for example, telephone menus now answer most of our questions automatically, without our hearing a human voice; clothing is bought and sold online via the computer without our ever touching the cloth in our hands for its feel. But our new world is also far more personal across very great distances than it once was, as the new technology allows us immediate intellectual and emotional communication with those we love that remained behind. Those sustained affective, emotional linkages also constitute a form of transnationalism, as Elizabeth Aranda and Elena Sabogal (2004) argued. They give evidence of the social networks across various nations that immigrants are embedded in, even though they do not entail sustained cross-border exchanges, as Portes et al. (Portes, Guarnizo, & Landolt, 1999) insisted on. For many immigrants in their new "home," this communication with their families and friends back in their old "home" represents the foundation of their emotional and economic well-being. As Waldinger (2004) concluded, "History involves change, which is why any particular historical constellation is distinct from other like developments encountered before." Thus, we do want to know how and why "now" differs from "then." However, as both David

Hollinger (1995) and Jose Moya (2004) stressed, the major differences are not necessarily between "then" and "now," but between groups who show remarkable variation in the development of diasporic identities and political and social involvement.

Like all social forms, transnationalism can have both positive and negative impacts—economically, politically, and socially. Transnationalism is not only salutary for the mental health of immigrants, but is also salutary for the economic health of the underdeveloped nations they came from. A recent survey of remittance senders conducted by Bendixen and Associates for the Inter-American Development Bank (2001), based on 1,000 interviews done with Latin American immigrants in the United States, asked them whether they had ever sent money to their family in their home country. The results showed that 65% of Mexicans had done so, as had 67% of Cubans, 74% of South Americans, 78% of Dominicans, and 82% of Central Americans. That in itself constitutes a good measure of the extent to which immigrants today are involved in transnationalism. In many Latin American countries today, immigrant remittances represent millions, even billions of dollars a year—the second or third largest source of foreign exchange, quite critical to the survival of those societies (Lora, 2003). This is true with respect to not only Mexico, Guatemala, El Salvador, Dominican Republic, and Venezuela, but also Cuba. Despite the insistence of a very vocal part of the Cuban American exile community, whose political task is to insist that no dollars be sent back to Cuba because that props up Fidel Castro's regime, another sizable part of the Cuban American exile community insists on putting their families back in Cuba first—and quietly sends dollars back to their families left behind, who need it—a moral task in which women are centrally involved (cf. Pedraza, 1991).

Not only does migration result in remittances, but remittances also result in migration. In her study of the cumulative causation of migration from Costa Rica, the Dominican Republic, Nicaragua, Mexico, and Puerto Rico to the United States, Elizabeth Fussell (2004) found that in all communities in these countries, except Puerto Rico, larger amounts of remittances sent to households in a given year were associated with higher migration prevalence ratios the following year, especially in places with older migration streams, such as Mexico and the Dominican Republic. As Fussell underlined, immigrants who send back remittances demonstrate the rewards to migration, thus enticing more members of the sending community to go to the United States. Puerto Rico was an exception because, as U.S. citizens, Puerto Ricans migrate freely to and fro—so much so that Jorge Duany (2000) investigated how a "nation on the move" constructs its identity in Puerto Rico (where 61% of Puerto Ricans live) and the diaspora (where fully 39% of Puerto Ricans now live). Although language (Spanish) and culture (Latin American) used to be the cultural markers of the Puerto Rican identity, such a large diaspora, many of whom do not speak Spanish and are rather American, challenges the very markers of that identity.

Moreover, although overall the impact of immigrant remittances is positive for buoying the sinking economies back home, it can also create certain imbalances. Sarah Blue's (2004) survey of Cuban families in Havana who received remittances from their relatives abroad showed that the remittances were relinking the family that both the Cuban government and the exile community had torn asunder, and that they certainly provided some measure of material comfort for those left behind, improving their lives; however, they also served to exacerbate racial inequality. Because the first two waves of the Cuban exodus (from 1959 to 1974) were predominantly White (cf. Pedraza, 1996a), Black and Mulatto Cubans in the island have fewer immigrant networks abroad they can rely on to send remittances to improve their household consumption or to sponsor their emigration.

Transnationalism has class as well as racial dimensions. Harriett Romo's (2004) study of the transnational lives of the Mexican elite in San Antonio, Texas, described the major influence they had on the cultural and artistic life in the city of San Antonio itself, as well as the role of "broker" they played between the Mexican community, on the one hand, and the Anglo elite, on the other, on behalf of the Mexican community.

Diasporic Citizenship

It is also important to recognize that yesterday as well as today, the immigrants' return migration and their involvement with life in the countries they left was due not only to their bonds of love and loyalty for the family and nation left behind, but also to their lack of acceptance in America. Michel Laguerre (1998) proposed the broader concept of diasporic citizenship—"a set of practices that a person is engaged in, and a set of rights acquired or appropriated, that cross nation-state boundaries and that indicate membership in at least two nation states" (p. 190). Laguerre underlined that thereby Haitian immigrants in the United States today "escape complete minoritization since the link with the homeland allows one to enjoy the majority status one cannot exercise in the adopted country" (p. 192). Thus Laguerre underscored the difference that race—being Black and immigrant—makes.

Moreover, as a social practice, diasporic citizenship is ahead of its legal expression. Laguerre argued that a new conception of dual citizenship is developing that is dual in two senses: first, in the sense it has always been for many immigrants—that while they are in the home country (Italy, Haiti) they are its citizens, while when they are in the United States they are Americans; second, in the new sense that the diaspora—those who are, as the etymology of the word indicates, scattered asunder like seeds—can now participate fully in the social and political life of both countries, exerting quite an influence on the course of the political life in the home country. Foner provides a telling example. In the last Dominican presidential election, many Dominicans residing in New York quickly flew to the island to vote. In the next elections, the trip will be unnecessary because, due to electoral reforms, it will be possible to vote while remaining in New York. This gives the diaspora (whether Haitian, Dominican, Mexican) a role in homeland politics that is much larger than ever before. Moreover, as Laguerre underscored, it removes the future of citizenship from its modern-day location in the nation-state. With Haiti's long history of political repression, the diaspora may well be playing the role of the missing political center—between the army and the government, siding with the people, thus helping the development of civil society and democracy in Haiti. Incidentally, that is precisely the role that the Cuban diaspora has never been able to play with respect to Cuba, at least in part because both the American and Cuban governments have drastically curtailed its involvement with life in Cuba, its transnationalism, much less its diasporic citizenship. As David Hollinger (1995) underscored, the new immigration, like the old, "displays a variety of degrees of engagement with the United States and with prior homelands, and it yields some strong assimilationist impulses along vivid expressions of diasporic consciousness" (p. 153). Governments will try to restrict the flows of communication involved in transnationalism. As of the Summer of 2004, President George W. Bush drastically curtailed the involvement of Cuban-Americans with their family and friends in the island by restricting their travel (only once every 3 years now) and the amount of money they may send back as remittances through formal channels, such as Western Union, as well as the goods they may send to the island. These restrictions will only temporarily reduce the flow of people, goods, and money, however. Cuban immigrants, like all other immigrants, will find a way to get around the government's restrictions. Try as governments might to stop the immigrants' transnationalism, however, they will not be able to do so. Transnationalism is a fact of the modern (or postmodern) world in which we live, it is a result of the spread of the new forms of communication.

Laguerre (1998) underscored that transnational Haitian Americans developed loyalty to their new country as well as to their homeland, loyalties that give rise "to a fragmented bi-polar identity that transcends national boundaries and is central to the social construction of the transnational citizen" (p. 173). He also saw such an identity as the result of transnationalism. Here I disagree with Laguerre, for to me such an identity (preferably called a bicultural identity) is not only fragmented but also sharper in its sensibility—not unlike that of Park's "marginal man" at the beginning of the 20th century. It is also both cause and consequence of transnational practices. To my mind, a bicultural identity not only is the result of transnationalism but also is that on which transnationalism first depends and ultimately (over the course of time and further investments) cements. Precisely because transnationalism depends on such a bicultural identity, it is unclear at present whether the second generation, the children of immigrants, can or will participate in such a transnational social field. Although that is the subject of future research, I believe that they can or will do so only to a rather delimited extent. However, it is possible for even a small group of the second and third generations to play an influential role, as they can transfer ideas and resources that can have important impacts in both places.

Last, participation in transnational practices and the exercise of a diasporic citizenship has consequences for the extent to which immigrants can engage in ethnic politics in American life. The emotional health the new transnationalism gives us may well come at the price of domestic political engagement, of creating institutions and lobbies that can improve their lives as immigrants, workers, ethnics. Transnationalism has consequences for the extent to which immigrants can assimilate—both culturally and structurally—in America. In the end, it may still be up to the second and future generations to play the ethnic politics game. Such, indeed, was the role the descendants of the old immigrants played in the past, when city-level political "machines" built on the support of various ethnic groups traded votes for city jobs and contracts. Hence, it is quite likely that the shift in concepts—from assimilation to transnationalism—will only be useful to describe the lived experience of the immigrant generation. That, however, is a necessity at a time like now when America is not only a "nation of immigrants"—whose history was written by immigrants—but is also an immigrant nation—whose present relies on immigration. Perhaps in the brave new world of this 21st century most nations will also become immigrant nations.

References

Alba, R., & Nee, V. (2003). *Remaking the American mainstream: Assimilation and contemporary immigration.* Cambridge, MA: Harvard University Press.

Aranda, E., & Sabogal, E. (2004, October). *Transnational capital and emotional livelihoods.* Paper presented at the meetings of the Latin American Studies Association, Las Vegas, NV.

Baltzell, E. D. (1964). "The immigrant's progress and the theory of the establishment." In E. O. Laumann, P. M. Siegel, & R. W. Hodge (Eds.), *The logic of social hierarchies.* Chicago: Markham.

Basch, L., Schiller, N. G., & Blanc, C. S. (1994). *Nations unbound: Transnational projects, postcolonial predicaments, and deterritorialized nation states.* Langhorne, PA: Gordon and Breach.

Barrera, M. (1979). *Race and class in the Southwest.* South Bend, IN: University of Notre Dame Press.

Blauner, R. (1969). Internal colonialism and ghetto revolt. *Social Problems, 16,* 393–408.

Blue, S. A. (2004, October). *The social cost of remittances: Race and income equality in contemporary Cuba.* Paper presented at the meetings of the Latin American Studies Association, Las Vegas, NV.

Bodnar, J. (1985). *The transplanted: A history of immigrants in urban America.* Bloomington: Indiana University Press.

Burawoy, M. (1976). The functions and reproduction of migrant labor: Comparative material from Southern Africa and the United States. *American Journal of Sociology, 81,* 1050–1087.

Corwin, A. F. (1978). *Immigrants—And immigrants: Perspectives on Mexican labor migration to the United States.* Wesport, CT: Greenwood.

Cowan, P. (1982). *An orphan in history: Retrieving a Jewish legacy.* New York: Doubleday.

Diner, H. R. (1984). *Erin's daughters in America: Irish immigrant women in the nineteenth century.* Baltimore, MD: Johns Hopkins University Press.

Duany, J. (2000). Nation on the move: The construction of cultural identities in Puerto Rico and the Diaspora. *American Ethnologist, 27,* 5–30.

Farley, R., & Alba, R. (2002). The new second generation in the U. S. *International Migration Review, 36*(Fall), 669–701.

Feagin, J. R. (1978). *Racial and ethnic relations.* Englewood Cliffs, NJ: Prentice Hall.

Foner, N. (1997). What's new about transnationalism? New York immigrants today and at the turn of the century. *Diaspora, 6,* 355–376.

Frazier, E. F. (1957). *Race and culture contacts in the modern world.* New York: Alfred A. Knopf.

Fussell, E. (2004, October). *Migration from central America and the Caribbean to the U. S.: The Role of cumulative causation.* Paper presented at the meetings of the Latin American Studies Association, Las Vegas, NV.

Galarza, E. (1964). *Merchants of labor: The Mexican Bracero story.* Santa Barbara, CA: McNally and Loftin.

Glazer, N. (1971). Blacks and ethnic groups: The difference, and the political difference it makes. *Social Problems, 18,* 444–461.

Glazer, N., & Moynihan, D. P. (1963). *Beyond the melting pot: The Negroes, Puerto Ricans, Jews, Italians, and Irish of New York City* (2nd ed.). Cambridge, MA: MIT Press.

Gold, S. J., & Phillips, B. (1996). Mobility and continuity among Eastern European Jews. In S. Pedraza & R. G. Rumbaut (Eds.), *Origins and destinies: Immigration, race, and ethnicity in America* (pp. 182–194). Belmont, CA: Wadsworth Press.

Gordon, M. M. (1964). *Assimilation in American life.* New York: Oxford University Press.

Higham, J. (1955). *Strangers in the land: Patterns of American nativism, 1860–1925.* New Brunswick, NJ: Rutgers University Press.

Hollinger, D. (1995). *Postethnic America.* New York: Basic Books.

Inter-American Development Bank. (2001). "Survey of Remittance Senders: U.S. to Latin America." Bendixen & Associates. Washington, DC: Inter-American Development Bank.

Laguerre, M. S. (1998). *Diasporic citizenship: Haitian Americans in transnational America.* New York: St. Martin's Press.

Lee, E. S. (1966). A theory of migration. *Demography, 3,* 47–57.

Light, I. (1983). *Cities in world perspective.* New York: Macmillan.

Lora, E. A. (2003). Changing patterns in the supply of labor. In *Economic and social progress in Latin America 2004* (chap. 3). Washington, DC: Inter-American Development Bank.

Martin, P., & Midgley, E. (2003). Immigration: Shaping and reshaping America. *Population Bulletin, 58,* 1–44. Washington, DC: Population Reference Bureau.

Martin, P., & Midgley, E. (2004). Number of foreign-born reaches all-time high in the U. S. *Population Reference Bureau.* Retrieved January 30, 2005, http://www.prb.org

Massey, D. S., Alarcón, R., Durand, J., & González, H. (1987). *Return to Aztlan: The social process of international migration from western Mexico.* Berkeley and Los Angeles: University of California.

Muller, T., & Espenshade, T. J. (1985). *The fourth wave: California's newest immigrants.* Washington, DC: Urban Institute.

Moya, J. (2004, November). *Diaspora studies: New concepts, approaches, and realities?* Paper presented at the meeting of the Social Science History Association, Chicago.

Ortiz, F. (1983). *Contrapunteo Cubano del Tabaco y el Azúcar.* La Habana, Cuba: Editorial de Ciencias Sociales. (Original work published 1963)

Park, R. E. (1928). Human migration and the marginal man. *American Journal of Sociology, 33,* 881–893.

Park, R. E. (1950). *Race and culture.* New York: Free Press. (Original work published 1913)

Park, R. E., & Burgess, E. W. (1921). *Introduction to the science of sociology.* Chicago: University of Chicago Press.

Pedraza, S. (1991). Women and migration: The social consequences of gender. *Annual Review of Sociology, 17,* 303–325.

Pedraza, S. (1996a). Cuba's refugees: Manifold migrations. In S. Pedraza & R. G. Rumbaut (Eds.), *Origins and destinies: Immigration, race, and ethnicity in America* (pp. 263–279). Belmont, CA: Wadsworth Press.

Pedraza, S. (1996b). American paradox. In S. Pedraza & R. G. Rumbaut, (Eds.), *Origins and destinies: Immigration, race, and ethnicity in America* (pp. 479–491). Belmont, CA: Wadsworth Press.

Pedraza-Bailey, S. (1985). *Political and economic migrants in America: Cubans and Mexicans.* Austin: University of Texas Press.

Piven, F. F., & Cloward, R. A. (1979). *Poor people's movements: Why they succeed, how they fail.* New York: Random.

Portes, A. (1978). Immigrant aspirations. *Sociology of Education, 51,* 241–260.

Portes, A., Guarnizo, L. E., & Landolt, P. (1999). Introduction: Pitfalls and promise of an emergent research field. *Ethnic and Racial Studies, 22,* 463–478.

Ramos, J. (2004, July 19). The three Americas. *The Miami Herald.*

Romo, H. (2004, October). *First class: Transnational lives of the upper middle class in San Antonio, Texas.* Paper presented at the meetings of the Latin American Studies Association, Las Vegas, NV.

Rouse, R. (1992). Making sense of settlement: Class transformations, cultural struggle, and transnationalism among Mexican immigrants in the United States. *Annals of the New York Academy of Sciences, 645,* 25–52. Special issue in N. G. Schiller, L. Bash, & C. Blanc-Szanton (Eds.), *Towards a transnational perspective on migration.*

Samora, J. (1971). *Los Mojados: The wetback story.* Notre Dame, IN: University of Notre Dame Press.

Thomas, W. I., & Znaniecki, F. (1927). *The Polish Peasant in Europe and America* (2 Vols.). New York: Alfred A. Knopf.

Turner, F. J. (1920). The significance of the frontier in American history. In *The significance of the frontier in American history.* New York: Holt. (Original work published 1893)

U.S. Bureau of the Census. (2001). *Region and country or area of birth of the foreign-born population, with geographic detail shown in decennial Census publications of 1930 or earlier: 1850 to 1930 and 1960 to 1990.* Retrieved January 30, 2005, http://www.census.gov/population/www/documentation/twps0029/tab04.html Last revised January 18, 2001.

Waldinger, R. (2004, November). *Immigrant transnationalism and the presence of the past.* Paper presented at the meeting of the Social Science History Association, Chicago.

Post-Reading Activities

1   Thinking about the definitions discussed in the introduction (Wagley & Harris (1967) and van Amersfoort (1978)), how well do the definitions apply to the discussion of race?

2   When pondering the American racial minorities, which article from the Universal Declaration of Human Rights most applies? Are there differences among racial and ethnic groups, meaning does one article better address the minority status of Asians and another article better address the minority status of Native Americans?

3   After discussing microaggressions in Reading 6, what are some microaggressions that pertain to Whites, Blacks, Native Americans, immigrants, and Asians?

Basic Lives, Minority and Majority

As discussed in Unit 3, much attention is placed on understanding the rights of racial and ethnic minorities. In Unit 4, we will discuss sex and gender minorities, sexuality minorities, and age minorities. Gurr and Naples (2014) provide an excellent overview of the sociology of sex and gender through the lens of understanding human rights of all minorities. Similarly, Bernstein takes a similar approach while reporting on the sociology of sexualities.

However, not typically included in a minorities book, this anthology introduces the discussion of aging and religion as minority groups. Typically, ageism is briefly discussed as "ageism" in some stratification or introduction to sociology books, and religion is incorporated into ethnicity. But, as the future shows a growing elderly population and a diminishing young child population, a renewed interest in age needs to develop when understanding age minority. The majority, or dominating, age population would typically be reflected as 25 to 65. These are working adults, making financial decisions. Achenbaum (2015) provides a brief history of ageism in the United States and stresses the importance of intersectionality while studying ageism. Again, intersectionality refers to the idea that a researcher cannot isolate just a person's age to study inequality. Rather, an aging individual will have differing experiences depending on one's race, class, gender, sex, and sexuality.

References

Achenbaum, W. A. (2015). A History of Ageism Since 1969. *Generations, 39*(3), 10–16.

Gurr, B. & Naples, N.A. (2014). Sex and Gender. In *Expanding the Human in Human Rights: Toward a Sociology of Human Rights*. London: Paradigm Publishers.

READING 10

Sex and Gender

Barbara Gurr and Nancy A. Naples

The intellectual history and topics of interest in the sociology of sex and gender are tied intimately to human rights scholarship and activism. The field was generated through the advocacy of activists inside and outside the discipline inspired by the women's movement of the late 1960s and early 1970s (Fox 1995). Recognizing that women's knowledge and experience had been either erased or diminished in importance by a discipline dominated by men and fueled by patriarchal assumptions of what counts as knowledge and who should be the primary conveyers of sociological insights, women sociologists challenged the gendered assumptions of the field (Smith 1987). In 1969, Alice Rossi, who would become one of the first women presidents of the American Sociological Association (ASA) in 1983, presented data at a business meeting demonstrating the underrepresentation of women and the discrimination they faced in the discipline. As a consequence, in 1971, feminist sociologists formed their own association, Sociologists for Women in Society (SWS), and produced a separate journal, *Gender & Society,* which is now one of the leading journals in interdisciplinary gender studies. SWS dedicated itself to establishing the importance of sex and gender research for sociology; ensuring that women's contributions to knowledge and other aspects of social, economic, political, and cultural life were acknowledged in academic literature; challenging sexist language in sociology journals; and increasing women's visibility in the ASA (Fox 1995). The ASA's Sex and Gender Section was formed in 1973 and is now one of the largest sections of the ASA. SWS members hold prominent leadership positions in the ASA, including the presidency. Since the Sex and Gender Section's founding, three new ASA sections have been added that developed directly from the feminist scholarship on sex and gender.

The topics that are prominent in the field of sex and gender are also at the heart of human rights scholarship. They include processes of discrimination and economic inequalities, the roles of social activism and law in challenging gender inequality, the sources of violence against women, and the role of culture in shaping gendered understandings and practices. Sociologists of sex and gender also address the gendered processes of economic development and migration as well as militarization and global capitalism, among other social structural and historical processes (Fukumura and Matsuoka 2002; Mendez 2005; Salzinger 2005). In this regard, sociologists of sex and gender argue that a gender lens offers a powerful tool for uncovering the social dynamics shaping all major institutions (Brush 2003; Coltraine and Adams 2008; Lorber 2002). To capture the diversity of these experiences, sociologists of sex and gender frequently approach their work from an intersectional perspective (Baca Zinn and Dill 1996; Collins 1990; Naples 2009), paying attention to the intersections of gender, race, class, sexuality, age, culture, and other factors that differentially shape social life rather than concentrating on a single dimension.

The Sociology of Sex and Gender

Examining Processes of Discrimination and Economic Inequalities

Sociologists of sex and gender focus attention on how sex and gender shape structures of inequality and power. Their research addresses structural factors that derive from gender inequality, including the wage gaps between men and women and other forms of discrimination in the labor force (Britton 2003; England 2005); the gender gap in electoral politics (Rossi 1983); and sexist and heteronormative assumptions embedded in law and social policy (Bernstein and Reimann 2001; Naples 1991).

Another dimension of this scholarship relates to understanding the contribution of global economic restructuring for gender dynamics and economic inequalities. Sociologists of sex and gender highlight the fact that globalization is a result of particular actions taken by identifiable actors and that globalization lands in particular places (Sassen 2006, 2007). Rather than view globalization as a process that occurs at a distance from the everyday lives and activities of particular actors, they demonstrate that global economic and political change is manifest in the daily lives and struggles of women and other members of communities in different parts of the world in ways that are often hidden from view in analyses of globalization that start from the perspective of multinational corporations, transnational organizations, and international political institutions (Naples and Desai 2002, vii).

Understanding the Role of Social Activism and Law for Challenging Gender Inequality

Until sociologists of sex and gender focused attention on women's political activism, especially the important roles they play in their communities, the extent and variety of women's political participation were ignored or unexamined (Naples 1998). Women's community work and activism, when noticed at all by academics, were understood primarily as a natural extension of their caretaking roles and as part of a maternalist politics in which women's engagement in the public sphere was justified through their identities as mothers (Koven and Michel 1993). In contrast to these assessments, women as community activists contribute countless hours of unpaid labor to campaigns to enhance the physical and environmental quality of their communities while tending to the emotional and social needs of other community members. Their approach to community development and leadership often involves collective and empowering strategies that encourage other women and other residents frequently left out of decision-making roles in formal voluntary associations and political parties to increase their political participation (Naples 2011). This scholarship also explores the role of transnational women's, LGBT, and social justice movements that challenge gender oppression, sexual violence, and other human rights violations (Adam, Duyvendak, and Krouwel 1999; Naples and Desai 2002; Tripp and Ferree 2006).

Analyzing the Sources of Violence against Women in Public and Private Spheres

One of the most important issues addressed by sociologists of sex and gender involves analyzing the many ways that women, minority men, and sexually nonconforming men become targets of violence. Studies of domestic violence were noticeably missing in early sociological literature on the family. With the recognition of the ways power inequalities in marital relations contribute to women's risk of violence in the family, as well as how women become targets of sexual harassment at work and in public spaces, sociologists of sex and gender revealed the daily costs associated with gender and sexual inequalities (Baker 2007).

In considering factors that contribute to violence against women, sociologists and other feminist scholars of sex and gender also brought attention to the roles of militarization and global capitalism in increasing risks of violence against women—for example, through the development of coercive sexual labor in military zones and gendered constructions of violence in armed conflict (Enloe 1990, 2000, 2007; Fukumura and Matsuoka 2002); the use of rape as a tool of war (Allen 1996); and the international crisis of sex trafficking and forced marriage, both of which have been centralized by international human rights groups (Gill and Sundari 2011; Zheng 2010).

Assessing the Role of Culture and Difference in Shaping Gendered Understandings and Practices

A main topic in the sociology of gender focuses on examining how cultural understandings of gender shape the norms of how a feminine or a masculine body should look and act (Connell 2002; Hughs and Witz 1997; Messner 1992; Witz 2000). This contributes to the attention that feminist sociologists have paid to standards of femininity and masculinity as they apply to evaluations of appropriate body size and shape for women and men, stigma attached to those who do not adhere to these standards, and the ways in which early childhood socialization and media serve to enforce these norms (Hesse-Biber and Nagy 2006). Sociologists of sex and gender also use an intersectional approach to explore the power dynamics between women of different racial and ethnic backgrounds (Becker 1994; Kang 2003) and with different abilities (Shakespeare 2006; Zitzelsberger 2005). Feminist scholars also analyze the role of the medical profession, pharmaceutical companies, and new technologies for providing the means by which women and men can reshape their bodies to fit into narrow definitions of appropriate gender and sexuality (Haiken 1999; Loe 2006).

Feminist sociologists of science are especially interested in new reproductive technologies and their ability to challenge the notion of the "natural" mother and father as older, infertile, or same-sex couples access alternative forms of reproduction (Mamo 2007). They point out the inequities in who can access new technologies and the expansion of "reproductive tourism," where wealthy couples travel to poorer countries to purchase reproductive services, including surrogacy arrangements (Purdy 1989). The new field of transgender studies further complicates analysis of the social construction and production of gender as well as the myriad of ways that gender shapes social policy—for example, by challenging hegemonic understandings of gender as a binary system that maps onto bodies that are understood as "male" or "female" (Currah, Juang, and Miner 2007; Valentine 2007).

Sociologists of sex and gender draw insights from postcolonial and third world feminist analysts who emphasize the ways that cultural diversity and other differences, including class, race, ethnicity, country of origin, age, ability, and sexuality, contour the lives of women and men, thus contributing to their different gendered expectations and experiences (Grewal and Caplan 1994, 2000; Alexander and Mohanty 1997; Mohanty, Russo, and Torres 1991). These complexities are particularly salient, for example, when we examine the lives of poor women, who are disproportionately women of color and disproportionately shoulder the burden of the economic and social dislocation resulting from gendered, racialized, and internationalized processes (Buvinic 1998; Sanford 2003; Women's Refugee Commission 2011). This insight relates to an approach that is at the heart of contemporary feminist sociological analyses, namely, intersectionality.

The call for intersectional analyses was first heard from feminists of color who critiqued approaches that constructed women's concerns without attention to the ways that race, class, and sexuality shaped the experiences of women (Baca Zinn and Dill 1996; Collins 1990). The most powerful approaches to intersectionality also include attention to the ways in which these interactions produce contradictions and tensions across these different levels of analysis and dimensions of difference (McCall 2001, 2005; Maynard 1994).

Research Methods for the Study of Sex and Gender

Prior to the intervention of feminist sociologists, when included at all, sex was merely considered as a variable in sociological studies. Feminists first argued for a distinction between the biological category of sex and the social construction of gender, then recognized that the biological category is also socially constructed (Lorber and Moore 2007). Beginning in the 1970s, researchers informed by a feminist call to describe women's experiences and perspectives in their own words began to make women's lives central in ethnographic and other qualitative accounts (Smith 1987). A gendered lens on men's lives and the development of men's studies was inspired by a growing sensitivity to the ways in which femininities and masculinities are coconstituted (Connell 1987, 2005; Kimmel 2005; Pascoe 2007). Since the 1980s, feminist sociologists who are influenced by postmodern analyses of power and knowledge have become particularly concerned with the role of discourse and the myriad of ways power shapes women's lives (Ferguson 1991). Differences in feminist epistemologies of knowledge influence what counts as data and how data should be analyzed; therefore, a postmodern feminist researcher would approach the collection and analysis of interviews differently from a scholar who draws on positivist or symbolic interactionist perspectives (Naples 2003).

Feminist sociologists have been particularly effective in identifying the processes by which power and "relations of ruling" are inherent in disciplinary practices (Smith 1990). Feminist sociologists have raised questions about the ethics of social research, especially as relates to power imbalances in fieldwork and interviewing (Stacey 1991; Wolf 1996). As one strategy, sociologists of sex and gender recommend addressing these inequalities through reflexive practice designed to interrogate how personal and situational factors contribute to power imbalances. For example, Nancy Naples explains that this form of reflexive practice "encourages feminist scholars to examine how gendered and racialized assumptions influence which voices and experiences are privileged in ethnographic encounters" (2003, 22). She also argues that a reflexive "approach also implies the development of more egalitarian and participatory field methods than traditionally utilized in social scientific investigations" (201).

Sociologists of sex and gender employ a number of research methods to better understand the complexities of sex and gender. Small-scale, locally focused studies such as those conducted by Patricia Richards (2005) in Chile and Vincanne Adams (1998) in Tibet often incorporate various interview methods, including in-depth interviews and focus groups, as well as observations of and, occasionally, participation in local communities, nongovernmental organizations, and state-sponsored organizations. Sociologists interested in larger demographic trends such as poverty levels, refugee status, education attainment, and maternal mortality and morbidity frequently employ statistical methods through censuses and surveys (Hafner-Burton 2005;

Hafner-Burton and Tsutsui 2005; Spirer 1990). Other quantitative approaches are used to capture aggregate patterns such as wage inequality and gender division of labor in employment across different regions (McCall 2001). Sociologists of sex and gender have also turned to policy and document analysis to better understand the bureaucratic and discursive development of instruments intended to identify and meet women's human rights needs (Merry 2006; Naples 2003; Wotipka and Tsutsui 2008).

Human Rights and the Sociology of Sex and Gender

Sex and Gender in Human Rights Documents

The Universal Declaration of Human Rights (UDHR) affirms the "dignity and rights" of all humankind. However, the near invisibility of sex and gender as specific categories for protection in the UDHR renders addressing the rights of women problematic, particularly in a global or transnational context (Bunch 1990; Freeman 1999; Gaer 1998; Binion 1995). Largely as a result of feminist scholarship and activism, particularly since the mid-1980s, human rights abuses based on or related to sex and gender have become increasingly noted; yet there is still no clear consensus as to how to understand these categories or appropriately address violations of women's and sexual minorities' human rights in an international human rights context. This lack of clarity continues to circumscribe the ability of activists and scholars to adequately frame gender-specific abuses as human rights violations in an international legal framework and also presents challenges to those seeking redress. However, progress has been made toward delineating women's and sexual minorities' human rights and demanding that they be formally recognized and protected. Sociologists of sex and gender contribute to this work through increasingly intersectional analyses of the interactions between gender and the state, citizenship, governance structures, and local and global political economies, among other factors.

Historical Perspective on Sex and Gender in Human Rights Discourse

Attention to sex and gender in human rights discourse and documents can be traced to the late nineteenth century (Lockwood et. al. 1998) and is more evident in the UDHR, which was adopted in 1948. The elaboration of concern for women's rights in particular was further evident in the efforts that resulted from the United Nations Decade for Women (1976–1985), during which women from many different geographical, ethnic, racial, religious, cultural, and class backgrounds took up the task of improving the status of women transnationally. The United Nations sponsored three international women's conferences during this time: in Mexico City in 1975, Copenhagen in 1980, and Nairobi in 1985. Several important human rights documents developed out of these conferences and the efforts of feminist activists and scholars.

The 1976 International Covenant on Civil and Political Rights recognized the equal right of men and women to the enjoyment of all civil and political rights set forth in the covenant (Article 3). This right was further codified in 1979 when the UN General Assembly adopted the

Convention on the Elimination of All Forms of Discrimination against Women. Some scholars note that its references to sex include sexual freedom, thereby offering protection to sexual minorities (Mittelstaedt 2008).

In 1990, following decades of concerted effort from feminist activists, organizations, and scholars, Dr. Charlotte Bunch published a foundational call for women's rights as human rights, criticizing the reluctance of states and international structures to address the needs of women and homosexuals from the legal framework of human rights. Three years later, the participants in the World Conference on Human Rights produced the Vienna Declaration and Program of Action, which specified a platform on women's human rights as inalienable from the individual and indivisible from universal human rights, noting that the eradication of sex discrimination is a priority for the international community.

The 1994 International Conference on Population and Development in Cairo featured discussions on sex, sexuality, and sexual health but linked these rights to heterosexual reproduction with no mention of freedom of sexual expression or sexual orientation. At the Fourth World Conference on Women in Beijing in 1995, sponsored by the United Nations, feminist activists finally saw the global emergence of the idea of "women's rights as human rights" (Bunch 1990). Developed by conference participants, the Beijing Platform for Action focused on removing obstacles to women's active participation in all spheres of public and private life through a full and equal share in economic, social, cultural and political decision-making. However, this platform failed to include support for the rights of lesbians and rejected the term "sexual orientation" (Bunch and Fried 1996; see also Baden and Goetz 1997).

Key Areas of Concern for Women's Human Rights

Sociologists have identified numerous areas of concern for the development and protection of women's human rights, and they generally understand these areas as linked globally (Naples and Desai 200; Reilly 2009). We offer here three brief illustrations: economic security, gendered violence, and reproductive health.

Economic Security

The United Nations asserts that women's economic security is at far greater risk than men's globally, and this is particularly true in rural areas that rely heavily on agricultural production (UNFAO 2010). Differential access to employment opportunities continues to reflect and reproduce gendered conceptualizations of women's domestic roles and to inhibit their ability to engage fully in civic life. Further, approximately 75 percent of the world's women are not entitled to property ownership and cannot receive bank loans due to underemployment, unemployment, and insecure employment (Moser 2007). These restrictions impact not only women but families and communities as well (Cagatay 2001).

Gendered Violence

Anthropologist Sally Merry points out that "the idea that everyday violence against women is a human rights violation has not been easy to establish" (2006, 2). Part of the difficulty lies in the tensions between global and transnational institutions and local structures. The translation of human rights laws and ideologies between multiple locations is complicated by cultural differences, questions of sovereignty, and access to resources, among other potential impediments (Bunch 1990). In this context, the role of intermediary institutions such as nongovernmental organizations is pivotal. Further complicating the ability of scholars and activists to address gendered violence as a human rights violation is the continuing construction of a public-private dichotomy in which violence against women is framed as a family issue in which state actors are reluctant to intervene (Clapham 2007; Tomasevski 1995). However, there has been some progress toward understanding gendered violence as an issue that transcends public/private dichotomies, particularly when this violence occurs in the context of war. In 2008 the UN Security Council passed Resolution 1820, which formally recognized the particular vulnerabilities of women and girl children to sexual violence during armed conflict and reaffirmed states' obligations to address sexual violence against civilians.

Reproductive Health

Maternal and child health continue to be a priority for women's human rights activists in the twenty-first century. Growing attention and increased resources from local, global, and transnational institutions over the last several decades—particularly since the 1994 International Conference on Population and Development explicitly linked the reproductive health and human rights of women to global efforts to reduce poverty—have resulted in important improvements in women's access to adequate health care (WHO 2010). However, globally women experience unequal access to health care. For example, according to the World Health Organization (2000), global maternal mortality and morbidity rates are highest in developing nations.

Guang-zhen Wang and Vijayan Pillai (2001) explain that sociologists have applied two general analytical frames to reproductive health: (1) identifying social-structural factors shaping reproductive health, and (2) examining a rights-based paradigm to elucidate states' obligations to provide reproductive health care. Utilizing these frames has enabled sociologists to offer critical analyses of the interactions between health and social environments that elucidate foundational causes for the disparities in health between sexes, genders, geographic locations, socioeconomic locations, and racial-ethnic identities, among other key factors (Doyal 1995, 2001; Warner-Smith, Bryson, and Byles 2004).

Key Sociological Questions and Insights in the Study of Women's Human Rights

A primary question emerging from the feminist sociological study of human rights is, What obstacles challenge universal recognition of women's human rights and prevent a comprehensive consideration of gender within the prevailing human rights frameworks? Findings in response to this question vary but often include the influence of religious groups, social and political constructions of a public-private gendered dichotomy, masculinized notions of citizenship, and the fact that the concept of "universal" human rights tends to mask the multiple dimensions of difference emerging from racial-ethnic, class, and cultural locations, as well as sex and gender differences, and to impose a Western conceptualization of individual rights.

Assessing the Influence of Religious Groups in Circumscribing Women's Human Rights

The lack of women's voices in the development of religious institutions and the concurrent influence of religious doctrine on state practices impose multiple and, at times, severe restrictions on women's freedoms (European Women's Lobby 2006; Winter 2006). For example, at the time of the Beijing Conference for Women, Roman Catholic authorities rejected what they considered the ambiguity of the term "gender" and noted that they understood "gender" to be "grounded in biological sexual identity" (UN Report 1995, 165), thus reinscribing an essentialist role for women that curtails women's opportunities (European Women's Lobby 2006). The role of religious doctrine in determining women's rights is complicated by these essentialist ideas about gender as they intersect with issues of cultural relativism and fundamental human rights (Sunder 2003; Winter 2006). These complications have led many scholars, such as Madhavi Sunder, to assert that "human rights law has a problem with religion" (2003, 1401; see also Reilly 2009).

Examining the Persistence of the Public-Private Dichotomy in Human Rights Discourse

Sociologists of sex and gender interrogate the social construction of a public-private dichotomy in which some aspects of human lives are conceptualized as occurring or belonging in a public sphere and others are deemed private and thus, in some measure, protected from surveillance or state control (Collins 1994; Okin 1989). Many violations of women's human rights, such as domestic violence, forms of sexual slavery, and child-preference practices that disadvantage girl children, are often considered "private" matters in which global and local states are reluctant to intervene (Bunch 1990; Freeman 1999; MacKinnon 1993). The occurrence of these and similarly gendered phenomena in what is constructed as the "privacy" of family and home constructs boundaries around how these issues are addressed and inhibits the abilities of international systems to intervene in such rights violations.

Gendering Human Rights Discourse and Practice

Sociologists of sex and gender point out that the dominant image of the political actor is male (Haney 2000; Bunch 1990; Yuval-Davis 1997), and most human rights institutions are male dominated (Freeman 1999). Therefore, women are largely invisible as human rights institutions deal with human rights violations on a large, public scale (for example, through the institution of democracies, fair housing, and economic security); "it is assumed that women benefit" (Freeman 1999, 515) as members of the larger populace. Failure to specify the needs of women as women presents an obstacle to recognizing the many ways their human rights can be and are violated through an imposed public-private dichotomy (Bunch 1990; MacKinnon 1993). Within this dichotomy, notions of citizenship become conflated with the presumably male political actor (Yuval-Davis 1997), and the human rights of women are subsumed or delegitimized under this rubric of masculinized citizenship.

Universalizing Notions of Human Rights and of Women

Citizenship for women is further complicated by political and cultural location, as the women's-rights-as-human-rights frame potentially implies a universalizing notion of women and of rights derived from Western conceptions of citizenship and the state. Sociological perspectives point out the ways in which this runs the risk of further masking local structures and institutions such as diverse family forms, law-enforcement practices, and religious beliefs (Bonnin 1995; Chow 1996; Howard and Allen 1996; Ray and Korteweg 1999). When theoretical space is allotted for the recognition of women outside a Western paradigm, it is often limited in scope. For example, as Chandra Talpade Mohanty argues, "Assumptions of privilege and ethnocentric universality (can) lead to the construction of a ... reductive and homogeneous notion of '... Third World difference'" (2006, 19), wherein third world and postcolonial women and U.S. women of color are produced as a "composite, singular 'Third World Woman'" (Narayan 1997). Women's human rights, therefore, potentially work from a binary framework of "West/not West" as well as "male/not male."

Redefining the Human Rights Paradigm from a Feminist Perspective

Gender requires a revisioning of human rights as a universal concept as well as a reconstruction of the systems used to create and ensure the sanctity of women's human rights (Staudt 1997; Binion 1995). This includes a blurring of imposed boundaries around "public" and "private" and recognition of the inherently political nature of the "private" lives of women, including domestic lives, religious beliefs and practices, and sexualities. Sociologists recognize that political borders are blurred in the transnational context of global economy, migration, and armed conflict (Freeman 1999; Naples and Desai 2002). Therefore, a feminist and intersectional sociological study of relevant social structures includes, but is not limited to, family and community; local, regional, and global political economies; culture, religion, law, and education; and national and transnational governance, including nongovernmental organizations.

Just as political boundaries are not permanently fixed, a human rights framework is not a static paradigm, as our local and global conceptualizations of what counts as human rights issues and what they require continue to evolve. Feminist sociologists' particular perspective on the intersections of social institutions and structures, such as the family, state, economy, and religion, and individual experiences of power and inequality renders visible the links between the lives of women and sexual minorities, violations of their human rights, and opportunities for protection and redress.

Sociological inquiry into gender and gendered structures and institutions has helped to reveal the ways in which definitions of citizenship; local, national, and transnational institutions and structures; and even the law itself are frequently informed by gendered notions of masculinity that exclude women and their experiences. Sociological analyses of gender thereby offer theoretical tools with which to understand, highlight, and advance an agenda of women's rights as human rights. Emerging emphases in feminist sociological work on the intersections of gender with race, class, sexuality, and other social and political locations (Collins 1994; Richards 2005) provide still greater space for consideration of women's diverse lived experiences under the rubric of human rights, allowing human rights scholars and activists greater opportunity to avoid essentializing women and imposing inadequate Western concepts of "rights."

Where Do We Go from Here?

Recognizing the diversity of women's and men's lives, yet striving to understand "women" and "men" as universal categories, produces a theoretical tension for sociology and for human rights praxis. Women constitute a "group" that exists everywhere; yet they are often differentiated by political, cultural, racial, economic, ethnic, religious, and other considerations. The specific needs of women and non-gender-conforming men for recognition and protection of their human rights share some similarities but vary in many ways. Sensitivity to the differences among women requires nuanced, locally grounded analyses of women's and men's diverse lived experiences; yet, as Gayle Binion asserts, "The facts and conditions of cultural diversity among societies cannot, from a feminist perspective, justify a failure to rectify the conditions in which women live worldwide" (1995, 522), conditions that include gendered violence, economic insecurity, and reproductive health concerns. The international instruments of human rights retain an uncomfortable relationship with culture and gender that requires ongoing reflexive practice and attention to local structures and cultural diversity as well as global economic and political processes that shape everyday life in different parts of the world.

References

Adam, Barry D., Dan Willem Duyvendak, and André Krouwel. 1999. *The Global Emergence of Gay and Lesbian Politics: National Imprints of a Worldwide Movement.* Philadelphia: Temple University Press.

Adams, Vincanne. 1998. "Suffering the Winds of Lhasa: Politicized Bodies, Human Rights, Cultural Difference, and Humanism in Tibet." *Medical Anthropology Quarterly* 12: 74–102.

Alexander, M. Jacqui, and Chandra Talpade Mohanty. 1997. "Introduction." In *Feminist Genealogies, Colonial Legacies, Democratic Future,* edited by M. Jacqui Alexander and Chandra Talpade Mohanty, xiii–xlii. New York: Routledge.

Allen, Beverly. 1996. *Rape Warfare: The Hidden Genocide in Bosnia-Herzegovina and Croatia.* Minneapolis: University of Minnesota Press.

Baca Zinn, Maxine, and Bonnie Thornton Dill. 1996. "Theorizing Difference from Multiracial Feminism." *Feminist Studies* 22: 321–331.

Baden, Sally, and Anne Marie Goetz. 1997. "Who Needs [Sex] When You Can Have [Gender]? Conflicting Discourses on Gender at Beijing." In *Women, International Development, and Politics,* edited by Kathleen Staudt, 37–58. Philadelphia: Temple University Press.

Baker, Carrie N. 2007. *The Women's Movement against Sexual Harassment.* New York: Cambridge University Press.

Becker, Anne E. 1994. "Nurturing and Negligence: Working on Others' Bodies in Fiji." In *Embodiment and Experience: The Existential Ground of Culture and Self,* edited by Thomas J. Csordas, 100–115. Cambridge, UK: Cambridge University Press.

Bernstein, Mary, and Renate Reimann, eds. 2001. *Queer Families, Queer Politics: Challenging Culture and the State.* New York: Columbia University Press.

Binion, Gayle. 1995. "Human Rights: A Feminist Perspective." *Human Rights Quarterly* 17: 509–526.

Bonnin, Debbie. 1995. "Road to Beijing." *Agenda* 27: 74–77.

Britton, Dana M. 2003. *At Work in the Iron Cage: The Prison as Gendered Organization.* New York: New York University Press.

Brush, Lisa D. 2002. *Gender and Governance.* Lanham, MD: AltaMira Press.

Bunch, Charlotte. 1990. "Women's Rights as Human Rights: Toward a Re-Vision of Human Rights." *Human Rights Quarterly* 12: 486–498.

Bunch, Charlotte, and Susana Fried. 1996. "Beijing '95: Moving Women's Human Rights from Margin to Center." *Signs* 22: 200–204.

Buvinic, Mayra. 1998. "Women in Poverty: A New Global Underclass." Women in Politics. http://www.onlinewomeninpolitics.org/beijing12/womeninpoverty.pdf (accessed April 11, 2011).

Cagatay, Nilufer. 2001. *Trade, Gender, and Poverty.* New York: United Nations Development Program.

Chow, Esther Ngan-ling. 1996. "Making Waves, Moving Mountains: Reflections on Beijing '95 and Beyond." *Signs* 22: 185–192.

Clapham, Andrew. 2007. *Human Rights: A Very Short Introduction.* New York: Oxford University Press.

Collins, Patricia Hill. 1990. *Black Feminist Thought: Knowledge, Consciousness, and the Politics of Empowerment.* New York: Routledge, Chapman and Hall.

_____. 1994. "Shifting the Center: Race, Class, and Feminist Theorizing about Motherhood." In *Representations of Motherhood,* edited by Donna Basin and Margaret Honey, 56–74. New Haven, CT: Yale University Press.

Coltraine, Scott, and Michelle Adams. 2008. *Gender and Families.* Lanham, MD: AltaMira Press.

Connell, Raeyn. 1987. *Gender and Power: Society, the Person, and Sexual Politics.* Stanford, CA: Stanford University Press.

Currah, Paisley, Richard M. Juang, and Shannon Price Minter. 2006. *Transgender Rights.* Minneapolis: University of Minnesota Press.

Doyal, Lesley. 1995. *What Makes Women Sick: Gender and the Political Economy of Health.* London: Macmillan.

———. 2001. "Sex, Gender, and Health: The Need for a New Approach." *British Medical Journal* (November 3): 323–331.

England, Paula. 2005. "Gender Inequality in Labor Markets: The Role of Motherhood and Segregation." *Social Politics* 12: 264–288.

Enloe, Cynthia. 1990. *Bananas, Beaches, and Bases: Making Feminist Sense of International Politics.* Berkeley: University of California Press.

———. 2000. *Maneuvers: The International Politics of Militarizing Women's Lives.* Berkeley: University of California Press.

———. 2007. *Globalization and Militarism: Feminists Make the Link.* Boulder, CO: Rowman & Littlefield.

Ferguson, Kathy E. 1991. "Interpretation and Genealogy in Feminism." *Signs: Journal of Women in Culture and Society* 16: 322–339.

Fox, Mary Frank. 1995. "From the President." *SWS Network News,* 2.

Freeman, Marsha. 1999. "International Institutions and Gendered Justice." *Journal of International Affairs* 52: 513–533.

Fukumura, Yoko, and Martha Matsuoka. 2002. "Redefining Security: Okinawa Women's Resistance to U.S. Militarism." In *Women's Activism and Globalization: Linking Local Struggles and Transnational Politics,* edited by Nancy A. Naples and Manisha Desai, 239–263. New York: Routledge.

Gaer, Felice. 1998. "And Never the Twain Shall Meet? The Struggle to Establish Women's Rights as International Human Rights." In *The International Human Rights of Women: Instruments of Change,* edited by Carol Lockwood et al., 41–69. Washington, DC: American Bar Association Section of International Law and Practice.

Gill, Aisha K., and Anitha Sundari. 2011. *Forced Marriage: Introducing a Social Justice and Human Rights Perspective.* Boston: Zed Books.

Grewal, Inderpal, and Caren Kaplan, eds. 1994. *Scattered Hegemonies: Postmodernity and Transnational Feminist Practices.* Minneapolis: University of Minnesota Press.

———. 2000. "Postcolonial Studies and Transnational Feminist Practices." *Jouvert: A Journal of Postcolonial Studies* 5. http://social.chass.ncsu.edu/jouvert/v5i1/con51.htm (accessed September 6, 2012).

Hafner-Burton, Emilie. 2005. "Right or Robust? The Sensitive Nature of Repression to Globalization." *Journal of Peace Research* 42: 679–698.

Hafner-Burton, Emilie M., and Kiyoteru Tsutsui. 2005. "Human Rights in a Globalizing World: The Paradox of Empty Promises." *American Journal of Sociology* 110: 1373–1411.

Haiken, Elizabeth. 1999. *Venus Envy: A History of Cosmetic Surgery.* Baltimore: Johns Hopkins University Press.

Haney, Lynn. 2000. "Feminist State Theory: Applications to Jurisprudence, Criminology, and the Welfare State." *Annual Review of Sociology* 26: 641–666.

Hesse-Biber, Sharlene Nagy. 2006. *The Cult of Thinness.* New York: Oxford University Press.

Howard, Judith, and Carolyn Allen. 1996. "Reflections on the Fourth World Conference on Women and NGO Forum '95: Introduction." *Signs* 22: 181–185.

Hughs, Alex, and Ann Witz. 1997. "Feminism and the Matter of Bodies: From de Beauvoir to Butler." *Body and Society* 3: 47–60.

Kang, Miliann. 2003. "The Managed Hand: The Commercialization of Bodies and Emotions in Korean Immigrant-Owned Nail Salons." *Gender and Society* 17: 820–839.

Kimmel, Michael S. 2005. *Manhood in America: A Cultural History.* New York: Oxford University Press.

Koven, Seth, and Sonya Michel, eds. 1993. *Mothers of a New World: Maternalist Politics and the Origins of Welfare States.* New York: Routledge.

Lockwood, Elizabeth, Daniel Barstow Magraw, Margaret Faith Spring, and S. I. Strong. 1998. *The International Human Rights of Women: Instruments of Change.* Washington, DC: American Bar Association Section of International Law and Practice.

Loe, Meika. 2006. *The Rise of Viagra: How the Little Blue Pill Changed Sex in America.* New York: New York University Press.

Lorber, Judith. 2002. *Gender and the Construction of Illness.* Lanham, MD: AltaMira Press.

Lorber, Judith, and Lisa Jean Moore. 2007. *Gendered Bodies: Feminist Perspectives.* New York: Oxford.

MacKinnon, Catherine. 1993. "On Torture: A Feminist Perspective on Human Rights." In *Human Rights in the Twenty-First Century: A Global Challenge,* edited by Kathleen E. Mahoney and Paul Mahoney. Boston: Springer Publishing.

Mamo, Laura. 2007. *Queering Reproduction: Achieving Pregnancy in the Age of Technoscience.* Durham, NC: Duke University Press.

McCall, Leslie. 2001. *Complex Inequality: Gender, Class and Race in the New Economy.* New York: Routledge.

_____. 2005. "The Complexity of Intersectionality." *Signs* 30: 1771–1800.

Mendez, Jennifer Bickham. 2005. *From the Revolution to the Maquiladoras: Gender, Labor, and Globalization in Nicaragua.* Durham, NC: Duke University Press.

Merry, Sally Engle. 2006. *Human Rights and Gender Violence: Translating International Law into Local Justice.* Chicago: University of Chicago Press.

Messner, Michael A. 1992. *Power at Play: Sports and the Problem of Masculinity.* Boston: Beacon Press.

Mittelstaedt, Emma. 2008. "Safeguarding the Rights of Sexual Minorities: Incremental and Legal Approaches to Enforcing International Human Rights Obligations." *Chicago Journal of International Law* 9: 353–386.

Mohanty, Chandra Talpade. 2006. *Feminism without Borders: Decolonizing Theory, Practicing Solidarity.* Durham, NC: Duke University Press.

Mohanty, Chandra Talpade, Ann Russo, and Lourdes Torres, eds. 1991. *Third World Women and the Politics of Feminism.* Bloomington: Indiana University Press.

Moser, Annalise. 2007. *Gender and Indicators: Overview Report.* Brighton, UK: Institute of Development Studies.

Naples, Nancy A. 1991, "Socialist Feminist Analysis of the Family Support Act of 1988." *AFFILIA: Journal of Women and Social Work* 6: 23–38.

_____. 1998. *Community Activism and Feminist Politics: Organizing across Race, Gender and Class.* New York: Routledge.

_____. 2009. "Teaching Intersectionality Intersectionally." *International Feminist Journal of Politics* 11: 566–577.

_____. 2011. "Women's Leadership, Social Capital and Social Change." In *Activist Scholar: Selected Works of Marilyn Gittell,* edited by Kathe Newman and Ross Gittell, 263–278. Thousand Oaks, CA: Sage Publications.

Naples, Nancy A., and Manisha Desai. 2002. *Women's Activism and Globalization: Linking Local Struggles and Transnational Politics*. New York: Routledge.

Narayan, Uma. 1997. *Dislocating Cultures: Identities, Traditions, and Third World Feminism*. New York: Routledge.

Okin, Susan Moller. 1989. *Justice, Gender, and the Family*. New York: Basic Books.

Pascoe, C. J. 2007. *Dude, You're a Fag: Masculinity and Sexuality in High School*. Berkeley: University of California Press.

Purdy, Laura. 1989. "Surrogate Mothering: Exploitation or Empowerment?" *Bioethics* 3: 18–34.

Ray, Raka, and A. C. Korteweg. 1999. "Women's Movements in the Third World: Identity, Mobilization, and Autonomy." *Annual Review of Sociology* 25: 47–71.

Reilly, Niamh. 2009. *Women's Human Rights: Seeking Gender Justice in a Globalizing Age*. Cambridge, MA: Polity Press.

Richards, Patricia. 2005. "The Politics of Gender, Human Rights, and Being Indigenous in Chile." *Gender and Society* 19: 199–220.

Rossi, Alice S. 1983. "Beyond the Gender Gap: Women's Bid for Political Power." *Social Science Quarterly* 64: 718–733.

Salzinger, Leslie. 2005. *Genders in Production: Making Workers in Mexico's Global Factories*. Berkeley: University of California Press.

Sanford, Victoria. 2003. *Buried Secrets: Truth and Human Rights in Guatemala*. New York: Palgrave Macmillan.

Sassen, Saskia. 2006a. *Cities in a World Economy*. 3rd ed. Boulder, CO: Pine Forge Press.

_____, ed. 2007. *Deciphering the Global: Its Spaces, Scales and Subjects*. New York: Routledge.

Shakespeare, Tom. 2006. *Disability Rights and Wrongs*. New York: Routledge.

Smith, Dorothy E. 1987. *The Everyday World as Problematic: A Feminist Sociology*. Toronto: University of Toronto Press.

_____. 1990. *Texts, Facts, and Femininity: Exploring the Relations of Ruling*. New York: Routledge.

Spirer, Herbert F. 1990. "Violations of Human Rights: How Many? The Statistical Problems of Measuring Such Infractions Are Tough, but Statistical Science Is Equal to It." *American Journal of Economics and Sociology* 49: 199–210.

Stacey, Judith. 1991. "Can There Be a Feminist Ethnography?" In *Women's Words*, edited by Sherna B. Gluck and Daphne Patai, 111–119. New York: Routledge.

Staudt, Kathleen. 1997. "Gender Politics in Bureaucracy: Theoretical Issues in Comparative Perspective." In *Women, International Development, and Politics*, edited by Kathleen Staudt, 3–36. Philadelphia: Temple University Press.

Sunder, Madhavi. 2003. "Piercing the Veil." *Yale Law Journal* 112: 1401–1472.

Tomasevski, Katerina. 1995. *Women and Human Rights*. London: Zed Books.

Tripp, Aili, and Myra Marx Ferree, eds. 2006. *Global Feminism: Transnational Women's Activism, Organizing, and Human Rights*. New York: New York University Press.

United Nations. 1995. *UN Report of the Fourth World Conference on Women*. New York: United Nations.

United Nations Food and Agriculture Organization (UNFAO). 2010. *Gender Dimensions of Agricultural and Rural Employment: Differential Pathways out of Poverty*. Rome: UNFAO, International Fund for Agricultural Development, and International Labour Office.

Valentine, David. 2007. *Imagining Transgender: An Ethnography of a Category.* Durham, NC: Duke University Press.

Wang, Guang-zhen, and Vijayan K. Pillai. 2001. "Women's Reproductive Health: A Gender-Sensitive Human Rights Approach." *Acta Sociologica* 44, no. 3: 231–242.

Warner-Smith, Penny, Lois Bryson, and Julie Ellen Byles. 2004. "The Big Picture: The Health and Well-Being of Women in Three Generations in Rural and Remote Areas of Australia." *Health Sociology Review* 13, no. 1: 15–26.

Winter, Bronwyn. 2006. "Religion, Culture, and Women's Human Rights: Some General and Theoretical Considerations." *Women's Studies International Forum* 29, no. 4: 381–394.

Witz, Ann. 2000. "Whose Body Matters? Feminist Sociology and the Corporeal Turn in Sociology and Feminism." *Body and Society* 6, no. 2: 1–24.

Wolf, Diane L., ed. 1996. *Feminist Dilemmas in Fieldwork.* Boulder, CO: Westview.

Women's Refugee Commission. 2011. *The Living Ain't Easy: Urban Refugees in Kampala.* New York: Women's Refugee Commission.

World Health Organization (WHO). 2000. *Maternal Mortality in 2000: Estimates Developed by WHO, UNICEF, and UNFPA.* Relief Web. http://www.reliefweb.int/library/documents/2003/who-saf-22oct.pdf (accessed January 20, 2012).

_____. 2010. *Global Strategies for Women's and Children's Health.* New York: Partnership for Maternal, Newborn, and Child Health.

Wotipka, Christine Min, and Kiyoteru Tsutsui. 2008. "Global Human Rights and State Sovereignty: State Ratification of International Human Rights Treaties 1965–2001." *Sociological Forum* 23, no. 4: 724–754.

Yuval-Davis, N. 2006a. "Intersectionality and Feminist Politics." *European Journal of Women's Studies* 13, no. 3: 193–209.

_____. 2006b. "Women, Citizenship and Difference." *Feminist Review* 57: 4–27.

Zheng, Tiantian. 2010. *Sex Trafficking, Human Rights, and Social Justice.* New York: Routledge.

Zitzelsberger, Hilde. 2005. "(In)visibility: Accounts of Embodiment of Women in Physical Disabilities and Differences." *Disability and Society* 20, no. 4: 389–403.

Sexualities

Mary Bernstein

T his chapter addresses two themes in the sociology of sexualities that are relevant to the study of human rights. First, the sociology of sexualities challenges the assumption that sexuality is "essentialist," a property of individuals, something that has its own truth and exists outside social forces, that is somehow presocial and biologically driven or perhaps divinely ordained. In contrast, sexuality is socially constructed. As Gayle Rubin explains, "Desires are not preexisting biological entities, but rather ... they are constituted in the course of historically specific social practices" (1984, 276). Second, sociologists of sexualities theorize the ways in which sexuality serves as an axis of domination and is part of every major social institution. As a result of studying how sexuality both influences and is influenced by major institutions, theorists reconceptualize the concept of power to understand how culture and discourse are constitutive of dominant institutions and produce new forms of knowledge and power that organize and regulate sexuality and provide sites of resistance. Thus, how we understand sexuality, what we define as normal or abnormal, and the types of sexual identities that exist in a given society are influenced by culture and discourse, institutions, and power. Understanding sexuality as an axis of domination and a site of resistance thus expands our study of human rights struggles.

The Sociology of Sexualities

Challenging Essentialism: The Body, Gender, and Sexuality

Sociologists of sexualities challenge essentialism by illustrating that our very understandings of what constitutes male and female bodies are socially constructed. Notions of what bodies should look like and the extent to which they should experience pleasure are used to justify regulating and disciplining them. Scholars also find that gender and age structure expectations about what is appropriate sexual activity.

The Body

Control over appropriate sexuality is linked to what Ponse termed "the principle of consistency" (1978)—that is, a view that biological sex (genes, genitals, hormones, secondary sex characteristics) is linked to gender (masculinity or femininity) and sexual orientation (whether one is attracted to men or women) in a straightforward manner, so that one is biologically male, masculine, and attracted to women or female, feminine, and attracted to men. Yet, in practice, these do not always align easily, as in the case of gay men, lesbians, bisexuals, and transgender people. Furthermore, control over this alignment starts from birth with the policing of genitals. In the early twentieth century, male circumcision was seen as a way to reduce the male sexual drive. Yet others see circumcision as a means to enhance, rather than reduce, male sexual pleasure (Ross 2009). Jewish rites of male circumcision are tied to men's covenant with god—a patriarchal rite from which women are excluded (Kimmel 2001). In short, views of appropriate genitals for men are bound to views of masculinity, male sexuality, and whether or not sexual pleasure is viewed as problematic, in need of reining in, or in need of enhancement.

Intersexed people who have "ambiguous genitals" are regulated as infants through surgical procedures designed to make their genitals appear to be either male or female (often accompanied later by hormonal treatment). Rather than chromosomes, whether or not a penis is big enough for sexual intercourse determines whether the child is surgically altered. Parents are instructed to socialize their child into the gender that matches the surgically altered genitals. Thus, appropriate views of sexuality and gender are used to justify medically unnecessary surgery on infants in order to support society's sex/gender system (Fausto-Sterling 2000a; Kessler 1990; Preeves 2003).

The desire to control adult sexuality and police gender is also apparent in cultures that practice female genital mutilation. These cultures place a strong value on virginity at marriage and do not believe in a woman's right to sexual agency or sexual pleasure. Thus, with removal of the clitoris and, in some places, the practice of infibulation, girls' bodies are irrevocably altered in ways that ensure they remain virgins and cannot enjoy sexual pleasure as adults (Hosken 1993). While debates over men's bodies concern enhancing male pleasure and sometimes reducing (but never eliminating) it, the assumption is that men will and should enjoy sexuality. Groups simply differ on how best to achieve this goal.

Whereas intersex infants are subjected to surgery without their consent, transgender people who wish to transition surgically are only allowed to do so after receiving a mental-illness diagnosis of gender identity disorder. Although this diagnosis, which is influential globally (GID Reform Advocates 2008), is useful for those whose insurance will pay for hormones and sex-reassignment surgery, others argue that the diagnosis contributes to societal stigma and harms the quest for legal rights and protection. Some transgender activists argue for reform of the diagnosis, facilitating access to surgery and hormones. Others avoid the issue of insurance coverage, advocating removal of the diagnosis coupled with acceptance of "genderqueer" individuals whose gender and physical body may not line up (Burke 2010).

Gender

Gendered expectations about sexuality result in a double standard for sexual behavior. Studies of US teenagers illustrate that girls' reputations suffer more damage than boys' due to their having sex and that girls are more likely to be condemned and considered "easy" for carrying a condom than boys are (Hynie and Lydon 1995; Levine 2002; Vanwesenbeeck 1997). In Mexico, González-López (2005) finds that a young woman's virginity provides her with a "capital feminino" that can be exchanged for social status for the family. Research in the United States also finds gendered differences in negotiations around sex. Boys initiate sex far more often than girls. As a result, the responsibility for saying no to sex falls disproportionately on girls. Beneke (1983) argues that this pattern of behavior, where boys are responsible for initiating sex and escalating sexual encounters, results in the development of a rape-like mentality among boys and men, so that boys learn not to listen when girls say no. Both boys and girls believe that a girl risks the loss of her relationship if she refuses to have sex with her boyfriend (Gavey, McPhillips, and Doherty 2001). In addition, boys are far less likely to raise the issue of safer sex than girls are (Holland et al. 1998; Kaiser Family Foundation 2002).

In explaining gendered differences in sexuality, sociologists challenge essentialist explanations. Essentialist models drawing on hormonal studies, brain studies, and sociobiology are methodologically flawed (Schwartz and Rutter 1998; Fausto-Sterling 2000b). Essentialist arguments also make analogies from animal behavior to explain human behavior such as violence, rape, and male dominance. But animals engage in a wide variety of sexual and social behavior, including homosexual behavior, anal and oral sex, and promiscuous sex (Bagemihl 2000), making it problematic to infer what does or does not constitute "normal" sexual behavior in humans. Furthermore, human behavior is based more on learning than on instinct, casting doubt on such analogies.

Instead, sociologists of sexualities posit a combination of factors to account for gender differences in sexuality. For example, fewer women masturbate than men because of the cultural messages they get about what is appropriate sexually for women. As a result, they may not know their bodies. Even for women who know what pleases them sexually, communication between partners may be poor, leading to less satisfaction for women (Schwartz and Rutter 1998). The sexual double standard inhibits women from developing their full sexual potential.

Socioeconomic conditions and rural/urban differences also explain sexualized gender inequality (González-López 2005).

Sexualities scholars also study heterosexuality as a social institution that has its own rules and norms that pattern behavior. Heterosexuality as an institution disadvantages heterosexual women, lesbians, and gay men. Ingraham (2008) argues that a romanticized view of heterosexuality symbolized by the big white wedding masks the gendered inequality that takes place within marriage. Others contend that heterosexuality is not only an institution but compulsory. Rich's (1980) concept of compulsory heterosexuality illustrates the ways in which men control female sexuality through physical force, economic inequality, punishment for lesbian sexuality, strictures against masturbation, and stronger punishments for female adultery than for male adultery, which makes women more financially dependent on men, leading women to marry for physical and financial protection (Eisenstein 1983).

Sexuality as an Axis of Domination

Sexualities scholars study the ways in which sexuality is entwined with larger systems of domination. In this section, I examine heteronormativity—that is, "the institutions, structures of understanding and practical orientations that make heterosexuality seem not only coherent—that is, organized as a sexuality—but also privileged" (Berlant and Warner 1998, 548)—through a discussion of sexual orientation, sex education, sexual health, and sex work. I also discuss how colonialism and racial and ethnic inequality are justified through understandings of appropriate (hetero)sexuality and gender.

Sexual Orientation

Psychologists dominate the study of homophobia (Adam 1998), defining it as an irrational fear of lesbians and gay men. These studies find that those who are older, less educated, single, or male tend to be more homophobic than those who are younger, more educated, married, or female (Britton 1990; Yang 1998). The few studies that examine race suggest that African Americans are more homophobic than white Americans (Herek and Capitanio 1996), though that may be related to higher levels of religiosity among African Americans (Egan and Sherrill 2009). Bernstein, Kostelac, and Gaarder (2003) find that African Americans are typically more supportive of civil liberties for lesbians and gay men than are white Americans. Explanations for these relationships stress that lesbians and gay men may threaten one's psychological sense of self in terms of sexuality, masculinity, and group identity. These approaches also stress the importance of contact with lesbians and gay men as a factor that minimizes prejudice and maximizes intergroup cooperation (Herek and Glunt 1993; Jordan 1997; Yang 1998).

Recent sociological approaches (Bernstein and Kostelac 2002; Bernstein, Kostelac, and Gaarder 2003; Bernstein 2004) pay closer attention to the interplay between the social construction of minorities and the role that organized groups play in fostering those constructions. Gay-rights opponents express status concerns when faced with lesbian and gay demands for equality. Dynamic interactions between diverse groups that have a stake in maintaining homophobia influence a group's sense of its proper position. From the group-position perspective, certain religions and social movements based on particular religious interpretations may indicate a commitment to group status based on self-interest as much as on psychological factors.

Sexuality scholars also examine the ways in which LGBT people of color may experience "secondary marginalization" (Cohen 1999) within the broader LGBT movement as well as within communities of color (Bennett and Battle 2001; Takagi 1994). This research is particularly important in examining the complex ways in which race, class, culture, and sexual identity influence the experience of sexuality, negotiations around sexuality, and family relations (Bernstein and Reimann 2001; Asencio 2009; Battle 2009).

Sexuality scholars also debate whether social movement strategies, identities, and goals challenge or support heteronormativity. For example, scholars question the value of the institution of marriage and debate the wisdom of pursuing same-sex marriage as a goal of the LGBT movement (Walters 2001; Warner 2000). For lesbian and gay rights activists, extending the right to marry to same-sex couples would simply give them the same rights and legitimacy as different-sex couples. In contrast, queer activists view extending the right to marry to same-sex couples as expanding current conceptions of what is normal to include same-sex married couples. Marriage equality would not ultimately challenge the very notions of normality that define LGBT people as other and would offer no support to people with nonnormative family structures.

Historical research on the emergence of the categories "lesbian," "gay," and "bisexual" finds that these categories, which are supposed to represent fixed sexual identities, are historically and culturally specific ways of organizing erotic desire and behavior. Even defining people in terms of sexual identity is a recent phenomenon (Katz 2007; Foucault 1978). Research on non-Western cultures finds that there are multiple ways of organizing same-sex desire and gender/transgender behavior. For example, sexual relations may be differentiated by biological sex, gender, and age (Herdt 1994, 1997; Drucker 2000). Western sexual and gender categories cannot be mapped onto non-Western configurations, such as the *aravani* or *hijras* of India (Herdt 1994; Waites 2009) or the *nahdle* of the Navajo/Dine culture, who are considered to belong to a third gender.

Studies of LGBT movements in the developing world show that homosexuality is often constructed as "Western," something that is not indigenous but is instead a colonial imposition (Adam, Duyvendak, and Krouwel 1999). These arguments are used as a way to deny basic human rights protection for intimate sexual behavior and other rights based on sexual orientation and point to the significance of discourse, culture, and colonialism for explaining inequality based on sexual orientation.

Sex Education and Sexual Health

In the United States, heteronormativity structures contemporary sex-education programs and research on sexual health. Rather than addressing how to empower women within sexual relations, research on sexual health and behavior focuses on sexuality as a social problem. As a result, such research centers on explaining what contributes to unwed motherhood, sexually transmitted infections (STIs), and adolescent sexuality with its presumed negative consequences, such as pregnancy, disease, and poor mental health. This is also reflected in battles over sex education (Irvine 2002; Luker 2006).

The United States has supported abstinence-only sex education since 1981. According to SIECUS (2010), "Moreover, many abstinence-only-until-marriage programs rely on fear, shame, and guilt to try to control young people's sexual behavior. These programs include negative messages about sexuality, distort information about condoms and STDs, and promote biases based on gender, sexual orientation, marriage, family structure, and pregnancy options." Sexualities research has shown consistently that abstinence-only education is ineffective in changing rates of vaginal intercourse or number of sexual partners (Underhill, Montgomery, and Operario 2007). In contrast, comprehensive sex-education programs present information on methods of birth control and discuss STIs, but these programs nonetheless present sexuality in terms of fear of pregnancy and risk of diseases. Ignored are discussions of how to empower girls around sexuality to say both no and yes. In other words, even comprehensive sex education fails to acknowledge that sexuality can be pleasurable, operating instead from the perspective of risk and fear. More recent work has focused on understanding "sexual subjectivity" (Horne and Zimmer-Gembeck 2005)—that is, on girls and women as sexual agents who can experience entitlement to sexual desire and pleasure (Tolman 1994; Martin 1996). In 2010, the United States dedicated money for comprehensive sexuality education. States may also choose to apply for funding for abstinence-only-until-marriage programs (SIECUS 2010).

The Sex Industry

Debates over the sex industry generally rest on the view that sex workers are either victims of male domination or are romanticized as the "happy hooker" (Weitzer 2000). Sociologists contend that neither view is correct. Instead, scholars examine the extent to which sex workers have agency in constructing their lives and work choices. By viewing sex work as an occupation, one can examine differences in terms of social status (e.g., street versus indoor prostitution), control over working conditions (e.g., the ability to choose or refuse clients, access to resources for safety and protection, independence or dependence on managers or pimps, and the ability to leave sex work), and experiences at work (prevalence of rape and assault and the risk of STIs) (Weitzer 2000). While some women may have more control over their working conditions in the sex industry, others may have no control, as in women who are victims of "sex trafficking," "a modern-day form of slavery in which a commercial sex act is induced by force, fraud, or coercion, or in which the person induced to perform such an act is under the age of 18 years" (US Department of Health and Human Services 2010).

Race, Ethnicity, and Sexuality

Sociologists of sexualities argue that sexuality is intimately linked to racialized systems of domination. For example, cross dressing and homosexual relations were commonplace among many indigenous peoples in the Americas (Terl 2000). European colonizers exported their views on such practices to the Americas as they worked to eradicate sodomy among indigenous people through terror and extermination. Viewed as an offense to their Christian god, the colonizers embarked on a campaign of mass destruction and appropriation of Native land, carried out partially in the name of abolishing sin (Fone 2000).

Slavery in the United States depended on sexualized and racialized stereotypes that provided whites with a convenient means of justifying exploitation. For example, stereotypes that Africans were overly sexual provided white slaveholders with a way to justify the rape of black women. Not only did this constitute sexual exploitation, but the children born of these rapes were considered slaves, thus providing an economic benefit to the slaveholder. This became particularly important economically after the transatlantic slave trade was abolished and reproduction became the only way to produce new slaves. Other racialized sexual stereotypes served to keep African and African American men in line. Viewing African and African American men as overly sexual and predatory justified lynching black men who even looked at a white woman or were simply accused of doing so. These stereotypes also served to keep white women afraid and dependent on white men for protection (Dowd 1993). Collins describes a series of sexual stereotypes of black women rooted in slavery that have "been essential to the political economy of domination fostering Black women's oppression" (2000, 67). Other sexual stereotypes linked to ethnicity are an integral part of nationalist discourse, colonization, sex tourism, and globalization (Nagel 2003).

Scholars of sexuality find that sexuality is linked to immigration. For example, Cantú (2009) examines why Mexican men who have sex with men (MSM) immigrate to the United States. Most research on immigration assumes that people immigrate for financial reasons but ignores the ways in which socioeconomic structures are linked to inequalities like sexuality, race, and gender. Men who have sex with men are marginalized and suffer discrimination and prejudice, which constrains their socioeconomic opportunities. MSMs who do not create a heteronormative family unit as an adult are subject to more discrimination. And thus, for some MSMs, sexuality contributes to a lack of financial opportunities, which pushes them to immigrate.

Studying Sexualities

The early study of sexualities was dominated by psychiatrists using the case-study approach, which was limited by not having control groups of people in nonclinical settings. Alfred Kinsey was the first researcher to conduct sexuality research on a large scale. However, his study did not employ random sampling techniques, likely skewing his findings (Kinsey, Pomeroy, and Martin 1948). In the mid-1950s, William Masters and Virginia Johnson conducted a major study of sexual physiology to measure exactly what human bodies do during sexual encounters. However, they limited their study to volunteers who were orgasmic and had experience masturbating and ignored the meaning of sexuality to the participants. The result is that sexual dysfunction, including diagnosis in the American Psychiatric Association's *Diagnostic and Statistical Manual of Mental Disorders,* is related to the failure of body parts to work appropriately. This has led to a view of sexuality that is not representative of female experience and ignores emotional attachment, which far more women than men define as key to their sexual satisfaction (Tiefer 2004).

Laumann et al. (2000) launched the National Health and Social Life (NHSL) Survey in the 1990s using a national random sample of adults and face-to-face interviews. Their study found Americans to be rather conservative in terms of sex. However, the accuracy of these findings has been questioned, based on the idea that respondents may "lie, or fudge, or mis-remember, or leave things out" and the fact that the study was done at a point in the AIDS scare where people were afraid that sex with the wrong partner could kill them (Adelson 2001, 63).

Large-scale, quantitative sociological research on adolescent sexuality emerged in a conservative context with public concern over teen pregnancy, the spread of STIs, and the reproduction of those deemed "undeserving," namely, the poor, immigrants, and racial minorities. For example, early incarnations of the National Longitudinal Study of Adolescent Health (Add Health) assumed that race and class differences, as well as biological factors such as hormones, accounted for differences in sexuality. Recent versions of Add Health focus on explaining teen sexual activity by looking at the impact of peers, family, religion, community, and schools (Cavanagh 2007; Wilkinson and Pearson 2009; Harding 2007; Bearman and Bruckner 2001). While important, these studies lack attention to the meaning of sexual activity and assume a framework of sexuality as harm. Some recent quantitative work, in contrast, has examined positive effects of sexuality as well as what contributes to female sexual empowerment (Horne and Zimmer-Gembeck 2005).

Sexuality research is difficult to fund, and it is always political (DiMauro 1995; Ericksen and Steffen 2001). The US government has canceled funding for many sexuality studies, including the NHSL survey, which was ultimately funded by private donors. There is a fear that simply asking people about sexual behavior or reporting on what others do will lead them to engage in those sexual acts and that findings will challenge some people's moral and religious views (Adelson 2001).

Qualitative research on sexuality typically focuses on the meaning of sexual activity, sexual development, and experience (Diamond 2006). Ethnography, indepth interviews, discourse, and content analysis are also important staples of sexuality scholarship. These methods provide insight into the symbolic meaning that sexual activity may hold for respondents and may uncover new sexual scripts (Bogle 2008) that develop in response to broader demographic and cultural trends. Many of these works question the universality of the categories that are used in the contemporary West to define gender and sexual orientation (Valentine 2007; Katz 2007). One of the most important implications of this work is that care must be paid when utilizing the categories "sexual orientation" and "gender identity" in international human rights advocacy and law.

What Can the Human Rights Paradigm Learn from the Study of Sexualities?

Sexualities research illustrates that the categories used to describe sexual orientation (gay, lesbian, and bisexual) and gender (male, female, transgender, gender identity) in the West are socially constructed. Scholars also illustrate that sexuality can be understood as fluid rather than fixed. While same-sex erotic behavior and attraction exist in every culture across time, how they are organized and whether they are used to define categories of persons is historically contingent (Rupp 2009; Greenberg 1988). Similarly, many cultures have had ways of instituting transgender behavior that differs from Western models (Kulick 1998). Therefore, human rights scholars and activists can work to identify indigenous forms of same-sex erotic behavior in order to sever the link that conservatives often make between "being gay" and the imperialism and excesses of Western bourgeois culture. As Waites (2009) points out, we must have a language to use, but care must be taken to ensure that "sexual orientation" and "gender identity" are understood in diverse ways.

Human rights activists have created a list of principles designed to protect people on the basis of sexual orientation and gender identity. The Yogyakarta Principles also outline the deleterious consequences that people suffer because of their sexual orientation or gender identity: "They include extra-judicial killings, torture and ill-treatment, sexual assault and rape, invasions of privacy, arbitrary detention, denial of employment and education opportunities, and serious discrimination in relation to the enjoyment of other human rights" (Corrêa and Muntarbhorn 2007, 6).

The sociology of sexualities also shows how practices such as female genital mutilation and surgery on intersexed children are rooted in views about appropriate genitals, bodily integrity, and sexual fulfillment. Surgeries on intersexed children and female genital mutilation often impair later sexual functioning, can curtail the ability to experience sexual pleasure, and can result in other health complications. Human rights groups opposed to male circumcision, female genital mutilation, and surgery on intersexed infants argue for children's rights to bodily integrity and to be free from unnecessary medical procedures.

Studies of sexual negotiations and sex education point human rights scholars toward understanding that strategies for preventing unwanted pregnancy and reducing the spread of STIs and HIV are linked not only to providing access to condoms, birth control, and education about safer sex but to women's becoming empowered in sexual encounters. If girls and women continue to be charged with saying no in sexual encounters, then old sexual scripts that perpetuate male dominance will linger.

The push for same-sex marriage and parental rights shows the importance of equality for those who want to enter into the institution of marriage, but the debate has also shown that the traditional family structure is not the only one deserving of state support. Human rights scholars and activists must push for recognition of a variety of family forms and policies that support the economic, emotional, and caretaking needs of all people.

What Happens When We Center the Human Rights Paradigm on Sexualities Research?

Centering the human rights paradigm pushes the sexual health literature away from focusing on models of disease and pregnancy prevention to ask more questions about sexual empowerment and control and how that is linked to basic issues of human rights and dignity. A human rights perspective should help sexuality scholars focus on how eliminating economic disparities between men and women will facilitate greater equality of power in negotiating sexual encounters.

Sociologists of sexualities need to incorporate a more global perspective on sexualities and incorporate human rights perspectives into their research. While it is important to be aware of how the goals of the LGBT movement may reinforce heteronormativity, as in the case of same-sex marriage, or reinstantiate the closet, as in the case of decriminalizing homosexuality based on a right to privacy, scholars must be aware that, according to the International Lesbian and Gay Human Rights Commission, "over 80 countries currently have sodomy laws or other legal provisions criminalizing homosexuality" (IGLHRC 2011). In such contexts, challenging heteronormativity may be neither desirable nor realistic. Obtaining basic human rights protections may be paramount.

In other ways, many sexualities scholars have already begun to link issues of sexual rights to the broader project of seeking fundamental human dignity. All too often, those who advocate rights for sex workers and those who advocate the abolition of sex work are speaking past each other, not acknowledging the variation that exists in the experience of sex workers. Chapkis (2000) offers a middle position, arguing that the best way to help women in the sex industry is by giving all women greater economic opportunities to do other types of work and by working to ensure that those who choose to be in the sex industry have control over their working conditions. So rather than take an abolitionist approach, human rights activists should work to improve conditions for all sex workers, eliminate forced sexual slavery, and increase economic opportunities for women and those who are transgendered, many of whom only turn to sex work as a means of survival. Sexuality scholars can also do much to link broader patterns of militarization to the sexual exploitation of women and global economic inequality that fosters sex tourism.

References

Adam, Barry D. 1998. "Theorizing Homophobia." *Sexualities* 1: 387–404.

Adam, Barry D., Dan Willem Duyvendak, and André Krouwel. 1999. *The Global Emergence of Gay and Lesbian Politics: National Imprints of a Worldwide Movement.* Philadelphia: Temple University Press.

Adelson, Joseph. 2001. "Sex among the Americans." In *Speaking of Sexuality: Interdisciplinary Readings,* edited by J. Kenneth Davidson Sr. and Nelwyn B. Moore, 57–63. Los Angeles: Roxbury Publishing.

Asencio, Marysol. 2009. *Latina/o Sexualities: Probing Powers, Passions, Practices, and Policies.* New Brunswick, NJ: Rutgers University Press.

Bagemihl, Bruce. 2000. *Biological Exuberance: Animal Homosexuality and Natural Diversity.* New York: St. Martin's Press.

Battle, Juan. 2009. *Black Sexualities: Probing Powers, Passions, Practices, and Policies.* New Brunswick, NJ: Rutgers University Press.

Bearman, Peter S., and Hannah Bruckner. 2001. "Promising the Future: Virginity Pledges and First Intercourse." *American Journal of Sociology* 106: 859–912.

Beneke, Timothy. 1983. *Men on Rape: What They Have to Say about Sexual Violence.* New York: St. Martin's Press.

Bennett, Michael, and Juan Battle. 2001. "'We Can See Them, but We Can't Hear Them': LGBT Members of African American Families." In *Queer Families, Queer Politics: Challenging Culture and the State,* edited by Mary Bernstein and Renate Reimann, 53–67. New York: Columbia University Press.

Berlant, Lauren, and Michael Warner. 1998. "Sex in Public." *Critical Inquiry* 24: 547–566.

Bernstein, Mary. 2004. "Paths to Homophobia." *Sexuality Research and Social Policy* 1: 41–55.

Bernstein, Mary, and Constance Kostelac. 2002. "Lavender and Blue: Attitudes about Homosexuality and Behavior toward Lesbians and Gay Men among Police Officers." *Journal of Contemporary Criminal Justice* 18: 302–328.

Bernstein, Mary, Constance Kostelac, and Emily Gaarder. 2003. "Understanding 'Heterosexism': Applying Theories of Racial Prejudice to Homophobia Using Data from a Southwestern Police Department." *Race, Gender and Class* 10: 54–74.

Bernstein, Mary, and Renate Reimann, eds. 2001. *Queer Families, Queer Politics: Challenging Culture and the State.* New York: Columbia University Press.

Bogle, Kathleen. 2008. *Hooking Up: Sex, Dating, and Relationships on Campus.* New York: New York University Press.

Britton, Dana M. 2003. *At Work in the Iron Cage: The Prison as Gendered Organization.* New York: New York University Press.

Burke, Mary C. 2010. "Transforming Gender: Medicine, Body Politics, and the Transgender Rights Movement." PhD diss., University of Connecticut, Storrs.

Cavanagh, Shannon E. 2007. "The Social Construction of Romantic Relationships in Adolescence: Examining the Role of Peer Networks, Gender, and Race." *Sociological Inquiry* 77: 572–600.

Chapkis, Wendy. 2000. "Power and Control in the Commercial Sex Trade." In *Sex for Sale: Prostitution, Pornography, and the Sex Industry,* edited by Ronald Weitzer, 181–202. New York: Routledge.

Cohen, Cathy. 1999. *The Boundaries of Blackness: AIDS and the Breakdown of Black Politics.* Chicago: University of Chicago Press.

Collins, Patricia Hill. 1990. *Black Feminist Thought: Knowledge, Consciousness, and the Politics of Empowerment.* New York: Routledge, Chapman and Hall.

_____. 1993. "Toward a New Vision: Race, Class, and Gender as Categories of Analysis and Connection." *Race, Sex and Class* 1: 25–45.

_____. 1994. "Shifting the Center: Race, Class, and Feminist Theorizing about Motherhood." In *Representations of Motherhood,* edited by Donna Basin and Margaret Honey, 56–74. New Haven, CT: Yale University Press.

Corrêa, S., and V. Muntarbhorn. 2007. "The Yogyakarta Principles on the Application of International Human Rights Law in Relation to Sexual Orientation and Gender Identity." The Yogyakarta Principles. http://www.yogyakartaprinciples.org/principles_en.htm (accessed July 21, 2010).

Diamond, Lisa. 2006. "Careful What You Ask For: Reconsidering Feminist Epistemology and Autobiographical Narrative in Research on Sexual Identity Development." *Signs* 31: 471–491.

DiMauro, Diane. 1995. *Sexuality Research in the United States: An Assessment of the Social and Behavioral Sciences*. New York: Social Sciences Research Council.

Dowd, Jacquelyn Hall. 1993. *Revolt against Chivalry*. New York: Columbia University Press.

Drucker, Peter. 2000. *Different Rainbows*. London: Gay Men's Press.

Egan, Patrick J., and Kenneth Sherrill. 2009. *California's Proposition 8: What Happened, and What Does the Future Hold?* San Francisco: Evelyn and Walter Haas Jr. Fund and the National Gay and Lesbian Task Force Policy Institute.

Eisenstein, Hester. 1983. *Contemporary Feminist Thought*. Boston: G. K. Hall.

Ericksen, Julia A., with Sally A. Steffen. 2001. *Kiss and Tell: Surveying Sex in the Twentieth Century*. Cambridge, MA: Harvard University Press.

Fausto-Sterling, Anne. 2000a. "The Five Sexes Revisited." *Sciences* 40: 18–23.

_____. 2000b. *Sexing the Body: Gender Politics and the Construction of Sexuality*. New York: Basic Books.

Fone, Byrne. 2000. *Homophobia: A History*. New York: Metropolitan Books.

Foucault, Michel. 1978. *The History of Sexuality: An Introduction*. Vol. 1. New York: Vintage Books.

Gavey, N., K. McPhillips, and M. Doherty. 2001. "'If It's Not On, It's Not On'—or Is It? Discursive Constraints on Women's Condom Use." *Gender and Society* 15: 917–934.

GID Reform Advocates. 2008. "GID Reform Advocates." Transgender Forum. http://www.transgender.org/gird (accessed November 11, 2011).

González-López, Gloria. 2005. *Erotic Journeys: Mexican Immigrants and Their Sex Lives*. Berkeley: University of California Press.

Greenberg, David F. 1988. *The Construction of Homosexuality*. Chicago: University of Chicago Press.

Harding, David J. 2007. "Cultural Context, Sexual Behavior, and Romantic Relationships in Disadvantage." *American Sociological Review* 72: 341–364.

Herdt, Gilbert. 1994. *Third Sex, Third Gender*. New York: Zone Books.

_____. 1997. *Same Sex, Different Cultures: Exploring Gay and Lesbian Lives*. Oxford: Westview.

Herek, Gregory M., and John P. Capitanio. 1996. "'Some of My Best Friends': Intergroup Contact, Concealable Stigma, and Heterosexuals' Attitudes toward Gay Men and Lesbians." *Personality and Social Psychology Bulletin* 22: 412–424.

Herek, Gregory M., and Eric K. Glunt. 1993. "Interpersonal Contact and Heterosexuals' Attitudes toward Gay Men: Results from a National Survey." *Journal of Sex Research* 30: 239–244.

Holland, J., C. Ramazanoglu, S. Sharpe, and R. Thomson. 1998. *The Male in the Head: Young People, Heterosexuality and Power*. London: The Tufnell.

Horne, Sharon, and Melanie J. Zimmer-Gembeck. 2005. "Female Sexual Subjectivity and Well-Being: Comparing Late Adolescents with Different Sexual Experiences." *Sexuality Research and Social Policy* 2: 25–40.

Hosken, Fran P. 1993. *The Hosken Report: Genital and Sexual Mutilation of Females*. 4th ed. Lexington, MA: Women's International Network News.

Hynie, M., and J. E. Lydon. 1995. "Women's Perceptions of Female Contraceptive Behavior: Experimental Evidence of the Sexual Double Standard." *Psychology of Women Quarterly* 19: 563–581.

Ingraham, Chrys. 2008. *White Weddings: Romancing Hetersexuality in Popular Culture*. New York: Routledge.

International Gay and Lesbian Human Rights Commission (IGLHRC). 2011. "Our Issues." IGLHRC. http://www .iglhrc.org/cgi-bin/iowa/theme/1.html (accessed November 11, 2011).

Irvine, Janice M. 2002. *Talk about Sex: The Battles over Sex Education in the United States*. Berkeley: University of California Press.

Jordan, Kathleen Casey. 1997. "The Effect of Disclosure on the Professional Life of Lesbian Police Officers." PhD diss., City University of New York.

Kaiser Family Foundation. 2002. *Sex Smarts Survey: Gender Roles*. Menlo Park, CA: Kaiser Family Foundation.

Katz, Jonathan. 2007. *The Invention of Heterosexuality*. Chicago: University of Chicago Press.

Kessler, Suzanne J. 1990. *Lessons from the Intersexed*. New Brunswick, NJ: Rutgers University Press.

Kimmel, Michael S. 2001. "The Kindest Un-Cut: Feminism, Judaism, and My Son's Foreskin." *Tikkun* 16, no. 1. http://www.cirp.org/pages/cultural/kimmel1/ (accessed September 6, 2012).

Kinsey, Alfred, Wardell B. Pomeroy, and Clyde E. Martin. 1948. *Sexual Behavior in the Human Male*. Philadelphia: W. B. Saunders Company.

Kulick, Don. 1998. *Travesti: Sex, Gender, and Culture among Brazilian Transgendered Prostitutes*. Chicago: University of Chicago Press.

Laumann, Edward O., John H. Gagnon, Robert T. Michael, and Stuart Michaels. 2000. *The Social Organization of Sexuality: Sexual Practices in the United States*.

Levine, J. 2002. *Harmful to Minors: The Perils of Protecting Children from Sex*. Minneapolis: University of Minnesota Press.

Luker, Kristin. 2006. *When Sex Goes to School: Warring Views on Sex and Sex Education since the Sixties*. New York: W. W. Norton.

Martin, Karin A. 1996. *Puberty, Sexuality, and the Self: Boys and Girls at Adolescence*. New York: Routledge.

Nagel, Joane. 2003. *Race, Ethnicity, and Sexuality: Intimate Intersections, Forbidden Frontiers*. New York: Oxford University Press.

Ponse, Barbara. 1978. *Identities in the Lesbian World: The Social Construction of Self*. Westport, CT: Greenwood Press.

Preeves, Sharon E. 2003. *Intersex and Identity: The Contested Self*. New Brunswick, NJ: Rutgers University Press.

Rich, Adrienne. 1980. "Compulsory Heterosexuality." In *Powers of Desire: The Politics of Sexuality*, edited by Ann Snitow, Christine Stansell, and Sharon Thompson, 177–205. New York: Monthly Review Press.

Ross, Lauren. 2009. "Contradictions of Power, Sexuality, and Consent: An Institutional Ethnography of the Practice of Male Neonatal Circumcision." PhD diss., University of Connecticut, Storrs.

Rubin, Gayle. 1984. "Thinking Sex: Notes for a Radical Theory of the Politics of Sexuality." In *Pleasure and Danger: Exploring Female Sexuality*, edited by Carol Vance, 267–319. London: Pandora Press.

Rupp, Leila J. 2009. *Sapphistries: A Global History of Love between Women*. New York: New York University Press.

Schwartz, Pepper, and Virginia Rutter. 1998. *The Gender of Sexuality*. Lanham, MD: AltaMira Press.

SIECUS. 2010. "Fact Sheet: State by State Decisions: The Personal Responsibility Education Program and Title V Abstinence-Only Program." http://www.siecus.org/index.cfm?fuseaction=Page.ViewPage&PageID=1272 (accessed September 5, 2012).

Takagi, Dana. 1994. "Maiden Voyage: Excursion into Sexuality and Identity Politics in Asian America." *Amerasia Journal* 20, no. 1: 1–17.

Terl, Allan H. 2000. "An Essay on the History of Lesbian and Gay Rights in Florida." *Nova Law Review* 24 (spring): 793–853.

Tiefer, Lenore. 2004. *Sex Is Not a Natural Act and Other Essays.* Boulder, CO: Westview Press.

Tolman, Deborah L. 1994. "Doing Desire: Adolescent Girls' Struggles for/with Sexuality." *Gender and Society* 8, no. 3: 324–342.

Underhill, Kristen, Paul Montgomery, and Don Operario. 2007. "Systematic Review of Abstinence-Only Programmes Aiming to Prevent HIV Infection in High-Income Countries." *British Medical Journal* 335: 248.

United States Department of Health and Human Services. 2010. "Fact Sheet: Sex Trafficking." Administration for Children and Families. http://www.acf.hhs.gov/trafficking/about/fact_sex.html (accessed December 21, 2010).

Valentine, David. 2007. *Imagining Transgender: An Ethnography of a Category.* Durham, NC: Duke University Press.

Vanwesenbeeck, I. 1997. "The Context of Women's Power(lessness) in Heterosexual Interactions." In *New Sexual Agendas,* edited by L. Segal. New York: New York University Press.

Waites, Matthew. 2009. "Critique of 'Sexual Orientation' and 'Gender Identity' in Human Rights Discourse: Global Queer Politics beyond the Yogyakarta Principles." *Contemporary Politics* 15, no. 1: 137–156.

Walters, Suzanna Danuta. 2001. "Take My Domestic Partner, Please: Gays and Marriage in the Era of the Visible." In *Queer Families, Queer Politics: Challenging Culture and the State,* edited by Mary Bernstein and Renate Reimann, 338–357. New York: Columbia University Press.

Warner, Michael. 2000. *The Trouble with Normal: Sex, Politics and the Ethics of Queer Life.* Cambridge, MA: Harvard University Press.

Weitzer, Ronald, ed. 2000. *Sex for Sale: Prostitution, Pornography, and the Sex Industry.* New York: Routledge.

Wilkinson, Lindsey, and Jennifer Pearson. 2009. "School Culture and the Well-Being of Same-Sex-Attracted Youth." *Gender and Society* 23, no. 4: 542–568.

Yang, Alan S. 1998. *From Wrongs to Rights: Public Opinion on Gay and Lesbian American's Moves toward Equality.* Washington, DC: National Gay and Lesbian Task Force Policy Institute.

A History of Ageism Since 1969

W. Andrew Achenbaum

> *Ageism predated Robert Butler, and remains in effect to this day.*

The term "ageism" was coined in 1969 by Robert N. Butler, M.D., then a 42-year-old psychiatrist who (among his other civic and age-focused advocacy responsibilities) headed the District of Columbia Advisory Committee on Aging. In partnership with the National Capital Housing Authority (NCHA), Butler used the term "age-ism" during a *Washington Post* interview conducted by then cub reporter Carl Bernstein. The *Post* story, "Age and race fears seen in housing opposition," described the apprehension of homeowners in Chevy Chase, Maryland, an affluent Washington, D.C., suburb, who were distressed by the NCHA's decision to turn an apartment complex into public housing (Bernstein, 1969). The project was intended to offer residences for the elderly poor—including African Americans—and was opposed by residents who feared Chevy Chase would never be the same.

"People talk about aging gracefully, which is what they want to do of course. So, naturally, they don't want to look at people who may be palsied, can't eat well ... who may sit on the curb and clutter up the neighborhood with canes," Butler told Bernstein. "Until our society builds [a] more balanced perspective about age groups, this lends to embittered withdrawal by old people" (Bernstein, 1969).

Ageism: The Greater Prejudice?

In Butler's opinion, long-standing racial prejudices and palpable class biases fueled an animus against age, a stigma that few Americans at the time acknowledged. "In the course of a *Washington Post* interview, I was asked if this negativism was a function of racism," Butler recalled (Butler, 1989). "In this instance, I thought it more a function of ageism."

Anger about age-driven injustices impelled Butler to engage in political activism on behalf of the old (and the young). As a delegate to the 1968 Democratic National Convention, Butler had witnessed clashes on the Chicago streets between age groups. This mayhem, to his mind, underscored a generation gap fomenting "in the political year 1968 [with] the elements of a counterrevolution by the middle-aged against both the young and the old" (Butler, 1969).

Elaborating upon his insights into ageism in *The Gerontologist*, he predicted that age bigotry would not soon fade. "Aging is the great sleeper in American life," he declared, noting that ageism permeated programs and resources meant to serve older Americans, such as Medicare, Social Security, and public housing, marginalizing older adults. "Age-ism might parallel (it might be wishful thinking to say *replace*) racism as the great issue of the next 20 to 30 years," he wrote (Butler, 1969).

Contempt, Down through the Ages

Butler was not the first to identify a seemingly universal, widespread contempt for old people. Negative attitudes toward age and aging have been, and remain, deeply rooted in global history. Men and women who no longer could contribute to communal survival in Neolithic cultures were cast aside, often left to die. "*Senectus morbidus est*" ("Old age is a disease"), the philosopher Seneca (4 BC–AD 65) said.

> Robert Butler declared that 'aging is the great sleeper in American life.'

By associating late life with disease and death, generations down the ages have justified the futility of granting the aged access to care (Achenbaum, 1978; Haber, 1983; Cole, 1992). Ageism is ubiquitous—evident in places as far-flung and with differing cultures as Japan (Gerlock, 2005) and east Africa (Ogonda, 2006)—and embedded in Western culture. The Roman poet Juvenal's *Satires* mock impotent and priapic septuagenarian satyrs alike; other classical authors disparaged mature women's disfigured grace and beauty. Unflattering imagery, like that in Keats' poem, "Ode to a Nightingale," permeates more modern works (de Beauvoir, 1971; Wyatt-Brown and Rossen, 1993). It is no wonder that post–World War II researchers, sampling respondents' attitudes about old people, reported stereotypically negative responses to age and aging (Barron, 1953; Rosow, 1962; Tuckman and Lorge, 1953).

Robert Butler's achievement was to give meaning to ageism as an affliction. (In 1969, "ageism" appeared in the *Oxford English Dictionary*; in 2003, "new ageism" showed up in the dictionary's electronic version.) For the rest of his career, Butler's critiques of ageism repeated themes enunciated when he had first introduced the subject:

Ageism can be seen as a systematic stereotyping of and discrimination against people because they are old, just as racism and sexism accomplish this with skin color and gender ... I see ageism manifested in a wide range of phenomena, on both individual and institutional levels—stereotypes and myths, outright disdain and dislike, simple subtle avoidance of contact, and discriminatory practices in housing, employment, and services of all kinds (Butler, 1989; Butler, 2005).

Whether working with the Veterans Administration, serving as founding director of the National Institute on Aging, and, subsequently, as the (first U.S.) chair of geriatrics at New York's Mount Sinai Hospital and Medical School, Butler constantly sought ways to rid eldercare of ageism. A top priority was training healthcare professionals to treat older patients with dignity and compassion (Butler, 1980; Achenbaum, 2013).

Combating ageism was the frequent goal of the publications and workshops of the New York-based International Longevity Center (ILC), which Butler founded and led during his last two decades of life. *Media Takes: On Aging*, an influential ILC report (Dahmen and Cozma, 2009), documented that much remained to be done to counter the insidious effects of age-based prejudice. The report claimed that 80 percent of Americans were subjected to ageism. A year before his death in 2010, Butler wrote:

The advent of possible means to delay aging and extend longevity is a great intellectual and social as well as medical achievement ... The very words we use to describe people are undergoing greater scrutiny. It is ironic, then, that at the same time Americans are beginning to see an unfolding of the entire life cycle for a majority, we continue to have embedded in our culture a fear of growing old, manifest by negative stereotypes and language that belittles the very nature of growing old, its complexities and tremendous variability (Butler, 2008).

Efforts to Define and Measure Ageism

The United States has always been an age-graded society. Its segmented age groups do not necessarily unify the populace, although most citizens claim to agree with Robert Wohl (1979) when he says, "the truest community to which one can belong is that defined by age and experience."

Intergenerational tensions flamed ageist rhetoric in the 1980s and 1990s, however. *The New Republic* depicted older people as "greedy geezers" who squandered their life savings and depleted Social Security funds (Fairlie, 1988). Younger Americans, struggling to obtain an education, a home, or a decent job blamed older Americans.

Debates over generational equity abated over time, without uprooting the perception that different age groups compete for diminishing resources in a zero-sum world. "Age-based social divisions, particularly in the current economic environment of budget deficits and fiscal tightening, threaten the sustainability of the American social compact" (Network on an Aging Society, 2012).

Scores of researchers have since followed Butler's lead in defining and measuring ageism. And scholars have deployed knowledge-building and consciousness-raising to mitigate, if not eradicate, the stigma. A fair number of investigators merit attention here.

The Researchers Go to Work

Donald McTavish (1971) prepared an exhaustive review of research methodologies and cumulative findings concerning perceptions of old people; he found the literature at hand mixed in terms of validity and usefulness.

Ageism became the cornerstone of Erdman Palmore's research while he was a graduate student in the 1950s. With Kenneth Manton, Palmore published the first systematic comparison of age-based inequality to racism (the pair reported small but significant gains at the time) and sexism (they claimed that women's inferior status was barely maintained). "Few people recognize the magnitude of age inequality in our society," they reported (Palmore and Manton, 1973).

In 1976, Palmore developed, and subsequently maintained, a twenty-five-point "Facts on Aging" quiz to help the public recognize the extent of their misinformation about older people's qualities—a bias that contributed to age discrimination (Bennett, 2004). In a guest editorial, Palmore (2000) offered usage guidelines for avoiding ageism in gerontological language. At age 82, he co-edited the *Encyclopedia of Ageism* (2005), wherein sixty authors reviewed 125 aspects of ageism, ranging from mapping elder abuse to assessing ageism among children.

Emerging Scholars Take Their Turn

A rising generation of scholars contributed to fresh understandings of ageism. Some validated insights by Butler and Palmore, while presenting novel approaches (McGuire, Klein, and Chen, 2008). Becca Levy (2001), for example, demonstrated how *implicit* ageism generated adverse health effects. Stereotypes previously aimed at African Americans or women were internalized by aging Americans, eliciting self-inflicted prejudice.

> 'Class still matters: Disenfranchised older people have less access to power, prestige, or property.'

Todd Nelson, in a collection of essays on ageism (2002) and a handbook on *The Psychology of Prejudice* (2005), sought to contextualize the syndrome by documenting the extent to which Americans' derogation of aging clashed with their views concerning youth, mobility, change, and fear of death. In *Agewise*, Margaret Morganroth Gullette (2010), in her analysis of the Fourth Age, provided a devastating critique of the "culture of decline" and the "systems of decline" (including those fostered by healthcare professionals and pharmaceutical firms) that distort how we view passages through the life course.

Other investigators tracked policies undermining ageism, such as changes in employment discrimination legislation, noting limitations in our country's landmark Age Discrimination in

Employment Act of 1967, which abolished mandatory retirement (Pampel and Williamson, 1992; Burchett, 2005).

International researchers—especially those in the United Kingdom—enriched the literature on ageism. Bill Bytheway (1995) surveyed the settings in which age biases compromised medical care, among other senior services. John Macnicol, who published a historical and contemporary analysis of age discrimination (2006) and also presented a think piece to the ILC (2010), argued that the British government took steps (not replicated in the United States) to encourage—even to force—older workers back into paid employment. Robin Blackburn claimed that poor public responses to older adults' vulnerabilities posed a societal risk (2006).

Exploring the nature of spirituality in the Fourth Age, Malcolm Johnson and Keith Albans (2013) recounted and interpreted stories of people's anxieties over declining capacities and fears of dying. Their treatment of ageism in late, late life recalled efforts by Nobel Laureate Elie Metchnikoff (1908) and psychologist G. Stanley Hall (1922), who linked gerontology and thanatology—a connection rarely pursued by investigators that is dedicated to probing "successful aging."

Parsing the Evolution (or Devolution) of Ageism

As ageism studies progressed, unresolved debates over definitional matters gave rise to measurement issues about ageism. Palmore acknowledged that his pioneering Equality Index was a useful but insufficient basis for such comparisons (Palmore, 1999). Synthesis is difficult (Aosved, Long, and Voller, 2009; Dittmann, 2003) because few researchers investigate intolerant beliefs simultaneously. Furthermore, as much survey data on ageism are self-reported; the negativity is likely to be implicit or unnoticed (as Becca Levy has shown). Ageism, after all, takes on various and nuanced forms, each with unique impacts: Making jokes at an older person's expense is vastly different from hitting one's grandparents or stealing their assets and resources.

And, times change: "Racism, sexism, homophobia, and other forms of discrimination don't look the way they used to" (Covert, 2014). Jim Crow laws may be history, but entrenched signs of disenfranchisement in African American communities remain—poverty, homelessness, incarceration, and violence. The status of women has improved due to greater opportunities in higher education and professional advancement, yet women are expected to interrupt their careers to be caregivers; and income disparities have not dissipated much since the passage of the Equal Pay Act of 1963, or with its amendment in 1974.

> 'We no longer limit comparisons of ageism to racism and sexism.'

Though few Americans gave much thought to the presence of Spanish-speaking immigrants in America in the late 1960s, this now burgeoning, diverse segment of our society has become a potent force in contemporary life and culture. The same might be said of immigrants from Asia and the subcontinent. And, since the Stonewall Riots of 1969, there has been a radical transformation of attitudes and public policies that support and affirm the rights of gays, lesbians, bisexuals, transgender individuals, and self-identified queers to participate in everyday affairs.

Much since 1969 remains the same about ageism. Then, as now, older Americans were a variegated group; their circumstances remain divergent in terms of financial resources and employment opportunities, mental and physical health, educational attainments, cultural diversity, marital status, religion, and region. Class still matters: Disenfranchised older people have less access to power, prestige, or property.

Ageism continues to bedevil segments of the older population in distressing ways. Most older African American women still embody a triple jeopardy (being female, African American, and old), which public agencies cannot fully ameliorate. Older Americans remain under-represented in the media. And gerontology's great irony persists—whereas most of us now live long enough to become old, ageism is the only prejudice that can diminish *everyone's* quality of life.

That said, ageism itself has taken on four new forms since Butler identified the prejudice:

- Older Americans benefit from age-based discounts and entitlements, which is a positive development, but the benefits still convey a scent of ageism. Many of these perquisites originated in the pervasive notion that older people, uniformly, were poor. That is no longer the case. As a group, the old, on average, have more income at their disposal than younger cohorts.

- The Baby Boom Generation has seen both sides of ageism. In their youth, they mocked people older than age 30. Now, they face job discrimination and competition from younger generations. And, they are taunted for their obesity and improvidence. Their very numbers fan worries that they might bankrupt Social Security and Medicare.

- We no longer limit comparisons of ageism to racism and sexism. New dyads have emerged, notably ones associated with the disabled and with lesbian, gay, bisexual, transgender, and queer (LGBTQ) individuals. Conjoining age with Alzheimer's Disease and related disorders, or recognizing the risk of HIV infections after age 60 arouses fears of loss of control and independence in late life and despair over prospects for a meaningful existence. Rates of dementia, sexually transmitted diseases, and drug use and abuse underscore the need to invest more in mental health and to provide greater access to older Americans to public health education and interventions.

- Elderly men and women who are feverishly committed to extending careers well into what had been considered retirement years rarely notice how ageism cripples peers. This is one reason Americans can postpone the 1960s version of age 65.

Ageism preys on vulnerability—fragility, frailty, and dependency at advancing ages—especially as dread of dying and death mounts.

Conclusion

Two ironies frame the history of ageism, both before and after 1969. First, ageism predates Butler's naming of a syndrome endemic over time and across space. Vulnerable elders feared physical and psychological abuse, regardless of their cohort's proportionate numbers in a given population. Second, ageism remains virulent amidst "the longevity revolution" (Butler, 2008).

The gift of extra years should afford time and opportunities to grow, to cherish bonds, to review life's meaning. Instead, older people often find themselves marginalized, which diminishes their capacities to contribute—and to matter.

References

Achenbaum, W. A. 1978. *Old Age in the New Land.* Baltimore, MD: The Johns Hopkins University Press.

Achenbaum, W. A. 2013. *Robert N. Butler, MD: Visionary of Healthy Aging.* New York: Columbia University Press.

Aosved, A. C., Long, P. J., and Voller, E. K. 2009. "Measuring Sexism, Racism, Sexual Prejudice, Ageism, Classism and Religious Intolerance." *Journal of Applied Social Psychology* 39(10): 2321–54.

Barron, M. L. 1953. "Minority Group Characteristics of the Aged in American Society." *Journal of Gerontology* 8(4): 477–82.

Bennett, R. 2004. "Professor Palmore's Amazing Facts on Aging Quiz." www.timegoesby.net/weblog/2004/09/dr_erdmans_amaz.html. Retrieved May 6, 2015.

Bernstein, C. 1969. "Age and Race Fears Seen in Housing Opposition." *The Washington Post,* March 7.

Blackburn, R. 2006. *Age Shock: How Finance Is Failing Us.* London, UK: Verso.

Burchett, B. M. 2005. "Employment Discrimination." In E. B. Palmore et al., eds., *Encyclopedia of Ageism.* Binghamton, NY: Haworth Press.

Butler, R. N. 1969. "Age-ism: Another Form of Bigotry." *The Gerontologist* 9(4, Part 1): 243–6.

Butler, R. N. 1980. "Ageism: A Foreword." *Journal of Social Issues* 36(2): 8–11.

Butler, R. N. 1989. "Dispelling Ageism: The Cross-cutting Intervention." *Annals of the American Academy of Political and Social Science* 503: 138–47.

Butler, R. N. 2005. "Ageism." *Generations* 29(3): 84–6.

Butler, R. N. 2008. *The Longevity Revolution: The Benefits and Challenges of Living a Long Life.* New York: PublicAffairs.

Bytheway, B. 1995. *Ageism.* New York: McGraw-Hill.

Cole, T. R. 1992. *The Journey of Life.* New York: Cambridge University Press.

Covert, B. 2014. "Racism and Sexism Look Different Than You Think." *ThinkProgress,* May 21. http://thinkprogress.org/economy/2014/05/21/3440209/discrimination-favoritism/. Retrieved May 8, 2015.

Dahmen, N. S., and Cozma, R., eds. 2009. *Media Takes: On Aging.* New York: International Longevity Center; San Francisco: Aging Services of California.

deBeauvoir, S. 1971. *The Coming of Age.* New York: G. P. Putnam's Sons.

Dittmann, M. 2003. "Fighting Ageism." *American Psychological Association Monitor on Psychology* 34(5): 50.

Fairlie, H. 1988. "Talkin' 'bout My Generation." *The New Republic*, March 28.

Gerlock, E. 2006. "Discrimination of Older People in Asia." Paper presented at the International Federation on Aging Conference, May 30–June 2, Copenhagen.

Gullette, M. M. 2010. *Agewise: Fighting the New Ageism in America*. Chicago: University of Chicago Press.

Haber, C. 1983. *Beyond Sixty-Five: The Dilemma of Old Age in America's Past*. Cambridge, UK: Cambridge University Press.

Hall, G. S. 1922. *Senescence: The Last Half of Life*. New York: D. Appelton & Co.

Johnson, M. L., and Albans, K. 2013. *God, Me and Being Very Old: Stories and Spirituality in Later Life*. London, UK: SCM Press.

Levy, B. 2001. "Eradication of Ageism Requires Addressing the Enemy Within." *The Gerontologist* 41(5): 578–79.

Macnicol, J. 2006. *Age Discrimination*. Cambridge, UK: Cambridge University Press.

Macnicol, J. 2010. *Ageism and Age Discrimination*. London, UK: International Longevity Center-UK.

McGuire, S. L., Klein, D. A., and Chen, S. L. 2008. "Ageism Revisited." *Nursing and Health Sciences* 10(1): 11–16.

McTavish, D. G. 1971. "Perceptions of Old People: A Review of Research Methodologies and Findings." *The Gerontologist* 11 (Supp.): 90–108.

Metchnikoff, E. 1908. *The Prolongation of Life: Optimistic Studies*. New York: G. P. Putnam's Sons.

Nelson, T. D., ed. 2002. *Ageism: Stereotyping and Prejudice Against Older Persons*. Cambridge, MA: The MIT Press.

Nelson, T. 2006. *The Psychology of Prejudice*. Boston: Pearson.

Network on an Aging Society. 2012. *Intergenerational Cohesion and the Social Compact*. Chicago: Mac-Arthur Foundation. www.agingsocietynetwork.org/sites/default/files/files/generational%20cohesion%20brief%20.pdf. Retrieved June 22, 2015.

Ogonda, J. 2006. "Age Discrimination in Africa." Paper presented at the International Federation on Aging Conference, May 30–June 2, Copenhagen.

Palmore, E. B., and Manton, K. 1973. "Ageism Compared to Racism and Sexism." *Journal of Gerontology* 28(3): 363–9.

Palmore, E. B., ed. 1999. *Ageism* (2nd ed.). New York: Springer.

Palmore, E. B. 2000. "Guest Editorial: Ageism in Gerontological Language." *The Gerontologist* 40(6): 645.

Palmore, E. B., Branch, L., and Harris, D. K., eds. 2005. *Encyclopedia of Ageism*. Binghamton, NY: Haworth Press.

Pampel, F. C., and Williamson, J. B. 1992. *Age, Class, Politics, and the Welfare State*. New York: Cambridge University Press.

Rosow, I. 1962. "Old Age." *The Gerontologist* 2: 182–91.

Tuckman, J., and Lorge. I. 1953. " 'When Aging Begins' and Stereotypes about Aging." *Journal of Gerontology* 8: 489–92.

Wohl, R. 1979. *The Generation of 1914*. Cambridge, MA: Harvard University Press.

Wyatt-Brown, A. M., and Rossen, J., eds. 1993. *Aging and Gender in Literature: Studies in Creativity*. Charlottesville, VA: University Press of Virginia.

Post-Reading Activities

1   Thinking about the definitions discussed in the introduction (Wagley & Harris (1967) and van Amersfoort (1978)), how well do the definitions apply to the discussion of sex and gender minorities, sexuality minorities, and age minorities?

2   When pondering the American minorities, which article from the Universal Declaration of Human Rights most applies?

3   After discussing microaggressions in Reading 6, what are some microaggressions that pertain to gender, sexuality, and age minorities?

4   Are there any additional minority groups that you have observed in the United States not reflected in the selected readings?

UNIT 5

Basic Outcomes, Minority and Majority

So, what do we do with this knowledge of minority-majority relationships in the United States? A lot of research has been conducted and presented in this book, but students reflect that a class on social issues oftentimes leaves them feeling like they are on the edge of something, but they cannot pinpoint exactly what to do next. This unit will provide examples and definitions of social policy and what can be done in the future. It is important to remember that the small things do add up. Students can overwhelm themselves with lofty dreams and goals, only to lead to immobilization and failure to do anything. As you read this concluding unit, think about what small things you can do as a student to help a minority group reach its potential of basic human rights.

As Merton (1936) warns social policy writers, we must be wary of the "unanticipated consequences" of social policy. Not all the consequences are negative; however, one must consider any inequality introduced by a social action. This means that if a positive effect is the outcome of a social action, the positive effect must apply to all groups equally, not just one single group. If only one group is receiving the benefit of a social action, then the social action is not equal and just, possibly violating a person's basic human rights. Later, he refers to the terms "manifest" and "latent" functions. Manifest functions are the expected outcomes of a social action. Latent functions are the unexpected outcomes of a social action. Both the manifest and the latent functions must be considered prior to social action or an introduction of a social policy. Latent dysfunctions are negative outcomes of a social action. These latent dysfunctions must be minimized and avoided. Some find this to be impossible to complete without a crystal ball; however, with careful consideration, planning, research, and monitoring, many of these issues can be addressed prior to implementation. It is important to understand all consequences (negative, positive, neutral) to social action. It is a foundation of the sociological ethics. As you move through Unit 5, think about the social consequences of your action plan to help minorities with human rights.

In Unit 5, first, Kenworthy (2012) provides an assessment of opportunity in the United States. He argues that the United States is no longer the land of opportunity because of too many obstacles that individuals at the bottom must face to reach high outcomes. Second, Titmuss (1974) provides possible guidelines on how to level the playing field, like what was described in Kenworthy. Third, Marcum and Perry (2010) provide an example of a social policy when addressing the rights of religious minorities in the United States.

References

Kenworthy, L. (2012). It's hard to make it in America: How the United States stopped being the land of opportunity. *Foreign Affairs, 91*(6), 97–109.

Marcum, T. & Perry, S. J. (2010). Dressed for success: Can a claim of religious discrimination be successful? *Labor Law Journal, 61*(4), 184–191.

Merton, R. K. (1936). The unanticipated consequences of purposive social action. *American Sociological Review 1*(6), 894–904.

Titmuss, R. M. (1974). What is social policy? In *Social Policy*. Oxford: Taylor & Francis Group.

It's Hard to Make It in America

How the United States Stopped Being the Land of Opportunity

Lane Kenworthy

For all the differences between Democrats and Republicans that were laid bare during the 2012 U.S. presidential campaign, the parties' standard-bearers, Barack Obama and Mitt Romney, do seem to have agreed on one thing: the importance of equal opportunity. In remarks in Chicago in August, Obama called for an "America where no matter who you are, no matter what you look like, no matter where you come from, no matter what your last name is, no matter who you love, you can make it here if you try." The same month, he urged the Supreme Court to uphold affirmative action in public universities, putting his weight behind what has been a mainstay of U.S. equal opportunity legislation since the 1960s. Days later, the Republican vice presidential nominee, Paul Ryan, echoed Obama's sentiment, saying, "We promise equal opportunity, not equal outcomes." Romney, too, argued that whereas Obama "wants to turn America into a European-style entitlement society," his administration would "ensure that we remain a free and prosperous land of opportunity."

It is no accident that both campaigns chose to emphasize equality of opportunity. It has long been at the center of the American ethos. And one of the United States' major successes in the last half century has been its progress toward ensuring that its citizens get roughly the same basic chances in life, regardless of gender or race. Today, women are more likely to graduate from college than men and are catching up in employment and earnings, too. The gap between whites and nonwhites has narrowed as well, albeit less dramatically.

Yet this achievement has been double edged. As gender and race have become less significant barriers to advancement, family background, an obstacle considered

Lane Kenworthy, "It's Hard to Make It In America: How the United States Stopped being the Land of Opportunity," *Foreign Affairs*, vol. 91, no. 6, pp. 97-109. Copyright © 2012 by Council on Foreign Relations, Inc. Reprinted with permission.

> The United States has lost its historical distinction as the land of opportunity.

more relevant in earlier eras, has reemerged. Today, people who were born worse off tend to have fewer opportunities in life.

Of course, there is no perfect way to measure opportunities. The best method devised thus far is to look at outcomes: college completion, gainful employment, and sufficient income. If the average outcome for one group far outpaces that for another, social scientists conclude that the first group had greater opportunities. Comparing outcomes is not foolproof, as differences in outcomes can result from differences in effort. But a person's effort is itself shaped by the circumstances he or she encounters.

To assess equality of opportunity among people from different family backgrounds, the measure of outcome that social scientists look at is relative intergenerational mobility—a person's position on the income ladder relative to his or her parents' position. Social scientists don't have as much information as they would like about the extent of relative intergenerational mobility, its movement over time, and its causes. The data requirements are stiff; analysts need a survey that collects information about citizens' incomes and other aspects of their life circumstances, then does the same for their children, and for their children's children, and so on. The best assessment of this type in the United States, the Panel Study of Income Dynamics, has been around only since the late 1960s.

Even so, there is general consensus among social scientists on a few basic points. First, an American born into a family in the bottom fifth of incomes between the mid-1960s and the mid-1980s has roughly a 30-percent chance of reaching the middle fifth or higher in adulthood, whereas an American born into the top fifth has an 80-percent chance of ending up in the middle fifth or higher. (In a society with perfectly equal opportunity, every person would have the same chance—20 percent—of landing on each of the five rungs of the income ladder and a 60-percent chance of landing on the middle rung or a higher one.) This discrepancy means that there is considerable inequality of opportunity among Americans from different family backgrounds.

Second, inequality of opportunity has increased in recent decades. The data do not permit airtight conclusions. Still, available compilations of test scores, years of schooling completed, occupations, and incomes of parents and their children strongly suggest that the opportunity gap, which was narrowing until the 1970s, is now widening.

Third, in a sharp reversal of historical trends, there is now less equality of opportunity in the United States than in most other wealthy democratic nations. Data exist for ten of the United States' peer countries (rich long-standing democracies). The United States has less relative intergenerational mobility than eight of them; Australia, Canada, Denmark, Finland, Germany, Norway, Sweden, and the United Kingdom all do better. The United States is on par with France and Italy.

So how did the United States get here? Why did it falter where other nations have not? And how can it fix the problem? On the right, a standard proposal is to strengthen families.

On the left, a recent favorite is to reduce income inequality. And everyone supports improving education. To know which proposals would work best, it helps to understand the roots of the new opportunity gap.

The Lost Opportunity Cost

Between the mid-1800s and the 1970s, differences in opportunity based on family circumstances declined steadily. As the formerly farming-based U.S. labor force shifted to manufacturing, many Americans joined the paid labor force, allowing an increasing share of them to move onto and up the income ladder. Elementary education became universal, and secondary education expanded. Then, in the 1960s and 1970s, school desegregation, the outlawing of discrimination in college admissions and hiring, and the introduction of affirmative action programs helped open economic doors for an even wider swath of Americans.

But since the 1970s, the United States has been moving in the opposite direction. A host of economic and social shifts seem to have widened the opportunity gap between Americans from low-income families and those from high-income families. First, family life has changed, at least for some. The share of poorer children growing up with both biological parents has fallen sharply, whereas there has been less change among the wealthy. About 88 percent of children from high-income homes grow up with married parents. That is down from 96 percent four decades ago. Meanwhile, only 41 percent of poorer children grow up in homes with married parents, down from 77 percent four decades ago. That has hurt poorer children's chances of success, since children who live with both of their parents are more likely, even accounting for income, to fare better in school, stay out of trouble with the law, maintain lasting relationships, and earn higher incomes as adults.

The modern culture of intensive parenting—a largely middle- and upper-class phenomenon—adds to the gap. Low-income parents are not able to spend as much on goods and services aimed at enriching their children, such as music lessons, travel, and summer camp. Low-income parents also tend to read less to their children and provide less help with schoolwork. They are less likely to set and enforce clear rules and routines for their children. And they are less likely to encourage their children to aspire to high achievement in school and at work.

Furthermore, a generation ago, most preschool-aged children stayed at home with their mothers. Now, many are enrolled in some sort of child care. But the quality of their experiences varies. Affluent parents can send their children to nationally recognized education-oriented preschools. Poorer parents might have little choice but to leave their children with a neighborhood babysitter who plops them in front of the television. Research by the economist James Heckman and others finds that much of the gap in cognitive and noncognitive skills between children from poor homes and those from affluent homes is already present by the time they enter kindergarten.

Things don't improve once children reach grade school. Funding for public k–12 schools, which used to vary sharply across school districts, has become more even in recent decades. Nevertheless, a large difference remains in the quality of education between the best and the worst schools, and the poorest neighborhoods often have the weakest schools. According to data compiled by Sean Reardon of Stanford University's School of Education, the gap in average test scores between elementary- and secondary-school children from high-income families and those from low-income families has risen steadily in recent decades. Among children born in 1970, those from high-income homes scored, on average, about three-quarters of a standard deviation higher on math and reading tests than those from low-income homes. Among children born in 2000, the gap has grown to one and a quarter standard deviations. That is much larger than the gap between white and black children.

Partly because they tend to be far behind at the end of high school, and partly because college has gotten so expensive, children from poor backgrounds are less likely than others to enter and complete college. The economists Martha Bailey and Susan Dynarski have compared the college completion rates of Americans who grew up in the 1960s and 1970s to the rates of those who grew up in the 1980s and 1990s. The share of young adults from high-income homes that got a four-year college degree rose from 36 percent in the first group to 54 percent in the second group. The share from low-income homes, however, stayed almost flat, rising only from five percent to nine percent.

When it comes time to get a job, the story is no better. Low-income parents tend to have fewer valuable connections to help their children find good jobs. Some people from poor homes are further hampered by a lack of English-language skills. Another disadvantage for the lower-income population is that in the 1970s and 1980s, the United States began incarcerating a lot more young men, including many for minor offenses. Having a criminal record makes it all the more difficult to get a stable job with decent pay—if, that is, good jobs still exist. A number of developments, including technological advances, globalization, a loss of manufacturing employment, and the decline of unions, have reduced the number of jobs that require limited skills but pay a middle-class wage—the very kind of jobs that once moved poorer Americans into the middle class.

> One solution would be to get more money into the hands of low-income families with children.

Finally, changes in partner selection have also widened the opportunity gap. Not only do those from better-off families tend to end up with more schooling and higher-paying jobs; they are more likely than ever to marry (or cohabit with) others like themselves, according to research by the sociologists Christine Schwartz and Robert Mare.

For all these reasons, the gap in opportunity between the United States' rich and poor has expanded in recent decades. Left unchecked, the trend threatens not only to offset the progress the United States has made on gender and racial equality but also to usher in a future of deep and hardened class divisions.

It might be tempting to shrug and conclude that the high and increasing opportunity gap in the United States is an unfortunate but inevitable consequence of economic and social shifts. The problem with this reaction is that other affluent democracies do better. The United States has lost its historical distinction as the land of opportunity. Yet there is at least some good news: the fact that other countries are more successful in this area suggests that with the right policies, the United States could do better, too.

Valuable Families

One simple, straightforward solution would be to get more money into the hands of low-income families with children. The education policy experts Greg Duncan, Ariel Kalil, and Kathleen Ziol-Guest have found that for children who grew up in the United States in the 1970s and 1980s, an increase in family income of a mere $3,000 during a person's first five years of life was associated with nearly 20-percent higher earnings later in life. The finding suggests that government cash transfers of just a few thousand dollars could give a significant lifelong boost to the children who need it most. Most other affluent countries, including those that do better on equality of opportunity, offer a universal "child allowance" that does exactly this. In Canada, for instance, a family with two children receives an annual allowance of around $3,000, and low-income families with two children might receive more than $6,000. The United States has only a weaker version of the benefit, the Child Tax Credit, which doles out a maximum of just $1,000 a year per child. Moreover, receipt of the money is contingent on filing a federal tax return, which not all low-income families do.

Other solutions involve Washington getting involved in home life. Fewer children in the United States grow up with both biological parents than in any other affluent country for which data are available. To remedy this, some, such as Barbara Dafoe Whitehead and David Popenoe, co-directors of the National Marriage Project at Rutgers, favor efforts to promote marriage. But research by the sociologists Kathryn Edin, Sara McLanahan, and Paula England and others suggests that this strategy is misplaced. Since women today need less from marriage and expect more from it than they used to, those who are better educated and better off tend to take more time to get established in their jobs and find good partners, which enhances the likelihood of a lasting marriage (or cohabitation). They delay childbearing as well. Among poorer and less-educated women, who see little prospect of a fulfilling and lucrative career, having a child in their teens or early 20s remains common. These women are less likely to stay with a partner: they have had less time to mature personally and to find a person with whom they are compatible, their partners are more likely to have weak financial prospects and a preference for traditional gender roles, and the presence of a child heightens financial and interpersonal tensions. Given all this, convincing more young low-income couples who get pregnant to marry is unlikely to produce many lasting relationships.

Genuine progress probably hinges on poor or less-educated women delaying childbirth. Eventually, this will happen; the teen birthrate has already been dropping for nearly two decades, albeit slowly. For its part, Washington (or any other government) has only limited tools to speed it up. The best might be an education campaign, as Ron Haskins and Isabelle Sawhill, policy experts at the Brookings Institution, have suggested, that focuses on the benefits of the "success sequence": first education, then a stable job, then marriage, and then children.

What about parenting practices, which have a clear effect on childhood development? Although few Americans support extensive government intrusion into home life, one potentially acceptable way that Washington and state governments could try to improve parenting is by paying for home visits by nurses or counselors and providing free or low-cost parenting classes. Getting people to change their behavior and routines is very difficult, so the benefits of such programs are inevitably modest. Nonetheless, in a recent review of existing research, the sociologist Frank Furstenberg found evidence that programs aimed at teaching better practices to parents of children at middle-school age or younger yield some improvements in school readiness and school performance.

Making the Grade

Given the difficulties of altering home life, improving schools remains the United States' main tool for assisting less-advantaged children. For all their inadequacies, public schools do help equalize opportunity by improving students' cognitive abilities. During summer vacation, the cognitive abilities of children in low-income families tend to regress, relative to those of their more advantaged peers. In other words, these children would lag even further behind if they never attended school.

A universal system of affordable, educational child care and preschool could help close the capability gap that opens up during the early years of life. Additionally, it would facilitate parents' employment and thereby boost household incomes, making it doubly helpful for children in low-income families. The Nordic countries offer some lessons: in the 1960s and 1970s, these countries introduced paid maternity leave and publicly funded child care. Today, early education teachers there have training and pay comparable to those of elementary school teachers. The cost of early education is capped at around ten percent of household income. In all these countries, a person's cognitive abilities, likelihood of completing high school and college, and eventual success in the job market tend to be less heavily determined by his or her family's wealth and makeup than in the United States.

There has been some movement to expand the United States' child-care and educational systems at the state level in the past two decades. Most states now have full-day public kindergarten, and some have added public preschool for four-year-olds. But the progress has been very slow, and in recent years, it has been set back by state revenue shortfalls. Assistance from Washington would be of considerable help.

The equalizing effects of college, too, cannot be overstated. Among Americans whose family incomes at birth are in the bottom fifth but who get four-year college degrees, 53 percent end up in the middle fifth or higher. That is pretty close to the 60-percent chance they would have with perfectly equal opportunity. Washington needs to do better at helping people from less-advantaged homes afford college. The average in-state tuition at an American four-year public university exceeds $8,000. In Norway, Sweden, Denmark, and Finland, attending four-year public universities is free. According to data from the Organization for Economic Cooperation and Development, in those nations, the odds that a person whose parents did not complete high school will attend college are between 40 and 60 percent, compared with just 30 percent in the United States.

Working on Labor

Employment is the next challenge. First, the low-hanging fruit: since a prison record impedes labor-market success, the United States should rethink its approach to punishment for non-violent drug offenders. According to the sociologist Bruce Western, states that have reduced imprisonment over the past decade, instead turning to alternative punishments, such as fines and community corrections programs, have experienced drops in crime similar to states that have increased imprisonment. If other states were to follow suit, the United States could avoid needlessly undermining the employment opportunities of a significant number of young men from less-advantaged homes.

Broader trends in the labor market since the 1970s present a stickier problem. Hourly wages at the median and below have not budged in inflation-adjusted terms. In the 1980s and 1990s, the United States created a lot of new jobs. These facilitated the movement of women into the work force and thereby helped many households enjoy rising incomes despite the stagnation in wages. But in the early years of this century, employment growth stopped, and the subsequent recession and slow recovery have dealt a crushing blow to the less skilled. The employment rate among men aged 25–54 who did not finish high school dropped by ten percentage points between 2007 and 2010.

Eventually, the U.S. economy will get back on track, but that will not automatically lead to more jobs and higher wages. The lone period of sustained wage growth at the middle rung and below occurred in the late 1990s. What distinguishes that period is that the Federal Reserve allowed the unemployment rate to drop to four percent, well below what many economists believed to be the level at which inflation would accelerate. If and when the United States returns to low unemployment, it will need the Federal Reserve to again be willing to allow wages to rise significantly before stepping on the brakes.

It would be foolish to count on this, though, so the United States would do well to consider alternative strategies. One useful tool might be the Earned Income Tax Credit. At the moment, the eitc provides an annual subsidy of up to $6,000 to households with less than $50,000 in earnings. That is helpful, but for a person with no children, the credit amounts to less than $500. That group—young adults with low earnings and no children—includes many Americans who grew up in disadvantaged circumstances. If the economy is growing but wages are not, the United States can and should offer a bigger boost to these people's incomes.

In the past year, a number of commentators, most notably Alan Krueger, chair of the White House Council of Economic Advisers, have suggested that reversing the rise in income inequality could improve economic mobility in the United States. After all, among the countries for which there are comparable data, those with less income inequality tend to have higher relative intergenerational mobility. The United States was already on the high end of the income-inequality scale a generation ago, and since then it has moved even further in that direction.

Yet general calls to reduce income inequality offer little help in identifying which policies to pursue. Consider three possibilities. First, imagine that Washington legislated a radical reduction in the pay differentials for various types of jobs. (Narrower pay differentials account for part of the smaller opportunity gaps in the Nordic countries.) This certainly would reduce income inequality. It would also reduce opportunity inequality: at least in the first generation, even if someone's capabilities matched perfectly those of his or her parents, his or her income would not. But such a drastic step is not likely to happen, in part because few Americans would support it. Second, suppose the United States were to raise income tax rates for the top one percent of households and lower them for middle-class households. Such a move would reduce income inequality, but it would do little to improve the opportunities of children in low-income families. Third, suppose the United States increased tax rates for all households and used the revenue to fund universal early education. (As the political scientist Andrea Campbell recently wrote in these pages, most other advanced democracies devote far more tax revenue to social programs.) That step would do little to counter income inequality, but it could substantially expand opportunity. A reduction in income inequality, in short, is neither necessary nor sufficient for achieving a reduction in inequality of opportunity.

Land of Opportunity

For all that other countries' experiences can teach the United States, there are also lessons the United States should take from its own history. The most direct way that Washington has made opportunity more equal in the past has been through affirmative action. Affirmative action is not a strategy that many other affluent countries have embraced, but it has a proven track record in the United States. Since the late 1960s, affirmative action programs for college admissions and for hiring have expanded opportunities for women and various minority groups.

Now, a number of observers from across the partisan spectrum, from Richard Kahlenberg, a senior fellow at the left-leaning Century Foundation, to Charles Murray, a fellow at the right-leaning American Enterprise Institute, favor shifting the focus of affirmative action efforts from race and gender to family background. Emphasizing family background would continue to disproportionately help African American and Latino children, since they are more likely to come from families with low incomes and other disadvantages. Indeed, it would do more to help poor black and Latino children than traditional race-based affirmative action programs, which have mainly benefited middle-class members of such minority groups.

In response to court rulings and ballot initiatives outlawing consideration of race in admissions decisions, some public university systems, including those of California and Texas, have already moved in this direction. One approach guarantees the top ten percent of students graduating from any public high school in a state automatic admission to a public university in that state. Sometimes, this is helpful; in schools where almost all the students are from poor families, the top ten percent of the graduating class will inevitably include low-income students. A more direct strategy would be for colleges and universities to consider family background as one of several kinds of disadvantages that applicants may have faced and to include that among the criteria by which applicants are ranked.

How might employers be persuaded to use this direct approach? Half a century ago, the federal government mandated the use of affirmative action in public agencies and in firms with which it contracted. It could do the same now in order to address the nation's new opportunity gap.

In the last half century, the United States has taken long strides toward equalizing economic opportunity. That progress did not happen on its own; it took place with a push from the government. In recent decades, however, the opportunity gap for Americans from different family backgrounds has started to grow. Fortunately, the United States' experience and that of other affluent nations suggest that the country is not helpless in the face of economic and social changes. There is no silver bullet; a genuine solution is likely to include an array of shifts in policy and society. Even so, a fix is not beyond the United States' reach.

What Is Social Policy?

Richard M. Titmuss

I n the chapters that follow we look first at the term 'social policy' and ask a good many questions about it. In doing so, we shall inevitably have to consider various definitions of associated concepts and categorised labels—social administration, social services, social welfare, social security, welfare states and so forth. We will have to ask ourselves why we should study social policy at all or, for that matter, society's response as it identifies or fails to identify social needs and problems. Are we concerned with principles and objectives about certain areas of social life and organisation—or with social engineering: with methods and techniques of action, management, organisation and the application of games theory?

Whatever the answer we arrive at, we cannot fail to become heavily involved in the issues of moral and political values. Indeed, political propaganda frequently masquerades under social policy labels.

What do we mean by social policy? Connected with this is the equally important question: whose social policy? For our purposes the word 'policy' can be taken to refer to the principles that govern action directed towards given ends. The concept denotes action about means as well as ends and it, therefore, implies change: changing situations, systems, practices, behaviour. And here we should note that the concept of policy is only meaningful if we (society, a group, or an organisation) believe we can affect change in some form or another. We do not have policies about the weather because, as yet, we are powerless to do anything about the weather. But we do have policies (or we can have policies) about illegitimate children because we think we have some power to affect their lives—for better or worse depending on whether you are the policy-maker or the illegitimate child.

The word 'policy' is used here in an action-oriented and problem-oriented sense. The collective 'we' is used to refer to the actions of government in expressing the 'general will' of the people—whether of Britain, Nigeria or China. The meaning and validity of a concept of the 'general will' is, of course, hotly debated.

The greatest semantic difficulty arises, inevitably, with the word 'social'. Nor is it made any easier today by the fact that so many disciplines, professions and groups claim it as a Christian name and, indeed, flourish it about as something distinctly different. We have, for example, social geography, social planning, social psychology, social psychiatry, social administration, social work, social law, social linguistics, social history, social medicine, social pathology, and so on. Even the Bank of America created in January 1972 a new post of executive vice-president in charge of social policy! Why not social theology? Is it really necessary to drive home so ponderously the fact that all these subjects and groups are concerned in some way with man in society—and particularly with the non-economic factors in human relations? Are they not all, in short, emphasising that man is a social being; that he is not solely Economic Man; and that society cannot be thought of in terms of mechanistic-organic models or physiological models? It may well be that much of the current fashion for 'social' is a reaction against the sillier models of man in society constructed in the past by economists, political philosophers, experimental psychologists and sociologists.

Take, for example, the attempts of the Victorian economists to establish a competitive, self-regulating total market economy, or Radcliffe-Brown's doctrine (as one of the 'fathers' of modem anthropology) that the organic nature of society is a fact. Such a doctrine implies that integration and solidarity must be 'natural' attributes of all social systems. 'Social structures', he wrote, 'are just as real as are individual organisms. A complex organism is a collection of living cells and interstitial fluids arranged in a certain structure....'[1]

This is what another anthropologist, a *social* anthropologist, Edmund Leach, had to say about this doctrine: 'If you feel certain, on *a priori* grounds, that all forms of social stress must produce a reaction which will tend to restore or even reinforce the solidarity (i.e. organic health) of society then you will quickly persuade yourself that war is peace and conflict harmony.'[2]

You might argue, if social stresses correct themselves automatically (on the analogy of the self-regulating market economy), then there is no place for an unpredictable concept like social policy.

But it can, of course, be argued that social policy (or, to be more precise, a system of social welfare) is simply part of the self-regulatory mechanisms built into a 'natural' social system. This would mean that the history of the development of the social services in Britain since the beginning of the twentieth century was, in a sense, predetermined; that it was bound to happen because of a 'natural' tendency in the social system toward equilibrium and order. Some part of the theory of Talcott Parsons sustains this equilibrium-order concept.[3] Fundamentally, it is a

1　Radcliffe-Brown, A. R., *Structure and Function in Primitive Society,* Cohen & West, London, 1952, p. 190.
2　Leach, E., 'Models', *New Society,* 14 May 1964.
3　See, for example, Talcott Parsons, *The Structure of Social Action,* Allen & Unwin, London, 1949; and *The Social System,* Routledge & Kegan Paul, London, 1964.

conservative ideology akin to the philosophy that 'All is for the best in this best of all possible worlds,'—or akin, to take another analogy, to neo-classical economic theory with its conception of the best possible self-regulating supply and demand private market (largely, as the Women's Liberation Movement has pointed out, a private market for men).

All this is a rather roundabout way of saying that these mechanistic theories of orderly man and society consign a minor subsidiary role to social policy; indeed, not a 'policy' role at all; a role similar to that assigned to the State in nineteenth-century Britain by Lassalle when he wrote about 'the Night Watchman State' (the 'Law and Order State' in the language of the 1970s). Only in a very restricted and contradictory sense could it be said that Night Watchmen have *policies*— unless it can be argued that to watch and keep order and not to act and change is a policy.

At the other end of the spectrum of values is the rejection of the notion of a mechanistic or residual role for social policy. Social policy can be seen as a positive instrument of change; as an unpredictable, incalculable part of the whole political process.

We must not, however, jump to the conclusion that social policy as conceived in this or any other way is necessarily beneficient or welfare-oriented in the sense of providing more welfare and more benefits for the poor, the so-called working-classes, old-age pensioners, women, deprived children and other categories in the catalogue of social poverty. A redistributive social policy can redistribute command over material and non-material resources from the poor to the rich; from one ethnic group to another ethnic group; from working life to old age within income groups and social classes—as, for example, in middle-class pension schemes—and in other ways.

There are social policies in South Africa today which many people would not regard as being beneficient or welfare-oriented. There are social insurance programmes in some Latin American countries, Brazil in particular, which function as concealed multipliers of inequality— they transfer resources from the poor to the rich. Hitler developed social policies in Nazi Germany—they were in fact called social policies—concerning the mentally ill and retarded, the Jews and other ethnic groups. World public opinion condemned these instruments of social policy which had as their ultimate ends the use of human beings for medical research, sterilisation and the gas chamber.

When we use the term 'social policy' we must not, therefore, automatically react by investing it with a halo of altruism, concern for others, concern about equality and so on. Nor must we unthinkingly conclude that because Britain—or any other country—has a social policy or has developed social services, that they actually operate in practice to further the ends of progressive redistribution, equality and social altruism. What is 'welfare' for some groups may be 'illfare' for others.

And, lastly, in guarding against the value implications of the term 'social policy', I should point out that it does not imply allegiance to any political party or ideology. We all have our values and our prejudices; we all have our rights and duties as citizens, and our rights and duties as teachers and students. At the very least, we have a responsibility for making our values clear; and we have a special duty to do so when we are discussing such a subject as social policy which, quite clearly, has no meaning at all if it is considered to be neutral in terms of values. Or as Nye

Bevan, the architect of the British National Health Service, was so fond of saying: 'This is my truth, now tell me yours.'[4]

Gunnar Myrdal has had much to say in his writings on economic and social policy about the dangers of deceiving ourselves and others about our values and biases. He has criticised sociologists and anthropologists for believing in the possibility of a value-free approach in their studies of social organisation.[5]

Hume once said that the true sceptic should be as diffident of his philosophical doubts as of his philosophical convictions. Can we then say that a true believer should be as diffident of his philosophical convictions as of his philosophical doubts—so a true sceptic and a true believer would be one and the same? Is such a paragon possible? Can a man temper his doubts with assertion, and his assertions with doubt, and yet act in pursuit of certain social policy goals? Is this what in the ordinary life of decision-making some people call wisdom—the power to be both critical and practical, both speculative and pragmatic?[6]

To return, however, to this tiresome business of defining social policy. Let us consider what some other writers have said on the subject. At one extreme, we can find the most comprehensive definition in the statement by Professor Macbeath in his 1957 Hobhouse Lecture: 'Social policies are concerned with the right ordering of the network of relationships between men and women who live together in societies, or with the principles which should govern the activities of individuals and groups so far as they affect the lives and interests of other people.'[7]

It would be difficult to be more sweeping than that. It could easily be read as a grand definition of the scope of sociology; indeed, a definition that includes economics and all the social science disciplines. However, one should point out that it was Professor Macbeath's purpose to state the central issue in social policy—or any policy determined by Government to intervene in the life of the community. As he saw it, the central issue was between the self-regarding (egotistical) activities of man and the other-regarding (altruistic) activities. Professor Ginsberg took much the same position. Arguing that some forms of social policy are based on the notion of moral progress, he then used criteria of moral progress which are to be found 'in the growing power of altruism over egoism'[8] brought about by a fusion of intelligence and concern for social justice and equality. *The Gift Relationship* was an attempt to provide a concrete illustration of this philosophical view from an international study of blood donor systems.[9]

---

4   'Life with Nye', Jenny Lee, *The Observer* Colour Supplement, 10 December 1972.

5   He did so first in his book *An American Dilemma: the Negro problem arid modern democracy,* Harper & Row, London, 1962, and more recently in *The Challenge of World Poverty,* Allen Lane, London, 1970 (see Ch. 1, 'Cleansing the Approach from Biases').

6   See Corbett, P., *Ideologies,* Hutchinson, London, 1965, p. 209.

7   Macbeath G., 'Can Social Policies be Rationally Tested?', Hobhouse Memorial Trust lecture, Oxford University Press, 1957, p. 1.

8   Ginsberg, M., *The Idea of Progress: a revaluation,* Methuen, London, 1953, p. 24.

9   Titmuss, R. M., *The Gift Relationship,* Allen & Unwin, London, 1971.

At the other extreme, let us take Professor Hagenbuch's definition of social policy. 'Stated in general terms', he said, 'the mainspring of social policy may be said to be the desire to ensure every member of the community certain minimum standards and certain opportunities.'[10] This I think is typical of many definitions offered by other writers in a large number of Western countries. It is similar also to the views expressed by the United Nations in a series of studies and reports in recent years: for example, in the *Report on the Organisation and Administration of Social Services*[11] published in 1962.

These and similar definitions, whether one views them as limited or broad, all contain three objectives—and, of course, value judgements. First, they aim to be beneficent—policy is directed to provide welfare for citizens. Second, they include economic as well as non-economic objectives; for example, minimum wages, minimum standards of income maintenance and so on. Thirdly, they involve some measure of progressive redistribution in command-over-resources from rich to poor.

Dissenting somewhat from these views is Professor Lafitte of Birmingham—the only professor in Britain with the title 'Social Policy'. He sees social policy as being more concerned with the communal environment—with the provision of social amenity (urban renewal and national parks, for example, and measures against pollution, noise, etc.) which the individual cannot purchase in the market as a lone individual. He puts less emphasis on individual transfer payments (like pensions) and argues that 'in the main social policy is an attempt to steer the life of society along channels it would not follow if left to itself'.[12] This is in some senses a more limited definition—but it does imply a substantial interventionist role by Government in the provision of a wide range of community facilities and safeguards.

Professor Marshall is more practical and down-to-earth: '"Social Policy" is not a technical term with an exact meaning ... it is taken to refer to the policy of governments with regard to action having a direct impact on the welfare of the citizens, by providing them with services or income. The central core consists, therefore, of social insurance, public (or national) assistance, the health and welfare services, housing policy.'[13]

Again, social policy is seen to be beneficent, redistributive and concerned with economic as well as non-economic objectives. Like many of the other definitions, social policy (as with economic policy) is all about 'what is and what might be'. It is thus involved in choices in the ordering of social change.

As an aid to our inquiries, it is helpful to examine three contrasting models or functions of social policy. The purpose of model-building is not to admire the architecture of the building, but to help us to see some order in all the disorder and confusion of facts, systems and choices

---

10   Hagenbuch, W., *Social Economics,* Nisbet, Welwyn, 1958, p. 205.
11   *Report on the Organisation and Administration of Social Services,* Report by Group of Experts to UN Secretary General (ST/SOA/44 and E/CN.5/360/Rev. 1), 1962.
12   Lafitte, F., *Social Policy in a Free Society,* Birmingham University Press, 1962, p. 9.
13   Marshall, T. H., *Social Policy,* Hutchinson, London, 1965, p. 7.

concerning certain areas of our economic and social life. Tentatively, the three models can be described as follows:

MODEL A *The Residual Welfare Model of Social Policy*

This formulation is based on the premise that there are two 'natural' (or socially given) channels through which an individual's needs are properly met; the private market and the family. Only when these break down should social welfare institutions come into play and then only temporarily. As Professor Peacock puts it: 'The true object of the Welfare State is to teach people how to do without it.'[14] The theoretical basis of this model can be traced back to the early days of the English Poor Law, and finds support in organic-mechanistic-biological constructs of society advanced by sociologists like Spencer and Radcliffe-Brown, and economists like Friedman, Hayek and the founders and followers of the Institute of Economic Affairs in London.

MODEL B *The Industrial Achievement-Performance Model of Social Policy*

This incorporates a significant role for social welfare institutions as adjuncts of the economy. It holds that social needs should be met on the basis of merit, work performance and productivity. It is derived from various economic and psychological theories concerned with incentives, effort and reward, and the formation of class and group loyalties. It has been described as the 'Handmaiden Model'.

MODEL C *The Institutional Redistributive Model of Social Policy*

This model sees social welfare as a major integrated institution in society, providing universalist services outside the market on the principle of need. It is in part based on theories about the multiple effects of social change and the economic system, and in part on the principle of social equality. It is basically a model incorporating systems of redistribution in command-over-resources-through-time.

These three models are, of course, only very broad approximations to the theories and ideas of economists, philosophers, political scientists and sociologists. Many variants could be developed of a more sophisticated kind. However, these approximations do serve to indicate the major differences—the ends of the value spectrum—in the views held about the means and ends of

---

14   Peacock, A., *The Welfare Society,* Liberal Publication Department, London, 1960, p. 11.

social policy. All three models involve consideration of the work ethic and the institution of the family in modern society.

The three contrasting models of social policy represent different criteria for making choices. [...]

Dressed for Success

Can a Claim of Religious Discrimination Be Successful?

Tanya Marcum and Sandra J. Perry

I. Introduction

Abercrombie & Fitch,[1] a trendy clothing store noted for its partially-clad models, is also becoming known as a target of the Equal Employment Opportunity Commission (EEOC) for alleged discrimination based on race and ethnicity and, now, for allegedly refusing to hire a 17-year-old female Muslim student who wore a black hijab, or headscarf, to her interview.[2] Abercrombie is defending on the basis of its "Look Policy,"[3] which requires associates to wear clothing consistent with its brand and prohibits head coverings and any clothes that are black.[4] In December 2009, Abercrombie & Fitch won a jury trial against the EEOC in a case questioning Hollister Company's (a subsidiary of Abercrombie & Fitch), efforts to reasonably accommodate an employee's request to wear below-the-knee skirts and shirts with three-quarter length sleeves in accordance with her conversion to the Apostolic faith.[5] On February 24, 2010, the Council of American-Islamic Relations filed a complaint with the EEOC on behalf of an Abercrombie & Fitch employee who was initially told she could wear the hijab, but was later told scarves were not allowed during work hours.[6]

In 2004, Abercrombie & Fitch[7] was sued by the EEOC for allegedly violating Title VII of the Civil Rights Act of 1964 by maintaining recruiting and hiring practices that excluded minorities and women and by adopting a restrictive marketing image, and other policies, which limited minority and female employment. On November 18, 2004, the EEOC announced the settlement of the case whereby Abercrombie & Fitch agreed to pay $50 million and to develop and implement hiring and recruiting procedures to ensure compliance with the settlement consent decree that enjoined the retailer from:

- discriminating against applicants based upon race, color, national origin which includes African American, Asian Americans, and Latinos;

- discriminating against women due to their sex; and,

- denying promotional opportunities to women and minorities.

Abercrombie & Fitch agreed to some changes in its practices to ensure that minorities and women are promoted into manager-in-training and manager positions without discrimination.

Employers are required to reasonably accommodate an employee's religious practice that interferes with an employer rule, unless accommodation would be an undue hardship for the employer. For example, in December 2009, the EEOC settled a case involving a discharged female housekeeper whose Muslim religion required her to wear the hijab outside her home, including during her work at an assisted living facility. The consent decree with the EEOC called for monetary damages of $43,000, equal opportunity training, reporting of any further religious discrimination complaints, and posting of an anti-discrimination notice.[8] However, employers with legitimate safety concerns may limit the type of attire employees may wear.[9] Public employers are permitted to have a strict dress code to promote cooperation and esprit de corps and to emphasize the hierarchal nature of a police or military force.[10] Abercrombie & Fitch will argue that an employee dress code may project a particular brand image, which is an integral part of the company's marketing plan. Would it be unreasonable to accommodate the hijab in this instance? This case is squarely within the gray area of the law.

II. The Requirement to Reasonably Accommodate a Religious Practice

Title VII of the Civil Rights Act of 1964[11] prohibits discrimination in all phases of the employment process on account of race, color, religion, sex, and national origin. With respect to religion, Title VII also requires reasonable accommodation of religious requirements or practices that may interfere with employment, unless accommodation would impose an undue hardship on the employer.[12] Undue hardship is defined as more than a *de minimis* cost, or burden to the employer, which the EEOC states is a much lower requirement than that for accommodation of disability under the Americans with Disabilities Act (ADA).[13]

Religion-based charges with the EEOC are increasing. The EEOC states that the number of religious discrimination charges filed with EEOC has more than doubled from 1992 to 2007.[14] From 1997 to 2000, religion-based charges to the EEOC (compared to all filings under Title VII, the Age Discrimination in Employment Act (ADEA), the ADA, and Equal Pay Act) represented about three percent of all filings.[15] From 2001 to 2005, religion-based charges to the EEOC represented about four percent of all filings and from 2006 to 2009, religion-based charges to the EEOC represented about five percent of all filings.[16]

A. Prima Facie Case

There are three elements[17] to the employee's prima facie case of failure to reasonably accommodate the employee's religious practice that conflicts with an employer-mandated rule:

- The employee has a sincerely held religious belief or practice that conflicts with an employer rule.
- The employee informed the employer of the conflict.
- The employee was disciplined for failing to comply with the conflicting requirement.[18]

At this point, the burden of production of evidence shifts to the employer to show that a reasonable accommodation was offered and not taken by the employee, or no accommodation was possible without undue hardship,[19] or the employee was discharged based on a legitimate non-discriminatory reason.[20] Once the employer has met the burden of production, the burden of proof remains with the plaintiff to show that the employer's articulated reasons are a pretext for unlawful discrimination.

B. No Reasonable Accommodation by Employer

In *EEOC v. Alamo Rent-A-Car*,[21] the U.S. District Court found Alamo liable for failing to reasonably accommodate a female employee's request to wear a head covering during Ramadan, a special one-month long religious celebration of the Muslim religion celebrated during the ninth month of the Islamic calendar. Alamo had a dress code called the "Dress Smart Policy," which promoted a favorable first impression with its customers.[22] While the policy did not expressly prohibit head coverings, Alamo contended that any item of clothing not specifically mentioned in the policy was prohibited. After the employee asked to wear a head covering during Ramadan, Alamo stated she could wear the head covering in the back office, but she could not wear it while working the rental counter.[23] However, she was not excused from working the rental counter. After several warnings, she was terminated from employment with Alamo.[24]

The employee made out a prima facie case that Alamo failed to reasonably accommodate her religious practice. The burden then shifted to Alamo to show a reasonable accommodation or that no accommodation was possible without undue hardship.[25] Alamo argued that it made a good faith effort to reasonably accommodate, although the employee was expected to remove her head covering when working the front counter. The court found that this failed as a reasonable accommodation.[26] Therefore, in order to prevail, Alamo would have to show that allowing the employee to wear the head covering would be an undue hardship to Alamo.

An Alamo supervisor testified that he did not believe that the head covering would affect the impression the employee would make on customers.[27] His primary objection to the head covering was his belief that allowing it would open the door for others to violate the uniform policy. As to this argument, the court stated that it represented a faulty understanding of Title VII accommodation for a religious practice.[28] Allowing the employee to wear a head covering would not allow everyone to deviate from the dress code.

There would have been no actual cost to Alamo if the employee was allowed to wear the head covering;[29] however, not allowing her to do so cost Alamo $287,000.[30]

III. Undue Hardship

In *Trans World Airlines, Inc. v. Hardison,*[31] the U.S. Supreme Court's seminal case on undue hardship, the Court held that more than a *de mimimis*[32] cost to the employer to accommodate an employee's religious requirement, or practice, is an undue hardship. An employee may not insist on any particular accommodation. In *Ansonia Bd. of Ed. v. Philbrook,*[33] the U.S. Supreme Court found "no basis in either the statute or its legislative history for requiring an employer to choose any particular reasonable accommodation."[34] The employer has met its burden when it demonstrates that it has offered a reasonable accommodation to the employee.[35]

It should be noted that the Workplace Religious Freedom Act[36] was introduced into both houses of Congress in 2005, although it has never passed either chamber. This proposal would overrule *TWA v. Hardison* by amending Title VII to change the current "*de minimis*" standard for establishing undue hardship. It would require employers to show that the accommodation would cause significant difficulty or expense.

A. Dress Code Required for Safety

When a dress code is implemented at the workplace due to safety concerns, any exception to the dress code for a particular employee will likely be considered an undue hardship. In *McCarter v. Harris County,*[37] the employee was told when hired that the dress code required navy blue pants and a blue front-button shirt. She wore the required uniform provided by the employer for several months. After the plaintiff's conversion to the Pentecostal church, she informed the employer that she could not wear men's clothing, including pants, pursuant to the tenets of her new faith. She requested that she be able to wear a long, tapered skirt. At that time, her supervisor allowed her request and accommodated her inability to climb ladders by assigning other employees to those tasks.

After the plaintiff's supervisor retired, the new supervisor told the plaintiff she should wear pants to work according to the uniform policy. The plaintiff continued to wear the long skirt, tripped, and fell a few months later while standing on a ladder to perform her job. While the plaintiff believed she fell because she became dizzy due to her eyeglass prescription, her supervisor and the safety coordinator believed that her uniform violation was a major cause of the accident. Subsequently, the employer sent a memorandum to the plaintiff reminding her of the safety risks that required wearing pants to perform the job functions. The memo suggested that if she was not satisfied with the county's decision, she could contact the county's Human Resources Department and apply for another position that would not require wearing pants.

All entry-level maintenance jobs required employees to work on ladders, and other entry-level positions required skills the plaintiff did not have, such as mechanical training or bilingual skills. She refused to return to work following the accident because she would not comply with the uniform requirement, and she was terminated.

While the plaintiff made out her prima facie case of discrimination based on the employer's duty to reasonably accommodate the plaintiff's religious requirement, the employer "produced ample evidence in support of its argument that demonstrates Plaintiff's uniform violation created an undue hardship as a matter of law."[38] The pants-only requirement was based on the required job duties of a building maintenance assistant, which included climbing ladders, cleaning around machinery, and stepping over large objects. The safety risks to the plaintiff, coupled with increased labor demands on the employer if others were assigned to perform her tasks, would clearly involve more than a *de mimimis* cost to the employer.[39] The court cited an unpublished opinion from the Fifth Circuit[40] on virtually identical facts holding that an employer did not discriminate when a woman was not hired as a stocker based on her refusal to wear pants for religious reasons.

In *EEOC v. Oak-Rite Mfg. Corp.*,[41] the court characterized the suit as "a conflict between the religious beliefs of a job applicant and an employer's safety policies."[42] Similar to the *McCarter* case, the employer required employees to wear long pants in its metal-working factory for safety reasons. The safety policy also prohibited sleeveless shirts and thin-soled shoes, and it required protective eyewear and gloves when needed. Employees worked with a variety of metals and manufactured large and small metal parts. Oak-Rite required all employees to be able to operate all the machines in the plant due to production demands. Many of the machines had foot pedals that required an employee to lift his/her leg knee-high from the ground, and other machines required the operator to straddle the machine, or work with the legs apart, to accommodate the machine. The pants-only component of the policy was intended to reduce skin exposure to sharp metal parts and avoid the risk that loose clothing could become entangled in machinery.

Brenda Enlow applied for a press operator job and was offered the job; however, she was not hired because of her refusal to comply with the pants only policy due to her religion. While her religious beliefs were not discussed in detail at the interview, she was a member of the Conservative Holiness faith, which has a dress code requiring women to wear skirts/dresses that extend below the knees and shirtsleeves below the elbow. Oak-Rite's uniform policy was facially neutral and a reasonable safety measure, according to the court. It was enforced regularly by sending employees home for wearing baggy clothing that could become entangled in machinery, and by prohibiting employees from entering the factory floor in shorts and sandals.

The EEOC presented a prima facie case that the employer failed to reasonably accommodate Enlow's religious attire requirement. Although the question of undue hardship is a question of fact, the court noted that some questions of undue hardship have been decided as a matter of law, particularly where the employer showed that accommodation would cause or increase safety risks or the risk of legal liability.[43] The EEOC offered an expert witness's testimony that Enlow might wear a close-fitting denim or canvas dress or skirt that extended to within a few inches above the ankle coupled with leather above-the-ankle boots. However, the expert acknowledged that it was not common for workers to wear skirts in industrial settings, and the court stated there was no evidence of production workers wearing the proposed outfit in any modern factory. Ultimately, the court granted summary judgment to Oak-Rite, stating that "[t]he few reported cases dealing with safety risks and legal risks make clear that an employer can be subjected to an undue hardship (a burden that is more than *de mimimis*) if the proposed accommodation would create any significant safety or legal risks."[44]

B. Police/Military Dress Codes

Uniform requirements for police officers, fire fighters, emergency personnel, and the military are designed to encourage "subordination of personal preferences and identities in favor of the overall group mission."[45] Officers in the military may not insist on wearing religious headgear in violation of the uniform policy.[46] Police officers may be required to remove religious pins from their official uniform when the policy prohibits pins of all types on the uniform.[47] In *Webb v. City of Philadelphia*,[48] the plaintiff was a practicing Muslim and a police officer with the city of Philadelphia. She had been so employed for at least seven years when she requested permission to wear a headscarf while in uniform and on duty, which would cover her head and the back of her neck. Her request was denied based on the department's uniform directive, which specifies the uniform in detail. Any item not listed in the directive was not permitted.[49]

> The EEOC presented a prima facie case that the employer failed to reasonably accommodate Enlow's religious attire requirement.

After filing her charge of religious discrimination with the EEOC, the plaintiff wore her headscarf to work with her uniform and was sent home when she refused to remove it. This happened two more days in a row. She was informed that a continuation of her conduct could result in disciplinary action. Thereafter, she reported to work without the headscarf although her earlier conduct resulted in a thirteen-day suspension.[50]

The plaintiff established a prima facie case of religious discrimination.[51] The burden then shifted to the department to establish that it offered a reasonable accommodation to the plaintiff, or that any accommodation would be an undue hardship. The department defended on the latter ground.[52] The police commissioner testified that uniformity "encourages the subordination of personal preferences in favor of the overall policing mission" and conveys "a sense of authority and competence to other officers inside the Department, as well as to the general public."[53] He also testified that "[i]n sum, in my professional judgment and experience, it is critically important to promote the image of a disciplined, identifiable and impartial police force by maintaining the Philadelphia Police Department uniform as a symbol of neutral government authority, free from expressions of personal religion, bent or bias."[54]

The U.S. District Court concluded that any accommodation would constitute an undue hardship, and the U.S. Court of Appeals agreed.[55] Although the plaintiff and another officer offered affidavits that other officers had worn religious symbols on their uniforms and had not been disciplined, neither could offer any evidence of the specific times or places that these incidents occurred, nor could they show that the police department was even aware of such incidents.[56]

B. Dress Code Required for Business Image

Employers may wish to convey a particular image to the public and to their customers. However, customer preferences cannot trump an employer's duty not to discriminate based on membership in a protected class.[57] According to the EEOC's Compliance Manual on Religious Discrimination, "[w]hile there may be circumstances in which allowing a particular exception to an employer's dress and grooming policy would pose an undue hardship, an employer's reliance on the broad rubric of 'image' to deny a requested religious accommodation may in a given case be tantamount to reliance on customer religious bias (so-called 'customer preference') in violation of Title VII."[58]

Perhaps the closest case on business image as the basis of the dress code is *Cloutier v. Costco Wholesale Corp.*[59] When Cloutier was hired by Costco, she had several ear piercings and tattoos, but no facial piercings.[60] In her position as a front-end assistant, the plaintiff's earrings were not a violation of the code. Her tattoos were covered by her work shirt and were not an issue in the case.[61] Cloutier transferred to the deli department in 1997.[62] The next year, Costco's dress code for food handlers was revised to prohibit all jewelry.[63] Rather than comply with the policy, Cloutier transferred back to the front-end position where she would be permitted to wear her jewelry.[64] She was later promoted to cashier.[65] She did not indicate any religious basis for her desire to wear jewelry at work.[66]

Over the next few years, Cloutier engaged in various forms of body modification including facial piercings.[67] In 2001, Costco modified its dress code again to prohibit all facial jewelry except earrings for all employees.[68] Cloutier did not remove her eyebrow piercing, but she was not challenged by management for several months.[69] When Costco began enforcing the no-facial piercing policy, Cloutier claimed for the first time that she was a member of the Church of Body Modification[70] and that wearing her piercing jewelry was a religious requirement.[71] The Church of Body Modification's Statement of Faith asserts its members' rights to alter their bodies as they wish with a purpose of education and inspiration.[72]

Cloutier provided information about the church to Costco. The church does not appear to require piercings to be visible at all times; that was Cloutier's individual interpretation.[73] Costco insisted that Cloutier remove her facial piercings. Cloutier filed her claim with the EEOC immediately.[74] Thereafter, she and Costco engaged in a series of meetings wherein she suggested some accommodations, such as covering the piercings with a flesh-colored band-aid or replacing the piercing jewelry with clear spacers to maintain the opening.[75] Costco did not appear to agree, but another employee began wearing the clear spacers with no objection from Costco. Cloutier was ultimately terminated from Costco for her unexcused absences.[76]

Through the EEOC's mediation process, Cloutier and Costco remained in contact. Costco offered to allow Cloutier to return to work with either of the accommodations she suggested— a band-aid over the piercings or clear retainers. Ultimately, Cloutier maintained that no accommodations would suffice; she was required to display her piercings at all times according to her interpretation of her religion.[77]

In the U.S. District Court, there was some concern that Cloutier's claim was not based on a bona fide religious practice.[78] The court avoided a determination of whether Cloutier made out her prima facie case by focusing on the undue hardship issue instead, finding that Costco had offered her a reasonable accommodation.[79] The U.S. Court of Appeals went further by holding that Costco would suffer an undue hardship if forced to grant Cloutier an exemption from the dress code for her piercings since Costco would lose control of its public image.[80]

In discussing an employer's interest in utilizing a dress code to present a particular image to the public and its customers, the court stated:

> It is axiomatic that, for better or for worse, employees reflect on their employers. This is particularly true of employees who regularly interact with customers, as Cloutier did in her cashier position. Even if Cloutier did not personally receive any complaints about her appearance, her facial jewelry influenced Costco's public image and, in Costco's calculation, detracted from its professionalism.

Costco is far from unique in adopting personal appearance standards to promote and protect its image. As the D.C. Circuit noted, 'Perhaps no facet of business life is more important than a company's place in public estimation ... Good grooming regulations reflect a company's policy in our highly competitive business environment. Reasonable requirements in furtherance of that policy are an aspect of managerial responsibility.'[81]

IV. Abercrombie & Fitch's Look Policy: Would any Exemption be an Undue Hardship?

In the pending case against Abercrombie & Fitch, Abercrombie will likely argue that its salespersons are models of the clothing sold in its stores and parts of a comprehensive marketing strategy.[82] In *EEOC v. Abercrombie & Fitch Stores, Inc.*,[83] a religious discrimination case based on Hollister Co.'s enforcement of its Look Policy, the employee requested that she be permitted to wear long skirts and sleeves that extended to the elbow in accordance with her recent conversion to the Apostolic faith. Hollister offered to allow her to wear short skirts with leggings underneath or skirts that would be consistent with her faith and the Hollister dress code if she could find any in other stores.

In a hearing on a motion by the plaintiff in the case to exclude expert testimony and expert witness reports, Abercrombie & Fitch offered the testimony of two expert witnesses to illustrate that adherence to and enforcement of the Look Policy is an essential function of the

MIT [Manager-in-Training] position, and deviations from the Look Policy would have a negative impact on Hollister's brand.[84] The jury found in favor of Abercrombie & Fitch.[85]

One difference between the Hollister case and the current case against Abercrombie & Fitch involves advertising. Hollister apparently does no advertising beyond its salesperson/models dressing in the brand's clothing.[86] However, Abercrombie & Fitch does advertise.[87] Nevertheless, based on the *de minimis* standard for undue hardship under Title VII and the company's successful argument to the jury in the Hollister case, the EEOC may have a difficult time winning their case.

V. Conclusion

It is commonly accepted by the courts that companies have the right to adopt personal appearance and dress code policies for their workforce, within reasonable limits. Common reasons for such policies include conveying a particular image to customers or clients, portraying a professional or business-like appearance, conveying a neutral public image with respect to religion, and enforcing safety standards. In developing and enforcing these policies, employers must be increasingly mindful of the likelihood of potential legal claims of religious discrimination, and they must make reasonable attempts to accommodate religious requests to deviate from those policies. However, it may be an undue hardship for an employer to accommodate any deviation from its dress code. If so, the employer should evaluate its reasons for the inability to accommodate and be able to articulate those reasons to the employee, and later to the EEOC and the court, if necessary.

Endnotes

1 Abercrombie & Fitch's main website is located at http://www.abercrombie.com/webapp/wcs/stores/servlet/home_10051_10901_-1 [last accessed February 7, 2010]; The website for associates/employees is located at https://associate.anfcorp.com/anf/intranet/site/extranet/[last accessed February 7, 2010]. The website for A&F's brand history is located at https://associate.anfcorp.com/anf/webdav/site/extranet/shared/docs/New%20Store%20Associate/Brand%20history.pdf [last accessed February 7, 2010].

2 EEOC Press Release, *Abercrombie & Fitch Sued by EEOC for Religious Discrimination Against Muslim Teen Applicant*, September 17, 2009, http://www.eeoc.gov/eeoc/newsroom/release/9-17-09b.cfm [last accessed February 7, 2010].

3 The Abercrombie & Fitch Look Policy can be found at https://associate.anfcorp.com/anf/webdav/site/extranet/shared/docs/New%20Store%20Associate/What%20to%20wear.pdf [last accessed February 7, 2010].

4 Sean Gregory, *Abercrombie Faces a Muslim-Headscarf Lawsuit*, Time, September 23, 2009, http://www.time.com/time/business/article/0,8599,1925607,00.html [last accessed February 7, 2010].

5 Donna Walter, *Verdicts & Settlements December 21, 2009: Hollister Co. Wins Suit*, Missouri Lawyers Media, December 21, 2009, http://findarticles.com/p/articles/mi_7992/is_20091221/ai_n45391641/ [last accessed March 13, 2010].

6 *Abercrombie & Fitch: Did the Store Fire Employee for not Removing Headscarf?* The Huffington Post, February 24, 2010, http://www.huffingtonpost.com/2010/02/26/abercrombie-fitch-did-the_n_478102.html [last accessed March 13, 2010].

7 EEOC v. Abercrombie & Fitch Stores, Inc., Case No. CV-04-4731 SI (N.D. Cal. 2004); http://www.eeoc.gov/eeoc/newsroom/release/11-18-04.cfm [last accessed April 17, 2010].

8 See http://www.eeoc.gov/eeoc/newsroom/release/12-18-09.cfm [last accessed February 7, 2010].

9 McCarter v. Harris County, 2006 U.S. Dist. LEXIS 26795 (S.D. Tex. 2006); EEOC v. Oak-Rite Mfg. Corp., 2001 U.S. Dist. LEXIS 15621 (S.D. Ind. 2001).

10 Webb v. City of Philadelphia, 2007 U.S. Dist. LEXIS 46872 (E.D. Pa. 2007), *aff'd,* 2009 U.S. App. LEXIS 7169 (3d. Cir. 2009).

11 42 U.S.C. § 2000e-2(a).

12 42 U.S.C. § 2000e(j).

13 EEOC Compliance Manual on Religious Discrimination, http://www.eeoc.gov/policy/docs/religion.html.

14 *Id.*

15 Religion-based Charges, http://www.eeoc.gov/eeoc/statistics/enforcement/religion.cfm [last accessed, March 13, 2010] and http://www.eeoc.gov/eeoc/statistics/enforcement/titlevii.cfm [last accessed March 13, 2010].

16 *Id.*

17 EEOC v. Aldi, Inc., 2008 U.S. Dist. LEXIS 25206 (W.D. Pa. 2008) citing Shelton v. University of Medicine & Dentistry of New Jersey, 223 F. 3d 220 at 224 (3d Cir. 2000).

18 Ali v. Alamo Rent-A-Car, Inc., 8 Fed. Appx. 156, 2001 U.S. App. LEXIS 3389 (4th Cir. 2001).

19 *See* fn. 17, *supra.*

20 Yehudah v. Bd. of Regents of the University System of Georgia, 2008 U.S. Dist. LEXIS 28407 (M.D. Ga. 2008).

21 432 F. Supp. 2d 1006, 2006 U.S. Dist. LEXIS 34674 (D. Ariz. 2006).

22 *Id.*, 432 F. Supp. 2d 1006 at 1008.

23 *Id.* at 1009.

24 *Id.*

25 *Id.* at 1012–13.

26 *Id.* at 1013.

27 *Id.* at 1015.

28 *Id.*

29 *Id.* at 1015–16.

30 Jennifer Carsen, *Avoiding Dress Code Lawsuits*, http://hr.blr.com/HR-news/Performance-Termination/Office-Dress-Codes/Avoiding-Dress-Code-Lawsuits/, last accessed March 5, 2010.

31 432 U.S. 63, 97 S. Ct. 2264 (1977).

32 *Id.*, 432 U.S. 63 at 84, 97 S. Ct. 2264 at 2277.

33 479 U.S. 60, 107 S. Ct. 367 (1986).

34 *Id.*, 479 U.S. 60 at 68, 107 S. Ct. 367 at 372.

35 *Id.*, 479 U.S. at 69, 107 S. Ct. at 372.

36 *See* H.R. 1431, 110th Cong. (2007).

37 2006 U.S. Dist. LEXIS 26795 (S.D. Tex. 2006).

38 *Id.*

39 *Id.*

40 Johnson v. Sears Roebuck & Co., 66 Fed. Appx. 523 (5th Cir. 2003).

41 2001 U.S. Dist. LEXIS 15621 (S.D. Ind. 2001).

42 *Id.*

43 *Id.*

44 *Id.*

45 Goldman v. Weinberger, 475 U.S. 503 at 508, 106 S. Ct. 1310 at 1313 (1986).

46 *Id.*, 475 U.S. 503 at 510, 106 S. Ct. 1310 at 1314.

47 Daniels v. City of Arlington, 246 F. 3d 500 at 501 (5th Cir. 2001).

48 562 F. 3d 256, 2009 U.S. App. LEXIS 7169 (3d Cir. 2009).

49 *Id.*, 562 F. 3d 256 at 258.

50 *Id.*

51 *Id.*, 562 F. 3d 256 at 261.

52 *Id.*

53 *Id.*

54 *Id.*

55 *Id.*, 562 F. 3d 256 at 264.

56 *Id.*, 562 F. 3d 256 at 262.

57 Wilson v. Southwest Airlines, 517 F. Supp. 292, 1981 U.S. Dist. LEXIS 12979 (N.D. Tex. 1981).

58 EEOC Compliance Manual, Religious Discrimination, http://www.eeoc.gov/policy/docs/religion. html#_Toc203359523 [last accessed March 15, 2010].

59 390 F. 3d 126, 2004 U.S. App. LEXIS 24763 (1st Cir. 2004).

60 390 F. 3d 126 at 128.

61 *Id.* at 129.

62 *Id.* at 128.

63 *Id.*

64 *Id.* at 129.

65 *Id.*

66 *Id.* at 128.

67 *Id.* at 129.

68 *Id.*

69 *Id.*

70 See, http://uscobm.com/ [last accessed March 16, 2010].

71 390 F. 3d 126 at 129.

72 See, http://uscobm.com/statement-of-faith/ [last accessed March 16, 2010].

73 390 F. 3d 126 at 129.
74 *Id.*
75 *Id.* at 130.
76 *Id.*
77 *Id.*
78 *Id.* at 131.
79 *Id.*
80 *Id.* at 137.
81 *Id.* at 135.
82 *See*, Claire Driessen, *Message Communication in Advertising: Selling the Abercrombie and Fitch Image*, UW-L Journal of Undergraduate Research VIII (2005). http://www.uwlax.edu/urc/JUR-online/PDF/2005/driessen.pdf [last accessed March 16, 2010].
83 Case No. 4:08CV1470 JCH, U.S. District Court (E.D. Mo.), filed September 25, 2008.
84 2009 U.S. Dist. LEXIS 99546 (October 26, 2009).
85 Donna Walter, *Verdicts & Settlements December 21, 2009: Hollister Co. Wins Suit*, Missouri Lawyers Media, December 21, 2009, http://findarticles.com/p/articles/mi_7992/is_20091221/ai_n45391641/ [last accessed March 13, 2010].
86 *Id.*
87 *See* fn. 82 *supra.*

Post-Reading Activities

1   After studying minorities, what is your definition of a minority? How do you incorporate all the facets of intersectionality? Do you utilize any previous definitions?

2   What is the top human rights issue in the United States? Write a social policy to address this issue.

3   How can social policy help the United States become the land of opportunity for the majority and the minority, simultaneously? Do you agree with Kenworthy's assessment of opportunity in the United States?

4   Realistically, what can you do to help the human rights of American minorities?

CONCLUSION

Thinking like Merton (see Unit 5), the manifest function of this book is to provide an overview of issues that some minorities face in the United States. The latent function of this book is to incite a passion in the reader to do something about the inequalities that minorities face. It is difficult when put in to practice to balance the rights of the majority with the rights of the minority. I am often asked in class whether it is okay to violate the rights of the majority to provide rights to the minority. Apparently, my message was not clear: ALL HUMANS deserve HUMAN RIGHTS! The majority do not need to give up rights so that the minority will have rights. Rights and privileges are not the same concept. Humans matter.

Using the information provided in this anthology, you have the research necessary to form an opinion, do more research on an area, and argue on behalf of a minority in need. The next time you see a minority individual presented in the news in a negative light, my goal is that you will think from a sociological perspective (see Unit 2) about what possible structural issues this individual may have faced that placed him or her in the situation. Think about how the outcome of this individual *might* have been different if all universal human rights were afforded. Humans matter.

While thinking about the riots following the death of Freddie Gray in Baltimore, Maryland, it does not take much research to see that the individuals in this neighborhood have the intersection of racial minority (primarily Black), social class minority (many are underemployed and undereducated), and age minority (young). This intersectionality provides a catalyst for explaining the inequality the minorities face. They are just walking distance from very wealthy and powerful politicians, but their lives are very different. Their basic human rights are different. We do not want to excuse any behavior; rather, our goal is to understand behavior. And, while we try to understand this behavior, we must keep in mind that humans matter. Human rights matter.